WHAT READERS SAY ABOUT

Turn Back Time

the earlier book in this series and winner of the *Benjamin Franklin Award for Popular Fiction*

"Do you enjoy historical romantic novels? Especially ones you could share with your daughter, granddaughter or mother? If so...get Turn Back Time by Lisa Kay Hauser and Philip Dale Smith... They combined storytelling skills and lyrical style to produce a warm, gripping and inspirational book. ... I started reading it on the plane and literally couldn't stop! I read on the plane, I read in the car coming home from the airport, and I read in my bed until I got to the last word on the last page and then I didn't want it to end.... Trust me, this is a book you'll share and share and share."

JoAnna Lund, The Healthy Exchanges Newsletter

"This romance, set in a Depression-era mining town, is about family (the good, the bad, and the ugly), faith (knowing God is there no matter what), and Christian living(love, acceptance, and forgiveness)....Hattie's stubborn faith and raw emotion is endearing. Her young daughter will charm any reader, and even Smith is more than likeable."

CBA Marketplace

"Turn Back Time. ... immediately involved me as a reader and made this a one-night read. ... Hauser and Smith have crafted a fine story.... characters are well-drawn and alive. ...even three-year-old Dulcie is a living, breathing person."

Anniesse Williams, Director, Muhlenberg County, KY Libraries

"This fast-paced story of family love, tragedy and endurance will touch the lives of readers everywhere. It is a delightful, uplifting read. The gentle humor is priceless."

Linda Howell, bookstore owner, Tacoma, WA

"The book held me spellbound! I started reading it at 11 PM. The next thing I knew, my husband stumbled in to interrupt my reading and call me to bed at 4:30 the next morning! The plot is well woven, the characters intriguing, the story moving and exciting."

Cindy Pavey, Billings, MT

What readers say about *Turn Back Time*...

"Looking for a model for today's families? The love, faith, and family ties that carry Hattie and friends through turbulent times deserve imitation. The Hauser/Smith writing team has created characters so real that I found myself thinking of them as friends and family. I can't wait for a sequel!"

Linda Sandlin, librarian and teacher, Sheridan, WY

"Ready to fall in love? Read this book and you will! There's warm, gentle Hattie and fiery, but caring, Smith Delaney. There's bubbly four-year-old Dulcie and the brusque, ancient Ma Richards. These are but a few of the memorable people who populate this spellbinding story. When I put the book down, I couldn't wait to pick it up again. I felt like I was part of the family and just had to find out where our adventure would lead."

April Dillon, librarian, Canadian, TX

"The present volume [Turn Back Time] is a fine example of recent coal literature...a compelling drama of Kentucky coal mining life of the Depression-ridden 1930s....any reader out there who says he's interested in learning about 'family values' this is your book."

Daily News, Bowling Green, KY

"This graceful, charming account of Hattie Crowe and her family is told in an easy-to-read style that quickly drew me into the center of the family's joys and sorrows. I very much appreciated the pure and simple qualiities so aptly blended into the story. It's the best book I've read in years!"

Loretta Sorensen, freelance writer, Yankton, SD

To learn about this and other books by the authors, including where to purchase them, see the order form and information sheets at the back of this book.

Sunshine & Shadow

 Contact: Golden Anchor Press, P.O. Box 45208, Tacoma, WA 98445 Phone 253 847-9441 Fax 253 537-5323 Email: Smithdale2@aol.com.

Publisher's Cataloging-in-Publication
(Provided by Quality Books, Inc)

Hauser, Lisa Kay.
Sunshine & Shadow : a novel / by Lisa Kay Hauser & Philip Dale Smith.
--1st ed.
p. cm. -- (The Stoneworth Chronicles ; 2)
Sunshine and shadow
LCCN 2002107216
ISBN 1-886864-04-7 (Hard Cover)
ISBN 1-886864-07-1 (Soft Cover)
ISBN 1-886864-13-6 (Series)

1. Coal miners--Kentucky--Fiction. 2. Wife abuse--Fiction. 3. Child abuse--Fiction. 4. Depressions--1929--United States--Fiction. 5. Muhlenberg Co. (Ky.)--Fiction. I. Hauser, Lisa Kay. II. Smith, Dale, 1932- III. Title. IV. Title: Sunshine and shadow

PS3558.A7586S86 2002 813'.54
QBI02-701642

Printed in the USA

02 03 04 05 06 07 08 09 - 8 7 6 5 4 3 2 1

Sunshine & Shadow

Stoneworth Chronicles - II

A NOVEL BY

Lisa Kay Hauser &
Philip Dale Smith

CHILDREN'S PICTURE BOOKS BY PHILIP DALE SMITH

Over is not UP!
Illustrated by Donna Brooks
(1995)

Nighttime at the Zoo
Illustrated by Gwen Clifford
(1997)

The Rabbit and the Promise Sign
Pat Day-Bivins, Co-Author
Illustrated by Donna Brooks
(1998)

Little Tom Meets Mr. Jonah
Pat Day-Bivins, Co-Author
Illustrated by Donna Brooks
(2000)

NOVELS BY LISA KAY HAUSER AND PHILIP DALE SMITH

Turn Back Time
(2000)

Secrets of Rebel Cave
(2002)

Published by Golden Anchor Press
PO Box 45208
Tacoma, WA 98445

Acknowledgments

We're aware that many people have contributed to our work. While we can't acknowledge all, some we must recognize.

Our longsuffering spouses, Richard and Mary Jo, and our families, have endured the effects of our being writers—with resulting deadlines, lack of sleep, and our quite common state of being present in body, but absent in mind and spirit.

Thanks to the Kentucky Skipworth, Rhoads, and Smith families we've tapped for inspiration, examples, stories, and occasional words, phrases, and snippets of conversation. And to their friends and neighbors, who've made similar contributions to our fiction.

Some who've been resources for information about the time and place of our story are: Bobby Anderson, Paul Camplin, Gayle Carver, Joanna Fox, Irene Jackson, Carl Lendle Mullins, Hope Neathamer, James Stewart, and Anniesse Williams and staff at Greenville's Harbin Memorial Library—especially Sandra Galyen, Carol Brown and Coni Wallace at the Local History Annex. Also thanks to the members of the Brodhead Historical Society who settled once for all our questions about how to start a '36 Chevy.

Thanks to our pre-readers: Jean and Bob Bell, Bill and Martha Brown, Sandra Dennings, Marla Estes, Darlene Mindrup, Dorothy and Johnny Shinn, and Rhea Nell Spurlin.

Our cheerleaders, in addition to the above: Bob and Carolyn Carpenter, Carolyn Cobble, Joyce Ewing, Pam Lewis, and the folks at Orchard Street church in Tacoma, WA, Deb Towns, Mary and Bob and Michelle at Living Word in Brodhead, WI. To Rock River Revival: Leon and Martha Mosley, Craig Bergum and Mary Monson, Gary and Terri West, Wayne and Monica Woodard: you stand in the gap like no one else!

Accolades to our production team: Sharon Castlen - consultant, George Foster – cover designer, Robert Juran – editor, Rowena Hanson – PageMaker specialist, and David Prentice and crew at Vaughan Printing. Special thanks go to artist Susan Vaughn for her pencil sketch of "The Old House at the Foot of the Hill."

PREFACE

What a joy writing this book has been! Response to *Turn Back Time*, the first novel in the Stoneworth Chronicles, has thrilled and overwhelmed us—and inspired us to continue the story.

We've found delight and challenges in this journey back to Muhlenberg County, Kentucky, during the era of the Great Depression. We wanted the story to be real in setting and circumstance, and hope our extensive research has made it as true to life as possible.

With the exception of the fictional Coaltown community and mine, all of the places are real. Yes, there really was a town named Paradise on the Green River. "Old Airdrie" was, and still is, just downstream. The abandoned furnace stack and stone engine house still rise below the bluff. Now owned by a coal company, it is, sadly, "off limits" to visitors. "Jockey Day," after decades of sharing circuit court day in Greenville, has long since been replaced by garage sales and Luke's Flea Market.

This book is inspired, as was Turn Back Time, by the lives of John Orville Smith and Ethel Skipworth Rhoads Smith, of Drakesboro and nearby Mondray, Kentucky. This is a novel, so much of it comes from our imaginations. But the personalities of those two people are woven into the story, along with numerous bits of history and family lore. With the exception of public figures, most of the people in the book are fictitious—but you may well recognize someone you know in many of them.

We hope you'll delight in this visit to a time when human struggles, while much like as those we face today, were set against a vastly different backdrop. Money was scarce. Life's pace was slower. And most significant of all, faith, family and friends were highest priorities. May they be so again.

Dedication

For my daughter Tracie and my granddaughter Mariah:

May the choices you make honor God and bring glory to Him.
May your lives be filled with others who love and respect you.
And may you enjoy enough sunshine to cast out the shadows.
Oh, and as the years go by and my memory gets fuzzy,
just in case I should ever forget to tell you:
remember who you are; be respectful;
and wear your seatbelts.

Sure do love my girls!

—Lisa Kay Hauser

For three men: Because children get much of their sense of worth from how adults treat them, I dedicate this book to a trio who made a difference for me and for many others:

Seaman Bowman – my brother-in-law was every kid's friend. He could shoot marbles, a slingshot, or a .22-rifle like no one I had ever seen. And could pinch with his toes! Seaman took me on my first trip to a zoo, a stage show, a circus, and on my first plane ride.

Doug Clark, Sr. – was a neighbor who always had time to help us build a ball field or put up a basketball goal. Or to teach us to throw a knuckleball or curve. Doug, in spite of his age, played the games with us—all out. And he must have been in his thirties!

Philip Cornette – this mail carrier didn't just deliver mail. Our scoutmaster taught us to tie bowline knots, build fires without matches, and so very much more. Our confidant, mentor, coach, role model, and cheerleader, Philip helped us find our way in life.

—Philip Dale Smith

Prologue

Hattie Stoneworth Crowe climbed the hill behind the small white house. Ahead, the sun broke over the edge of the horizon just as she reached the top of the rise. Turning back, and peering down through the orchard, she let her eyes wander from one side of the property to the other. A fine wisp of smoke rose from the chimney, and soft lamplight glowed from the windows. Every stick of wood and lump of stone had been joined or mortared with love. From where she stood, Hattie couldn't see the walk coursing across the front yard, but each carefully laid brick there had once warmed in the palm of her father's hand.

A lone tear trickled down Hattie's cheek. Unmindful of it, she watched the sun come up over this small piece of earth in Mondray, Kentucky. It was where she belonged. Her roots ran deep here—as deep as the roots of the azaleas and rhododendrons her mother had planted beneath the windows, as deep as the pear tree that shaded the north side of the house, as deep as the massive oaks that stood sentinel in the front yard.

Now it was Hattie's home—the home where she and Jack had labored to build their lives together—to twine two souls into one. And then, he was gone. Senselessly, achingly gone.

Life in the moment of his passing had horribly changed, forever.

Hattie had loved Laughing Jack Crowe since childhood. She'd watched him silently from under her black lashes, and adored him from afar until the day he noticed that the shy little girl with the ebony braids had become a striking young woman—quiet in her faith, and in her nature. He'd told her once, in one of those quiet, precious moments when husbands and wives lie together whispering in the dark, that when he realized she was all grown up, she'd taken his breath away. That strong man who labored every day in the underground workings of the coal mines of Muhlenberg County, swinging a pick and hauling tons of coal, had weakened and faltered under her sweet smile.

A memory tickled and wriggled out of the dim past. Hattie in her favorite school dress, watching her older brothers, Forrest and Berk, swimming with Jack in Pond Creek. Standing on the bank and wishing he would notice her. She saw her little-girl self laying down her books and stepping out onto the large sycamore limb that stretched low and flat over the water. The cries of the big boys to be careful and get down. The warnings—and then the plunge. The sickening embarrassment that she'd made an utter fool of herself, trying to show off for Jack. And dragging her sodden humiliation to the bank. Then—gloriously then—Jack Crowe rising from the creek, the afternoon light glistening on the beads of water running down his chest, throwing his sun-warmed shirt around her shoulders, and walking her home.

Hattie shivered at the deliciousness of that moment. The halting conversation that skipped and started, and then purred as they walked the half-mile to the small white house under the hill. The sidelong glances that showed he was watching her face, listening to her soft words….

Now she leaned against the gnarled trunk of an ancient apple tree. Another tear traced the path of the first. Hattie brushed it away and turned her thoughts from memories of the past. Today was the present—tomorrow the hope for the future. But today, April 14, 1934, was special.

I'm getting married today, Jack. Can you believe it? I never thought I could love another man after you died. Never. I reckon it came as much of a surprise to me as anyone, but I love him.

Hattie smiled softly. *Smith Delaney's not like anyone I've ever known before. He's sure not like you were. He's all rough edges and elbows, but he's got a heart as big as all outdoors. He loves me, Jack! An' he loves our children. Dulcie puppy-dogs around after him like he's the king of the world. You should see her. I didn't know she was so hungry for a daddy 'til I saw 'em together. An' he's gentle with Jackie, too. Just like you would have been. I think you'd be proud of the way he takes to 'em, Jack.*

Hattie brushed her hair back off her forehead and closed her eyes. A warm spring breeze kissed her cheeks.

He's good to me, Jack. Just so good. I know there's folks who say it's too soon—it's only been a year—but I know it's right. He's the right one. ...An' if you could only know him, in my heart, I b'lieve you'd want this for me and the children. God brought him to me when I didn't even know how bad I was gonna need him. Guess that's just the way He works. Fittin' the puzzle pieces together when we can't even see the picture....

The rooster crowed in the chicken coop, and Hattie lifted her eyes back toward the house. *It's comin' on day, now, so I need to go back to the house, but I wanted you to know, Jack. I wanted to tell you myself.*

Hattie retraced her steps through the orchard slowly, letting her right hand trail along the tips of the branches of the apple trees as she passed. She gazed back at the house her father had built and knew it was ready for the wedding. She and her five sisters had taken down all the curtains, washed and starched them and rehung them. The floors gleamed with new polish and wax. The porches and walks were swept. She'd deadheaded all the flowers in the beds scattered in the yard herself, finding peace in the simple joy of watching things renew themselves in the earth. Two of her three brothers had helped Smith repaint the buildings. Everything was clean and fresh. All was ready.

A clatter startled her from her reverie. She looked down the lane toward Jacksontown and saw a strange procession marching toward her house. A woman and four children with two wagons followed the rutted route. Hattie quickened her pace and went to meet them.

"Mamie, what have you got there?"

Mamie Dunford ducked her head and smiled her gentle

smile. "I think every bride needs fresh flowers, Hattie. I brung you some of mine."

Hattie's mouth dropped open. She glanced toward the wagons. Each was loaded down with large tin cans stuffed with moss-covered earth. From each can shy purple and pink violets peeked out of the moss, and shooting upward in waving banners were cut branches of flowering dogwood and redbuds pressed down into the dirt.

Hattie clapped her hands in delight. "Oh, they're beautiful! But when did you do all this? How?..."

Mamie bit her lip around a giggle. "Are you surprised, Hattie? I hoped you would be. I started transplantin' the violets a couple weeks ago, an' then I got up early this mornin' to cut the dogwoods and the redbuds. They won't last long, but they're so purty..."

Hattie grabbed Mamie and hugged her tight. "They're perfect! Just perfect! We'll line the walk leading up to the steps. That's where we're havin' the ceremony. An' just you wait, Mamie. I bet you'll get more compliments on your flowers than I will on my dress!"

Mamie's gaze dropped to her shoes. "I...I won't be comin' for the weddin', Hattie. I...I wanted, to, but Deke...Well, he thinks I need to be at home today."

Hattie sobered at the mention of Deke Dunford. "Are you sure? I mean, maybe you could come for a little while—especially when he knows how much work you put into the flowers..."

Mamie twisted a corner of her apron in one rawboned hand. "No, it just won't work out today." She glanced toward the rising sun, then back toward Jacksontown. "In fact, I need to be gettin' back quick now. I just wanted you to know I'd be thinkin' about you when you say your vows."

The two women silently pulled the wagons through the yard and placed the cans of flowers in two neat rows down the brick walk while the three older children watched. The oldest girl balanced her two-year-old little sister on one jutting hip.

Hattie and Mamie talked quietly while they worked. After she had put the last of the flowers in place, Mamie straightened up and brushed the dirt off of her hands.

"I watered 'em good this mornin' so they should stay fresh all day," she said, turning to walk back home.

"Mamie, wait," Hattie called. "Th.... thank you!"

Mamie stopped and grabbed Hattie in a crushing hug.

"I hope you'll be happy, Hattie," she whispered fiercely. "Just...just so happy..."

She wheeled around and walked briskly down the road with her children at her side, dragging the wagons behind them.

In that split second before Mamie turned away, Hattie thought she saw tears trickle down her friend's life-worn face.

❧

The wedding was a moment out of time. Dulcie in her pretty pink ruffles, and Jackie, bouncing in the arms of an aunt. All of Hattie's brothers and sisters, even Berk, who came all the way from Louisville with his wife and children. Smith's family, stoic mountain folk, like dignified old souls, watching from the edge of the crowd.

Hattie walked on Eldon's arm. His lined face was peaceful as he escorted his youngest sister up the walk to place her hand in Smith's. Smith's slate-blue eyes were shining into hers. A few quiet words, and they were married. Together forever, or as long as God would allow.

1

Becky Dunford's face was that of an old woman, not of a ten-year-old girl. She looked out at the world with eyes that seemed to have seen the worst of what life has to offer and didn't expect any different. "M...Miz Delaney? Is my Mama gonna be all right?"

Hattie didn't look at the child, but wrung out the cloth she had dipped in cold water from the wash basin by the bed and placed it against Mamie Dunford's bruised cheek.

"Becky, where did you say your brother and sisters are?"

"I...I took 'em up to the old cabin. They'll wait for me to come get 'em. They won't come out 'til I tell 'em to." Becky's bare toe rubbed a pattern against the bare wood floor. "If you think Mama'll be all right, maybe y...you should be g...goin' now."

Hattie glanced away from the badly beaten face of Becky's mother to the little girl.

"I'm not leavin' yet. I want to see her open her eyes first. How long d'you say she'd been like this before you came to get me?"

"Um... well... she *fell* last night and I couldn't wake her up this mornin'."

"Becky, where was your daddy when she *fell?*"

"D...daddy? He weren't here. She just tripped and fell."

The little girl nervously twisted one blond braid around her finger.

"You know how clumsy she is, Miz Delaney. Always fallin' down..." Her voice cracked and faded.

Hattie gritted her teeth. *Tripped and fell, my foot! Deke*

Dunford beat her again.

She sat up straight on the edge of the bed. "Honey, I'm thinkin' maybe you should run for Ma Richards. This time, it looks like your mama's hurt purty bad. Ma'll know what to do better'n me."

Becky's face radiated pure terror. "Oh no, ma'am! I cain't do that. Daddy don't hold none with that ol' midwife. Says she's always meddlin' in other folks' business. I reckon Mama'll be all right. You… you can prob'ly go on home now. I shouldn't of come after you, but…It's just, I was a little scared when she wouldn't wake up. An' one time Mama said, if anything was to happen, you'd be the best one to help out." Becky hardly spoke above a whisper.

Hattie reached for the child. When Becky cringed and ducked her head, Hattie let her hand fall back in her lap.

"Becky, listen to me. However your mama hurt her head, it's bad hurt. I don't know what to do. See how black her eyes are gettin'? They wasn't that black two hours ago. She's bruisin' up on the inside of her head an' I don't know how to stop it. I need help, honey."

"Miz Delaney, I cain't go get Miz Richards. Daddy'd…I just cain't. Ain't there no one else?"

Hattie closed her eyes for a minute as a wave of nausea washed over her. She hadn't had problems this late in her pregnancies with Dulcie and Jackie, but this time, it seemed like she was sick constantly.

"Miz Delaney, you all right?"

"I'm fine, honey. Just a little dizzy. That happens sometimes." Hattie swallowed hard. "Could you just bring me a glass of water? That'll help."

Hattie lifted her heavy dark hair off the back of her neck and pressed the cold cloth to the back of her own neck for a moment. She glanced around the small room. Everything was neat as a pin. The Dunfords might be poor, but they were clean, she'd grant them that. Mamie Dunford's floors were clean enough to eat off of. There were none of the little frills that Hattie had in her own little house. No music box. No pretty little framed embroidered Bible verses hung from the walls. The only adornment was the beautiful quilt that lay folded across the bottom of the bed where Mamie Dunford lay, made by her own hand, no doubt. "Sunshine and Shadow" was the pattern. It was one of Hattie's favorites, but oh, the stitching. It was tiny and flawless.

Hattie ran her small hand across the squares. *I'm a purty good quilter, but, my land! I could never make such a pretty running stitch! She musta put hours and hours in that coverlet!*

"I fetched it cold from the well, Miz Delaney." Becky handed Hattie a tin cup. Already the heat of early June had caused condensation to bead up on the outside. Hattie took a careful sip.

"Oh! That's just what I needed. Listen, Becky. I want you to run up to Ma Richards' house and fetch her. If anybody can help your mama, she can. I'll tell your daddy it was my idea. I'll make sure he understands it was my doin' and not yours."

"Miz Delaney, please don't make me. I'm purty sure Mama's gonna be all right. I just cain't go after Miz Richards. Daddy, why he'd…" Becky gulped hard.

"He'd what, Becky?"

The little girl looked at the floor. "He…he just wouldn't like it none and he might get mad at M…Mama 'cause she went an' got herse'f hurt again. 'Sides, I can't leave, I got to go get the young'uns, an' I got to get supper goin'. If it ain't ready when he gets home…"

You'll be in for it, too. Hattie looked at the misery on the little face before her.

"Tell you what I'll do. I'll walk over to Ma's house, tell her about your mama and see if she can tell me what to do. Then I'll come back and check on her and help you get supper on."

Relief poured off the child like a vapor. "I'm much obliged, Miz Delaney."

❧

"He pert' near beat her to death, sounds like to me." Ma Richards glared out the window into the yard. "He's gonna kill her one o' these days and ain't nobody gonna know it 'til she's dead and gone."

Hattie sat on a small wooden chair at the old midwife's kitchen table. Strings of dried herbs hung from the rafters and sent a mixture of scents wafting around the room.

"I just don't know what to do, Ma. Her face is swollen, and her arms are just black where he must've jerked her around. There's a soft spot of swellin' on the back of her head. It's almost mushy. Her eyes are gettin' blacker by the minute."

"Mercy! She may not live through the night, if'n you're right about that swellin' on her head. I better go down there."

"Ma, I don't know why, but Becky Dunford's in mortal fear of you bein' there. She said her Daddy wouldn't stand for it. Cain't you just tell me what to do? I'll do exactly like you say."

Ma snorted. "If you had done like I said, you'd be at home with your feet up, not runnin' all over the county tryin' to fix everybody's troubles. You ain't in no condition to be seein' to other folks. You got your own garden to tend to! 'Sides, seein' somethin' like that in your condition could mark the baby. Don't you have no sense?"

Hattie ducked her head. "No, ma'am, not when a young'un comes to my door tellin' me her mama won't wake up, I don't. Especially when it's Mamie. You know it's just a matter of time before he..." Hattie's shoulders slumped and her eyes filled with tears. "How could he do it to her? How could he beat her like that? I just don't understand it!"

"'Course you don't, honey. I don't neither. Makes me so mad I could spit." Ma paced back and forth the length of her kitchen. "Tell you what let's do. You reckon your man'd let you bring Mamie and them young'uns down to your place? We could go get 'em and then I could see her down there and Deke Dunford wouldn't have no say."

"I...think so. We could put 'em upstairs and..."

"You ain't climbin' no stairs to wait on her. I'm tellin' you right now you ain't! You got that room up in the smokehouse where Smith stayed when he worked for you. We'll put her in there. The young'uns, we can put on pallets on the floor. It's clean. I remember it."

"I reckon that would be all right."

"Think Carrie'd come get 'em in her Ford?"

"I think so."

"Well, what are we waitin' for? Let's call her."

❧

Hattie stood at the stove in her kitchen and stirred the pot of stew she'd made to feed the crowd that had landed on her doorstep. She jumped when two strong arms wrapped around her, then relaxed against the familiar body pressed against her back. She tipped her head back to look up at her husband's face.

Smith Delaney's blue eyes twinkled. "Honey, there's a buncha long-faced young'uns out there on the smokehouse porch that don't look like they belong to us."

Hattie smiled. "They're the Dunford kids. Mamie's up in the smokehouse."

Smith's smile softened. "Guess that explains why none of 'em called me 'Daddy.' You savin' the world again, Hattie?"

"Just my little corner of it."

Hattie explained how Becky Dunford had come to the door that morning begging for help and how she'd gone to the house and found Mamie. By the time she finished, Smith's face was grim.

"I couldn't just leave her there, Smith. I had to bring 'em down here."

"You did the right thing. Only thing is, sooner or later Deke's gonna come lookin' for 'em." Smith's face hardened. "I'll deal with him when he shows hisself."

Hattie fisted her left hand on her hip and shook the ladle

she held in her right hand.

"You'll do no such a thing. You gave up your fist fightin' and wild ways and you're not goin' back to 'em now! If there's any dealin' to be done with Deke Dunford, I'll do it myself."

Smith threw up both hands in mock surrender and backed up a step or two. "Honey, he don't know it yet, but somehow I think ol' Deke's met his match."

❧

Hattie shifted her weight carefully as she clambered up onto the smokehouse porch, carrying the covered tray of food she'd brought for Ma Richards. Mamie's children stood watching silently as she crossed the porch. Reaching the wooden door, she balanced the tray against her hip and softly pushed the door open, then closed it behind her.

"How's she doin'?" Hattie asked quietly.

"She ain't doin' good," Ma answered, her face grim in the darkened room. "She ain't doin' good at all. You was right about the soft spot on the back of her head. He whupped her bad this time."

Hattie looked at Mamie's still face. Her eyes were circled with black bruises. Her left cheek was swollen and discolored. Hattie shook her head. "Ma, you reckon this coulda been an accident—any way this coulda happened without Deke doin' it?"

"Land sakes, Hattie! Open your eyes an' look at her."

"I know, Ma. I guess I was just hopin'. It don't seem possible a man could beat the woman he loves like that! It just don't seem possible!"

Hattie set the tray on the small table next to the bed.

Ma Richards rose stiffly from the straight-backed chair where she sat vigil beside Mamie. "Looka here, girl." Ma raised the loose sleeves on Mamie's nightgown, exposing her upper arms. "Look here at the those bruises. Those are handprints. He grabbed ahold of her and slung her around like a sack of flour, then he bashed her head against the wall or the floor. That's why the back of her head's like that. I b'lieve he busted her skull. She's hurt bad, Hattie."

"Is she gonna…" Hattie paused, swallowed hard and continued. "Will she live?"

"I wish I knew. I just ain't certain yet."

❧

"Well?" Becky Dunford blocked Hattie's path as she left the smokehouse. "Is she awake yet? When we goin' home, Miz Delaney?"

Porter Dunford stood behind Becky, his eyes wary. Dorie and little Mary Claire silently watched the interchange between Becky and Hattie.

Hattie sighed and started to put her arm around the child, then let her arm drop to her side when Becky twisted away. Hattie leaned against one of the uprights holding up the porch roof. "Becky, you and your brother and sisters are gonna have to stay here awhile. It looks like it could be some time before your mama's ready to go home."

Becky's eyes flickered with something like fear, then quickly hooded. "No, ma'am, I got to get these young'uns on home. I'm much obliged to you for takin' care of mama. I'll just take these kids an' go on."

Hattie reached out and cupped Becky's chin before the child could duck away. "Becky, y'all are stayin' here. Now, I've made a good supper for us and we're gonna eat it together. Then I'm gonna put you to bed. Tomorrow we'll decide what else we're goin' to do, but for right now, you, Porter, Mary Claire and Dorie are stayin' put with us. Do you understand?" Hattie said gently but firmly.

Becky shuddered under Hattie's hand, and drew back. This time her fear was obvious. "Yes, ma'am," she whispered.

The other three children backed away as Hattie stepped down off the porch.

Porter's hands fisted as he followed Hattie and the little girls into the house. He paused at the back door.

Smith folded the newspaper he was reading and smiled at the band of children as they took the one step down from the porch into the kitchen. "Come on in." He stood and limped toward them and extended his hand to Porter.

Porter looked at Smith's hand for a long second, then reached out and shook it.

"Digger, how you been?" Smith asked, calling the boy by his nickname.

"Tolerable, I reckon," answered the boy.

"You been takin' care of your sisters?"

"Tryin' to, but they're a handful, Mr. Delaney." Digger sounded like a small adult.

Smith laughed. "I 'magine keepin' up with 'em can be a trial, but they look like good girls to me."

"Most the time, Mr. Delaney." Digger's face was expressionless, his eyes darting around the neat kitchen.

"Hattie, you ready to feed this bunch?" Smith asked.

"Just about. Let's get 'em washed up while I set the table, then we'll be ready. While I show 'em the bucket, will you call Dulcie and get Jackie for me?"

Smith disappeared into the front room and came back with Hattie's children, six-year-old Dulcie and two-year-old Jackie. Jackie wrapped his arms around Smith's legs and hid behind him when he saw the children.

Dulcie skipped into the kitchen and hugged Hattie. "I'm hungry, Mama."

Hattie smiled down at the little girl and reached to hug her back. "Get washed up and we'll eat. You show Dorie how we do it here, all right?"

"Okay, Mama. Hi Dorie."

Dorie was as fair as Dulcie was dark. Blue eyes shone from her round face. "Hi Dulcie."

Dulcie led the little girl to the washpan and the bucket of clean water that sat on the white enamel table and soon little girl giggles were floating like the soap bubbles they made in the washpan.

Becky shushed her sister with a quick look over her shoulder at the adults. She took Mary Claire by the hand and took her to the other end of the kitchen by the back door. She moved as far from Smith as she could get and still stay in the same room. She gestured to Digger with her head to get Dorie and move out of Smith's way. Digger grabbed the little girl by the arm and yanked her toward the door. "C'mon! Get over there." He shoved the little girl down on the step.

"Don't you move," he said, shaking his finger in her face.

"Whoa, Digger." Smith walked toward the children. The three girls recoiled. Digger clenched his fists.

Smith stopped in his tracks. He looked at Hattie, then back at the children, "Uh, we don't mind a little laughin' around here, son." He smiled. "In fact, we sort of plan on it most days. Little girls are s'posed to giggle. That's their job."

"Beggin' your pardon, Mr. Delaney, but you got to stay on top of these girls. My daddy says that if'n you don't take a firm hand they'll even be thinkin' they got the right to vote."

Digger lifted his chin and looked Smith right in the eye. "I ain't tellin' you your bizness, but that's the way womenfolk is—born into sin. They get real prideful if'n you don't keep a firm hand."

Hattie covered her mouth and coughed to cover the soft gasp that tried to erupt.

Smith picked up Jackie and said, "Son, women already have the right to vote. It's a constitutional right, given to 'em by the United States government."

"No, sir," Digger said. "My daddy says womenfolk ain't got no legal rights, exceptin' the right to obey their husbands. Oh, they's some that think they do, but they don't know no better. They're gettin' above themselves. No, sir. It'll be a cold day in— "

"Digger! Would you like to help me with the table?" Hattie interrupted, her face beet-red.

"Becky, get over there and grab them beans," commanded Digger. "Dorie, you get the biscuits. Mary Claire, sit up there on that chair and don't talk 'less'n your spoke to."

Somehow, Hattie and Smith got through the meal with six silent children. After the prayer, even her own children didn't make a peep as the food was passed and eaten. Smith tried to start a conversation with Becky, but she refused to meet his eyes. Her only response was a shrug. Finally they gave up and finished the meal in silence.

As soon as the last bite was eaten, Digger ordered Becky, Dorie, and Mary Claire to clear the table. It was done quickly and quietly until Mary Claire dropped a saucer. It shattered the silence. The four Dunford children froze in place, staring at the pieces of broken china. Mary Claire's eyes darted from the saucer to Smith to Becky and back to Smith again.

Digger was the first to move. He grabbed the three-year-old by the arm and shoved her toward Smith. "Well, go on. You broke it, you gotta take what's comin' to you. You know the rules. Go ahead, Mr. Delaney. She knows she done it. Do what you need to do."

Mary Claire gulped hard, terror written all over her small, round face.

Smith glanced at Hattie, then crouched down in front of Mary Claire. "Honey, did you drop that saucer on purpose?"

"N...no, sir," she whispered.

"Come here, Mary Claire," Smith coaxed.

The little girl slowly moved a step closer to Smith. He reached out and pulled her to him. "It was an accident, Mary Claire. Accidents happen. It's all right."

Mary Claire's body shuddered against him. He hugged her tighter. "It's all right."

Becky, Dorie and Digger stood against the back wall of the kitchen. The looks on their faces were a mixture of relief and confusion.

Digger spoke up. "You better tell her to hush that snivelin'.

She ain't allowed to snivel."

Hattie reached for Digger, but he jerked away. Once again Hattie let her arm drop to her side. It was going to be a long night.

❧

As Hattie got ready for bed that night, she prayed for Mamie Dunford and her children. *Lord, these young'uns are scared to death. Help us to find a way to show 'em that touch doesn't have to hurt.*

She ain't allowed to suffer."

Hattie reached for Dinah, but he jerked away. Once again [illegible] her attention to [illegible] it was going to be a long night.

As Hattie got ready for bed that night, she prayed for Mamie, Paul and her children, [illegible]

2

Under a blanket of stars and a pale moon, Hattie walked up the rise to the smokehouse. Ma Richards nodded at her from the chair beside the bed as Hattie slipped into the small room.

"What are you doin' up here this time of the night?" Ma asked.

"I couldn't sleep. How's she doin'?"

The old woman shook her head sadly. "She ain't. Come daylight, you better send your man for Doc Wilson. I don't b'lieve there's much he can do for her, but it might set folks' minds at ease knowin' we done everything we could."

"You mean she's gonna die?" Hattie's eyes filled with tears.

"Yes, child. She's gonna die."

Ma reached out and took one of Hattie's hands. "Hattie, I cain't save her. The only one who could is the Lord, and I b'lieve He's callin' her home. Ain't no sense in healin' her so Deke can kill her another day."

Hattie raised Ma's hand to her cheek and kissed the soft papery skin. "You sure have seen your share of heartache, haven't you?"

Ma smiled softly. "Yes, ma'am. I've seen more'n most, I reckon. I've watched a lot of good folks die—like your mama and daddy. And bad ones, too. But I've seen more joy than sorrow over the years. That's what I hold onto, honey. Not the hurtin'."

"How do you do it, Ma? How do you watch 'em die and not let a little bit of you die with 'em?"

Ma knew Hattie was thinking of her first husband, Jack Crowe. His death after a mine accident had crushed Hattie.

"Well, I reckon a little of *me* does go with 'em. But you

know, I think more of *them* goes on with me. As long as I got memory to recollect 'em by, they ain't really gone, now are they?"

"I... I guess not," Hattie answered slowly.

"Look here, you an' Carrie and Eldon and the rest of the Stoneworth clan all got the memories of your mama and daddy to pass on to your young'uns. They all gonna know what a fine family they come from, 'cause you remember, and 'cause you're livin' out the things they taught you. Right?"

"Yes, ma'am."

"Well then, that's what I'm sayin'. As long as there's a Stoneworth, or a body that remembers a Stoneworth, they'll keep right on bein' here with us. Right here."

Hattie smiled. "I like that, Ma. Thinkin' about how the family will go on passing the stories down from generation to generation, like in the Bible."

Ma Richards grinned her gummy smile. "Honey, y'all ain't exactly the Old Testament prophets, but with all the begetting your mama done, them stories should go on a good long while. I don't think there's too much danger of your side of family bein' forgot any time soon. Shoot, y'all are spread all over Muhlenberg County."

"And if you count Berk and Nan bein' up in Louisville, we're beginnin' to spread over the state of Kentucky," added Hattie.

"You go on back to bed now, girl. I don't like the circles under your eyes, nor the swellin' in your ankles, neither." Always the midwife, Ma Richards looked Hattie up and down. "You still feelin' poorly of a mornin'?"

"Of a mornin' and afternoon and nighttime, too. It just don't seem to quit," Hattie admitted.

"When did we decide your baby was comin'?"

"You said you figured around the middle of September."

"An' you're still feelin' poorly. Hmmm... mebbe I got some tea that'll ease you a mite. I'll check my bag in the mornin'. Go on now, go to bed."

The old woman stood up from the chair and flapped her apron at Hattie as she shooed her toward the door.

Hattie turned back one last time to look at Mamie's still face. "I'll tell Smith what you said about goin' after the doctor."

"Hattie, tell him to bring the sheriff, too."

❧

Doc Wilson ran practiced hands lightly up Mamie's face and around the back of her head, pausing to gently press the mass at the back of her skull. He lifted her eyelids and peered into the lifeless blue eyes. Then he moved down to press his hands over Mamie's chest, stopping to probe her ribs. Finally, he backed away and turned to face the small group of observers who waited for his judgment.

"Fractured skull, orbital fractures around her left eye, three broken ribs that I'm sure of, maybe more. She's in a coma. It's just a matter of time."

"Do you want me to help you move her into my car for the ride to the hospital?" Sheriff Westerfield asked.

The doctor ran a hand over his face and glanced back at Mamie. "No, I don't see any point in moving her. She's not in any pain—and I don't know but that any move might…"

Hattie's hands flew to her mouth. "Did bringing her here hurt her? Make her worse?"

"No, Hattie. I don't think so. From what Ma Richards told me, it wouldn't have made any difference. At least here, there's folks watching after her."

"Isn't there any hope? I mean, couldn't she…?" Hattie asked.

"Hattie, look here. You too, Ma Richards, Sheriff." The doctor leaned over Mamie again and pulled her nightgown smooth against her abdomen. "See how she's breathing?"

Mamie's stomach sucked back deep under her ribs and then released. "That's called 'agonal breathing' in the textbooks. It's a sign that her body is failing."

"But why is she havin' trouble breathin', if it's her head

that's hurt?" the sheriff asked.

"I don't know all the ins and outs of the brain, Sheriff. I'm a country doctor, not a neurologist. All I know is, there's a part of the brain that controls when to breathe and when not to breathe. Looks to me like the bleeding in her head is putting pressure on that part of her brain. Her eyes don't react to light, so she's got swelling in there somewhere."

The doctor picked up his bag and walked to the door. Ma Richards went to Mamie's side and drew the quilt up over her, reaching down to smooth Mamie's fair hair back from her battered face.

"I'll stay with her, Doc. Much obliged for you comin'," she said.

Hattie accompanied Sheriff Westerfield and the doctor out to the waiting car.

"The children..."

"I'll take em' to the county home," the sheriff interrupted.

"No!—I mean, can't they stay with us until...well, until..." Hattie paused.

Smith limped out of the house and joined the three solemn-faced people standing at the car. Seeing Hattie's stricken face he put an arm around her. "Leave 'em here, Sheriff. We got room. And they know us."

The sheriff hesitated, then nodded his assent.

Smith reached out his hand to shake with the sheriff and the doctor. "You goin' after Deke now, Sheriff?"

"Cain't do that Smith. I don't have enough to go on," he answered. "I know we got a badly hurt woman up there, but I don't have any witnesses that Deke did it."

Smith clenched his jaw and snarled, "What do you mean you don't have any witnesses? You saw her!"

"I mean that the young'un's said their mama fell. I can't arrest a man for his wife fallin' down." The sheriff looked shamefaced at his feet. "I don't like it no more than you do."

The nausea that Hattie had been fighting all morning finally reached the boiling point. She clapped a hand over her mouth and hurried toward the outhouse.

Smith looked after her.

Doc Wilson climbed into the passenger seat of the police car and leaned out the window. "You better see to your wife, Smith. She's not well."

The sheriff walked to the other side of the car and opened the door.

"Listen, Delaney. I know he done it. You know he done it. I cain't prove it. That's all there is to it. I'm sorry."

❧

Smith walked up the road toward town. Dulcie and Dorie hung onto his hands. They were going to Radburn's store to buy a sack of flour and a tin of baking soda. Hattie had counted out the coins from her purse and handed them to Smith before he left the house. The little girls skipped along beside him, chattering like magpies.

"I'm gonna be a princess when I grow up," said Dulcie.

"I'm gonna be a princess, too," said Dorie.

"Daddy, can Dorie be a princess, if I'm a princess?" asked Dulcie.

Both little faces looked up expectantly for Smith to declare their future. "Well, now, lessee. I reckon there's enough room in the world for two princesses," he answered.

"Did you ever go to the movin' picture show?" Dulcie asked her friend.

"No! My daddy says they're powerful wicked! We don't have no truck at all with the movin' pictures," Dorie answered.

"Wicked? I don't think they's wicked. Do you, Daddy?" Dulcie asked.

"Hmmm. I guess it depends on what movin' picture you are goin' to see. Your mama and I would never take you to a show that wasn't fit for your eyes."

"My daddy says if'n you go to one, you might as well go to all of 'em—might as well play with gamblin' cards an' drink hard liquor and go to dances, too." Dorie said.

Smith chewed on his lower lip in an effort to keep from laughing out loud. "Well, now, I don't know that I agree with your daddy, but I guess everyone's got their own opinion."

The bell over the door tinkled as they walked into the store.

"Miz Annie, I'm here!" Dulcie called to the woman behind the counter.

"Well, honey, I guess you are. Come here to me and hug my neck!" Annie Radburn smiled and came around from behind the counter and opened her arms to Dulcie.

"How you doin', sugar?"

"I'm fine. I brung Dorie with me, an' Daddy."

"I see that. Mr. Radburn, come out here and just see who come in the store today!" Annie called to her husband.

Harwell Radburn looked around the corner from their living quarters. His eyes twinkled when he saw the little girls. "Well, who are these lovely young ladies darkenin' our door, Annie?"

"You know me, Mr. Radburn, I'm Dulcie Crowe!"

"No, you ain't. Dulcie Crowe's just a little girl. Here you are comin' in here all grown up, an' with company to boot."

"That there is Dorie. You know her, Mr. Radburn." Dulcie giggled.

Dorie hung back behind Smith. This kind of exchange was new to her. She'd never gone anywhere alone with her daddy. And going to the store with her mama was a quiet affair. She would never have been allowed to banter with an adult the way Dulcie was.

Dulcie ran back and grabbed Dorie's hand and pulled her forward. "See, you know Dorie. We go to Sunday school together. Remember?"

Harwell Radburn rubbed his chin and contemplated the girls. "Well, lemme see, now." Suddenly he slapped his knee and laughed. "Yes, that's right. I know you both. Just can't get over how much you've grown since last Sunday!"

Both girls giggled this time. It was only Wednesday.

"Annie, I'm gonna get these girls a penny candy." Harwell lifted both little girls up onto the stools that sat before the long wooden counter and pointed at the candy jars.

"What kind do you want today, girls?"

While the girls carefully made their selections, Annie Radburn took Smith by the arm and led him to the table set at the back of the store. "All right, cousin, tell me about Mamie."

Smith sat down with Annie and, keeping his voice low, told her what the doctor had said that morning. "It's only a matter of time."

"Aw, that's a cryin' shame! I just don't ken how a body could hurt that sweet Mamie." Annie twisted her apron between her hands and glanced over at the girls.

"What's gonna happen to the children?" she asked. "Has Deke been down to see 'em?"

"No, and he better not be comin' to the house any time soon. I ain't feelin' real kindly toward Deke Dunford right now."

"But, Smith, he's their daddy! Sooner or later he's gonna come get 'em."

"Best be later, than sooner," Smith growled under his breath.

"Smith, don't you be talkin' that way," Annie whispered. "Hattie'd have your head. 'Sides, you already been tried for murder once. I don't think we can live through another trial."

The year Hattie and Smith got married, he'd been framed for the murder of two mine foremen. He was found innocent, but it had been a horrible time for them all.

"I ain't plannin' on doin' nothin'. But I tell you, Annie, it sure sticks in my craw to let that man walk around, knowin' he killed his wife."

"Shhhhh! She ain't dead yet. You never know what could happen. She might..."

Smith interrupted. "No, Annie. Doc Wilson said she's dyin'. Ma Richards, too."

"You mean to tell me there ain't no hope at all?" Annie was shocked.

"That's what they're sayin.'

"Oh, those poor little young'uns. What's gonna happen to 'em?"

"I think Hattie's plannin' on keepin' 'em." Smith smiled at the thought of his sweet little Hattie. "You know how partial she is to children."

The bell over the door rang and Annie got up to wait on a customer. Smith watched the little girls sitting at the counter. Dark-eyed Dulcie was playing hostess to blue-eyed Dorie as if she owned the store. Dorie had relaxed under the kind attention of Harwell Radburn. She giggled at something he said. Both little girls swung their bare feet from the stools. *They're like little bookends,* Smith thought. *One light and one dark. Both of 'em purty as pups!* He smiled at their antics.

Annie finished with her customer and came back to sit with Smith. She followed his gaze to the little girls and smiled with him.

"They're awful sweet, Smith. It fair breaks my heart to think of them young'uns."

"Me too, Annie."

"Won't the sheriff make y'all give 'em back to Deke?"

Smith grinned. "You wanna take bets over who'd win, with Hattie fightin' for 'em?"

Annie whooped with laughter. "Smith, don't you let her hear you talkin' 'bout takin' no bets. I'd lay odds you'd find yourse'f in the woodshed."

"Might be worth it, Annie," he replied.

3

Digger Dunford slumped against the outside wall of the smokehouse, his skinny arms curled around his knees, one cheek resting on his arms. Inside, Hattie, Smith, and Ma Richards stood around his mother's bed.

Earlier that day, just as the sun was going down, Hattie had called all the Dunford children together and told them their mother was dying—that she probably would not live through the night. Dorie and Mary Claire had cried. Even his big sister Becky had cried. He didn't cry. He'd stood there, jaw set, chin held high.

Now he muttered to himself, "I ain't gonna cry for you, Mama. I ain't like them pitiful girls. I ain't cryin' for you."

Without raising his head, he reached one hand down to the hole in the right knee of his worn overalls, pulling one scraggly thread, then another, like a love-struck teenage girl plucking petals from a daisy.

Each thread brought a new murmured statement. "What'd you have to go an' do it for, Mama?" He yanked a thread. "It's your own stupid fault for trying to get away from him." Another thread. "You shoulda just stood there and taken what was coming to you."

He wrapped a long thread around his finger and toyed with it for a moment, then pulled. The hole around the knee grew larger. "It never would have got so bad if you'da just..."

Letting his hand drop from the now-tattered hole, he kicked his curled knees out straight, and threw his head back against the wooden wall. He whispered into the night sky, "Why'd you have to go and run, anyway? You shoulda took it like a man. It woulda been over quick that way. You shoulda just took it!" He knuckled white-hot tears from his eyes. "I ain't cryin' for you, Mama! You hear me?"

Digger Dunford scrambled to his feet, leaped from the smokehouse porch, and disappeared into the dark orchard behind the house.

❧

In the gloomy light of the lantern, Ma Richards leaned closer to Mamie, listening to the irregular, labored breathing. "Won't be long now. She's failin'."

Hattie reached up and took Smith's hand. He squeezed his fingers gently around hers. Together they watched as Mamie took one last tortured breath. Her chest rose, fell, then stilled.

In the ensuing silence, Hattie turned her face to Smith's chest and wept. She wept for her friend, for her friend's children, and for the senselessness of it all. Smith pressed his cheek against her dark hair and held her until the storm passed.

It was Ma's wrinkled, aged hands that pulled the quilt up over Mamie's face. She paused a moment, eyes closed. Then she looked over her shoulder at Hattie. "Send for the preacher. I'll prepare the body."

"No, Ma," answered Hattie. "You've done enough. I'll take care of her. You should sleep. You've been up with her for three days. Let me take you to the house."

Ma straightened up from bending over the bed. She pushed a loose strand of steel-gray hair back into the tight bun she wore on top of her head.

"I brung her into the world twenty-seven years ago. I'll see her out." She turned from the bed and sat back down in the straight-backed chair. "I know you must be pert' near wore out by now, Hattie, but I'll need clean water and soap, soft cloths, and reckon come daylight we'll have to send to the house for a dress for the buryin'."

"Ma..." Hattie began.

"Smith, if'n she won't he'p me, you'll have to," the old

woman snapped.

"'Course she'll help you, Ma. It's just that you've hardly left this room since you got here. Please let us do for Mamie. We weren't much help while she was livin'. Least we can do..."

"Guess I'll get the water m'self." Ma pushed herself up from the chair and would have headed out to the well had Smith not laid a hand on her arm.

"I'll get it, ma'am. I'll do it." Smith went into the dark night. Hattie followed to find the other items Ma Richards had asked for.

When they were gone, Ma walked to the door. She latched it with shaking fingers, then leaned her forehead against the rough wood and sobbed.

❧

Smith left for town shortly after the sun came up. Hattie had given him a list of instructions: report the death; go by her sister Carrie's house to ask for help with the funeral; call preacher Fenton; don't go after Deke Dunford.

Smith smiled grimly to himself at the thought of his little wife, round with the baby that was coming, tapping her foot, shaking her finger, a warning in her look when she added that last item to the list.

He'd already been to the sheriff's office. Sheriff Westerfield had shaken his head at the news and promised to keep looking for Deke. He'd also been stern in his warning to Smith not to go seeking out the man who was responsible for Mamie's death. He'd reminded Smith there wasn't enough evidence to prove Deke had killed her.

Now Smith drove the blacktop road back from Greenville toward Drakesboro; past Pond Creek, past the rise in the road where the murders he'd been accused of committing had taken place, past Ebenezer Baptist Church. He knew every bend in this road—had been down it a thousand times.

He sat straight in the cab of his old truck, his left arm resting on the window frame. That arm was browner than the other from the many times it had rested right there, out the truck window into the heat of the Kentucky sun.

At the edge of Drakesboro sat the neat, white house of Hattie's oldest sister, Carrie, and her husband, Gene Beckwith. Carrie and Gene had raised Hattie, her sister Lalie, and brother, Berk, in that house after their parents died when Hattie was ten years old.

Carrie stood on the front porch shaking a small rug over the railing into the yard. At the sound of the truck, she raised a hand to shade her eyes from the bright morning sun. Seeing Smith emerge from his truck, she called a hello.

"Well, look what the cat dragged in," she laughed. "How's Mamie?"

Mounting the steps to the porch, Smith pulled his cap off his head and stood with it between his hands. "She died about four o'clock this mornin'. Real quiet. She just stopped breathin'," he said.

Carrie's shoulders slumped. "Oh, Smith. You better come on in." She pulled the wood-framed screen door open and led Smith into the neat kitchen. "Sit down and tell me. How're the kids takin' it?"

Smith pulled out one of the wooden chairs and sat down at the table while Carrie took two heavy china cups from the cupboard above the sink and poured coffee for them both from the gray-blue speckle-wear pot on the stove.

"The little girls are confused. The oldest one's tryin' to mother-hen 'em, and the boy… well, I think the boy's just plain angry."

Smith nodded a thank-you for the cup of coffee Carrie placed on the table before him.

Carrie sat down across from him and looked into her cup. "What can I do to help?"

"Would you call the preacher? Hattie said he'd better hear about it as soon as possible. I could run over there, but I'm thinkin' I ought not be away too long. Deke still ain't showed his face. I don't want to be away from the house when he finally does."

Carrie's plump face settled into hard lines at the mention of Deke's name. "Yes, you better get on home. I'll take care of the preacher, then come on down to the house. Do y'all need anything?"

Smith shook his head. "Don't think so. We're fine. Oh, Ma Richards said somethin' about Mamie needin' a dress for the buryin'. I'm warned off goin' to Dunford's house, so maybe you could stop there on the way to our place?"

He took a sip of the hot coffee. "If you go, though, don't go alone," he added.

"No, I won't. I'll stop and get Willa. She'll go with me," Carrie said over the rim of her cup.

"You might ought to take one of the men, Carrie. I don't like the idea of you sisters goin' without a man with you."

Carrie gave a short, humorless laugh. "Deke Dunford ain't gonna mess with us, Smith. You know how he is, always tryin' to impress folks with how wonderful he is. He'll be too busy oozin' oil and playin' the grievin' husband."

Smith thought about that for a moment, then replied, "You may be right, Carrie, but unless Sheriff Westerfield's already found him, he don't know he's a grievin' husband. He may be settin' down there getting' madder by the minute, thinkin' his wife and young'uns have run off on him."

Smith shook his head. "No, you better take Gene, or your brother, Forrest."

Carrie had been the one to go with Ma Richards and Hattie to get Mamie and drive her to Hattie's house when Ma Richards called. She had seen the black eyes and swollen face. She'd helped lift Mamie's limp body into the back seat of her car. She shivered, then agreed. "All right. I'll find one of the boys."

They talked for a few more minutes, then Smith stood up to leave. "Thanks for the coffee. I'm sorry to be burdenin' you like this."

Carrie smiled softly and slipped her hand through his arm, walking him to the door. "Honey, that's what we do when we're family," she replied. "That's what we do."

❧

Dulcie Crowe sat between Dorie and Mary Claire Dunford on the porch swing that hung from the roof of the side porch. They kicked their legs to make it move gently back and forth. Little Jackie played in the dirt next to them. He piled up small rocks, knocked them down, and piled them up again.

Dorie glanced at the two-year-old and said, "That's why we call my brother 'Digger.' 'Cause he was always diggin' in the dirt when he was little. My mama says he got up of a mornin', headed outside, and played 'til she called him in at night. Had to drag him out of the dirt to make him come in."

Dulcie looked at her little dark-headed brother and laughed. "I s'pose we could call Jackie that, too."

Dorie's eyes grew big. "You cain't call Jackie 'Digger.' There's only one Digger, an' he's ours," she said.

Jackie moved one of the rocks, pushing it through the dirt, making "errrrr errrrr" noises, like a truck shifting gears.

"Guess you're right. We could call him "Errrrr Errrrr" instead," Dulcie said.

All three little girls laughed.

They watched the toddler for a moment, then Dorie rested her head against the high back of the swing. "You reckon it hurt my mama to die?"

Dulcie's face scrunched up as she appeared to think about the question. "I don't think so. My first daddy died. Mama said he just went to sleep, real easy-like. An' he didn't wake up any more. She said your mama did the same thing."

"So you don't think it hurt her none?"

Dulcie shook her head slowly. "If she went all quiet-like, I don't think it coulda hurt. I reckon she'd have been hollerin' otherwise."

Dorie wadded up the skirt of her dress, then smoothed it

out with her hands. "We can ask her when she comes back," said the six-year-old.

Digger walked out from where he'd been listening behind the screened porch. "Dumb baby!" he shouted. "She ain't comin' back, you dummy! She's dead! Dumb! Dumb! Dumb!"

"Whoa now." Smith pushed open the screen door from the kitchen. "What's all this? Who's dumb?" He looked from the girls to Digger.

Digger stood red-faced at the edge of the side porch. He kicked at the grass growing around the edge of the fieldstones. "Dumb girls," he muttered.

Dulcie hopped off of the swing and took Smith's hand, pulling him forward.

"Dorie said when her mama comes back, she's gonna ask her if it hurt to die," she explained. "Then Digger got all mad an' started callin' her names."

"Oh, I see." Smith rubbed his chin. "Well now, first off, we don't call names at our house—even when we think we're in the right," he directed to Digger. "It hurts a person's feelin's. That's not the way we treat each other."

"So?" Digger muttered, "She's just a dumb girl—thinkin' Mama's just gonna waltz back in here. That's just dumb!"

Smith fumbled for the right thing to say. "She's little, Digger. She don't have your knowledge of the world yet. By the time she's nine like you, she'll understand more. 'Til then, you got to be patient with her. Maybe try teachin' her the things you know. You understand?"

The look on Digger's face clearly said he didn't understand, but he gave an automatic 'yessir' in the face of Smith's male authority. He turned and walked away, shoulders curled up around his ears, hands jammed deep in his pockets.

Smith sat down between the Dunford girls and pulled Dulcie up on his lap. He turned to the middle Dunford girl. "You'd like your mama to come back, huh, Dorie?"

Dorie nodded her head.

"That would be fine, wouldn't it?"

Another nod.

"But you know, once a person dies, they're gone. They ain't comin' back—you know that—don't you?"

This time a sniffle accompanied the nod. Dorie looked at Smith's face, tears slipping from her blue eyes.

"It's hard losin' someone you love," Smith said.

"I want my mama!" Dorie wailed.

Hattie flew through the kitchen door and scooped the sobbing child into her arms. Mary Claire, crying now, too, leaned against Smith.

Becky Dunford watched it all from the door of the kitchen where she and Hattie had been making lunch and listening to the conversation outside. Silent tears ran down her cheeks.

Hattie glanced up and saw her. She opened one arm from around Dorie and held it out to Becky. Becky banged out the door and ran into Hattie's embrace. They stood together, rocking and crying while Hattie murmured gently to them. Smith wrapped one arm around Mary Claire and pulled her to his chest. He rested his chin on her blond curls. Dulcie reached down from her perch on his lap and gently patted Mary Claire's back.

Jackie pushed a rock. "Errrrr errrrr," he said.

❧

Far behind the house, Digger heard Dorie's cry for their mother. He turned and took a hesitant step toward the agonizing sound of his little sister's grief. He could see them below; Becky and Dorie in Hattie's arms, Smith Delaney rocking and holding Mary Claire. A dull ache, starting in his belly and rising to his throat, choked him until he almost couldn't breathe.

He turned his back and walked on.

4

Hattie said, "And Jonah knew he had to preach to the people of Nineveh. Since God gave him a second chance, Jonah had to give them one, too."

Hattie sat on the edge of the bed where Dorie and Dulcie were tucked together upstairs under the eaves. Becky and Mary Claire were in a bed set under the opposite side of the sloping roof, and Digger lay on a pallet on the floor at the end of the room. All five of the children had listened with rapt attention while Hattie told the story of Jonah and his disobedience. How he'd run from God and been swallowed by the great fish; how he'd been spewed out on dry land and gone on to Nineveh, but pouted when the people repented. He didn't want them to straighten up. Instead, Jonah wanted God to rain down His wrath and destroy the city. And he wanted to watch."

Across from Hattie, Smith sat on the bed with Becky and Mary Claire.

"God didn't like the fact that Jonah was so set in his ways," said Smith. "He had to teach him who was really in charge before Jonah would change. When Jonah repented, God forgave him. Just like He forgives us today."

"Mr. Delaney?" asked Dorie, knuckling a sleepy eye.

"Yes, Dorie," he answered.

"Do... do you think God forgives *every*one?"

Smith seemed to think about that for a moment, then said, "He forgives everyone who's really sorry—and is willin' to let God be in charge. He can't forgive those who ain't sorry and ain't willing to try to mind Him, now can He?"

"He could if He wanted to..." came the quiet answer.

Hattie said, "God made rules for His people to live by. He gives us the opportunity to choose whether we'll do things the right way or the wrong way. When we make poor choices we can come back to Him and ask for His forgiveness. Just like when Dulcie is naughty…"

"Mamaaaaa!" Dulcie cried.

Hattie smiled at her outraged daughter. "When *we* are naughty, or even just thoughtless, we need to go to the person we've wronged and ask their forgiveness. It makes them feel better about what happened, and it also makes us feel better. We can go to bed at night and not have those bad thoughts bothering our consciences."

'What's a con…conscience?" asked Dorie.

"It's that little voice in your heart that tells you when you are doin' something you shouldn't," Hattie answered. "When you get angry with your sisters, or Digger, and say mean things, don't you feel bad about it?"

"Most of the time," agreed Dorie, "less'n they was mean to me first. Sometimes, they's mean to me an' Mary Claire, just 'cause we're the littlest."

Hattie nodded solemnly. "I know how you feel then, 'cause I'm the littlest one of all my brothers and sisters. They even call me 'Least'un' to remind me I'm the smallest. But instead of just one big brother and sister—like you have—I have eight of 'em! Five sisters and three brothers. They pick on me all the time."

"They do, Miz Delaney?" asked Dorie.

"They sure do. But I don't mind 'cause I know they love me, and I love them. And because we're family and we love each other, I know they'd never really do anything that would hurt me."

Digger rolled over and faced the wall.

Smith cleared his throat. "Let's get back to God and forgiveness. When we do something wrong, the right thing to do is seek God's forgiveness. Because Jesus died for our sins,

God will forgive us every time. It's just like it never happened." Smith stood up. "Bedtime. Y'all say your prayers."

Hattie bent over to kiss the little girls beside her and then stepped across to the other bed and kissed the older two. "Sweet dreams," she said as she smoothed Mary Claire's hair back off the child's forehead.

She knelt beside Digger and patted his back, then stood. Smith took her hand and led her down the steep steps and out the kitchen door to the porch swing. He sat and pulled her down next to him.

"Now, don't you go frettin' about sayin' that about families lovin' and not hurtin' each other. They need to hear that what they came from ain't normal."

Hattie rested her head against Smith's shoulder. "I know that, but did you see Digger's face before he rolled over? I could have bitten my tongue in half!"

"I could tell." Smith lifted Hattie's chin and spoke to her softly. "Honey, you can't solve all their problems in one night. You hear me? It's gonna take time."

"I hear you, Smith." Hattie pushed up from the swing.

"Come back here, you. I'm not finished with you yet," Smith said with a tease in his voice.

"Yes, you are. There's too much to do before tomorrow. I need to put the ham in to soak, and the beans. I need to press the tablecloth, your good white shirt and those pitiful clothes Carrie brought down for the children when she brought Mamie's dress."

Hattie turned back to Smith and whispered angrily, "It makes me so mad I could spit. Did you see those dresses and the shirt and pants for Digger? They're not much more'n rags. Oh, Mamie patched 'em neat as a pin and they're clean, but..."

Smith furrowed his brow. "Hattie, we all have to make do. You mend our kids' clothes, too. Not too many folks can afford to buy new, when you can fix what you already have. And the Dunford kids always looked just fine."

Hattie blinked at him in the dim light. "'Course they did. It's just...I know that suit Deke wears to church on Sundays cost every bit of fifteen dollars! In fact, I'm sure it was one of those I saw that Cohen's advertised in the *Greenville Leader*—'Worsted Wool—Latest Style—$14.95.' Can you imagine?—while his wife and children go around in patched clothes!"

Smith stood to open the door for Hattie. "Honey, he didn't respect his wife enough not to beat her. Did you really expect anything different?"

Hattie looked at her hands. "No, I guess not. But look at this."

She picked up a small dress and turned it inside out, exposing a neatly mended tear. "Mamie was such a wonder with a needle. I never would have guessed if I hadn't looked at it up close." She flipped the dress over and pointed. "See how Mamie made tiny little pin tucks all across the bodice to cover it up? It doesn't show at all."

Hattie laid the dress aside and picked up the next one on the pile. "And Dorie's dress has these deep flounces in the skirt where her mama must have spent hours hemming it in rows so it would be short enough for her. It has to be a hand-me-down from Becky."

Hattie brushed hot tears from her eyes. She reached for her flatirons and placed them on the stove. "Becky's is made over from one of Mamie's old dresses. I don't know how she did it—but I remember when Mamie wore it. I could never have made it look as good as she did."

She raised her tear-filled eyes to the ceiling and blinked hard. "She loved those children, Smith. She loved 'em."

"Nobody ever questioned that, Hattie." Smith poked wood into the stove to heat the irons.

"Then why didn't she leave? Why did she stay with Deke, knowin' how he was?"

Smith closed the firebox and turned to Hattie. "I don't know. But it would'a been mighty hard on her to make it on her own with four kids. Ain't enough jobs rights now for able-bodied men. Sure ain't many for women. Reckon that's why. She didn't have no one to turn to."

"She could've come to *us!* Or...or the church ...or *someone.*"

Smith smiled gently at his wife. "Guess she didn't see it that way."

Hattie pressed the clothes while Smith polished his shoes and the small pair Carrie had brought for Digger. When he'd finished the shoes, he went to the smokehouse to bring in a salt-cured ham and set it in a bucket of water.

Smith tucked a large burlap bag of dried beans between his feet on the floor. He scooped a cup of beans out onto the tabletop and in the lamplight sorted them into a pile, discarding the ones that were discolored or misshapen and watching for small rocks that might have been mixed with the beans. He swept the sorted pile into a blue ceramic bowl. He repeated the process until the bowl was full.

Finally Hattie set the flatirons on the windowsill above the table and stepped back. "All finished here," she said.

She poured water from the drinking bucket into a large pan and took the bowl of sorted beans from Smith. She dumped the beans into the pan of water and set them on the work surface of her hutch. "They'll be ready to cook come morning. Thanks for your help," she said, brushing her hand down the side of his face.

Smith stood up. "You're welcome. Ready for bed?"

"Just about. I think I'll sit out on the porch and read my Bible for a little bit. I'll be in soon." Hattie raised up on her tiptoes and kissed him on his cheek.

"Make sure it's real soon, honey. You're 'bout done in," Smith said gently.

Hattie watched him walk into the bedroom, then picked up her Bible and carried it and a lantern to the table set out on the screen porch. She pulled out a chair and sat down.

She hadn't read more than a chapter when she heard Smith's

gentle snores coming from the house. She smiled and continued to read.

Car lights shone down the hill, then lit up the interior of the porch when it pulled up the drive. Hattie walked to the screen door and pushed it open.

Deke Dunford stood directly in front of the door. "Miz Delaney? I'm here to get my young'uns."

Hattie's heart hammered in her chest. She glanced back toward the inside of the house, then took a half dozen steps out into the yard. Deke had no choice but to back up.

"Mr. Dunford, I'm awful sorry about Mamie. We did everything we could to save her. She was too far gone by the time we got there," Hattie said.

"It's a shame all right." Deke shook his head. "Just don't know what I'll do without that woman. She was the light of my life." He pulled a blue handkerchief from his pocket and swiped at his eyes. "I heard how she fell and hit her head. She was all the time fallin' over something…"

Hattie cut him off. "The children are asleep. They are doin' as well as can be expected with things like they are, but I think it'd be better if they stay here with us tonight."

Deke looked startled at her polite but firm refusal to turn his children over to him. His face hardened. "No. They need to be gettin' on home. I'll be needin' 'em around the place more'n ever now that their mama's gone."

Hattie stood as tall as her almost-five-foot frame would allow. "That may be so, but I'm not gonna wake 'em up. They're stayin' here tonight. And I'm thinkin' maybe they ought to stay a while after tonight, too."

"What do you mean? Now you listen here, them are my young'uns and they're comin' home with me," Deke growled.

Hattie prayed silently for patience and the right words to change the angry man's mind.

"Mr. Dunford, your wife's funeral is tomorrow. Sheriff Westerfield couldn't find you anywhere—or any next of kin, except the children. The county judge told him to go ahead with arrangements. So it's gonna be here at the house. Brother Fenton's out of town, so his son Conroy from the church over at Beech Creek is comin' to preach the service. He's married to my sister Marva, you know."

Hattie went on telling Deke about the arrangements they had made for Mamie's funeral and the burial at Ebenezer afterward. "Hope that's all right," she said. From the look on his face, Hattie could tell it wasn't all right. It wasn't all right at all.

Hattie rushed on as though she couldn't see the angry face glaring at her in the dim light. "If there's something special you want us to do, a certain hymn you want sung, or a certain Scripture, it's not too late. We can add whatever you want, or take something out if you don't like it."

Deke took a step toward Hattie. "Now look here, Miz Delaney, you Stoneworths can sing over Mamie all you want. You can even bury her in the back yard if you want to, but *I* want them young'uns and I want 'em *now.*"

Hattie stood her ground. "We'll talk about what happens to the children after the burial tomorrow. You come on back around two o'clock. The service is set for three. After we come back from the cemetery we can talk about it then. We're goin' to have supper here afterwards, so that would be a good time. Now, I'm tired an' I'm goin' to bed. You might ought to think about doin' the same, Mr. Dunford. Tomorrow's gonna be a long day for all of us."

Deke reached out a large hand and clamped it around Hattie's left arm. "Wait just a minute, woman…"

A slight movement caught his eye. He glanced toward the window behind Hattie. There, silhouetted in the lamplight from the kitchen, stood Smith, lazily rubbing a cloth up the barrel of a shotgun. Up the cloth went, and down again. Then the shadowy form put the gun to his shoulder and sighted down the barrel out into the yard.

Deke dropped Hattie's arm as if he'd been burned. "I…I just want to th…thank you for everything you done for Mamie. And for my kids, too. I'm much obliged. Two o'clock, you say? I'll be here. Thanks again."

He never took his eyes off the shadow in the window over Hattie's right shoulder. Deke backed slowly away from Hattie until he bumped into his car. He reached around behind him to unlatch the door and climbed in. Carefully he backed down the drive and then pulled up the hill and out of sight.

Hattie's shoulders slumped and her head dropped to her chest. She blew out a long breath, then looked at the sky. *Thank you, Lord. Thank you for changin' his mind like that! I was scared, but I knew you were hearin' my prayers. You answered 'em too, didn't you? Thank you, Father.*

Hattie walked back into the house. She blew out the lantern and slipped out of her dress and into her nightgown. Smith's snores were a little louder now. She smiled to herself. Pulling back the covers, she slid into bed beside him.

"Huh? Wha…? That you, Hattie?" Smith leaned up on one elbow and rubbed his eyes with his other hand.

"Shhhhhh. 'Course it's me. Were you expectin' someone else?" Hattie laughed softly, still giddy with her triumph over Deke. "Guess what! Deke Dunford came to the door, not five minutes after you went to sleep. Said he was goin' to take those children home tonight. I told him he couldn't."

"How'd he take that?" Smith yawned hugely.

"He wanted to argue about it, but I told him he couldn't have 'em. He got a little heated, but nothin' I couldn't handle."

If Smith noticed that Hattie had left out the part about Deke grabbing her arm, he didn't let on. He rubbed a hand across his beard-stubbled chin.

"That's good, Hattie. I figured you'd be able to take care of ol' Deke when the time came." Smith punched his pillow to make a soft spot for his head.

Hattie snuggled as close to Smith as her expanding belly

would allow. "I thought he was goin' to argue with me, so I was praying my way through it, but all of a sudden he stopped, thanked me for everything we've done for Mamie and the kids, got in his car and left! It was the strangest thing."

Smith reached over and stroked her hair. "Nothin' strange about it, darlin'. He knew you were right, that's all."

"I reckon, but…" Hattie reached up and grabbed Smith's hand and sniffed. "Smith Delaney, why do you smell like machine oil?"

"Go to sleep, Hattie." He yawned.

5

Hamie Dunford's body was dressed and laid out in the front room. Cars and trucks, and children playing quietly in the yard, surrounded the house. The adults, all the Stoneworths, their wives and husbands, Ma Richards, and a few of the good citizens of Drakesboro and Mondray sat or stood in small groups when the woman on the mule came down the long hill.

A blue, shapeless dress hung on bone-thin shoulders. In her arms, a young baby cried. She kicked the mule in the ribs and he trotted up between the cars. She slid down, tossing the reins over the headlamp of the nearest vehicle.

At the screen door of the porch she stood, uncertain. Marva Fenton, Hattie's sister, opened it for her.

"I come to see the little boy," the woman said, looking embarrassed and not a little afraid. "I come to see if he can cure my baby."

Marva glanced at the baby, wrapped in a dingy dishtowel, nodded, then led the woman into the house.

Hattie rose from her chair at the kitchen table.

"This is Hattie Delaney," Marva said. "She's Jackie's mama. It's up to her," she added kindly.

"Ma'am, I'm Darlin McBride from over Belton way. The lady that lives up the road from us said you had a young'un' borned after his daddy died."

Darlin shoved the baby toward Hattie, "My boy, Levi here, he got the thresh awful bad. He can't hardly eat. He's gonna die if'n he don't get the cure."

The baby's dull eyes stared at Hattie, then he yawned. White film coated the inside of his mouth and tongue. Thrush—its typical symptoms.

Smith, and Hattie's brother, Forrest, came to stand at the door of the kitchen that led from the dining room. Hattie glanced at Smith. "Honey, would you find Jackie for me?"

"Hattie, not today," Smith said.

"Yes, I want you to go get Jackie and bring him on in the house. This baby's sufferin'. Anything we can do, we'll do." Hattie looked hard into Smith's eyes, begging his understanding. When he'd nodded and walked out the door, she turned back to Darlin.

"We have a buryin' today. It's not a good time, but there's plenty of food. Marva, fix Miz McBride a plate," she said.

"That ain't necessary, Miz Delaney..."

"You had a long hot ride, why don't you let me take that baby, and you set down here a minute." Hattie ushered Darlin to the chair she had vacated a moment before and took the baby from her arms.

"Carrie, this baby's warm. Would you bring me a cool cloth?"

Ma Richards came around the corner from the bedroom where she'd been lying down. "Let me see that boy," she ordered.

Hattie moved aside and gave the old midwife room to examine the baby.

"This is Ma Richards, Mrs. McBride. She's the best granny-woman in these parts."

The young mother, hardly more than a child herself, nodded shyly.

Ma stripped off the baby's ragged clothes and turned him over, running her hand down his spine. She peered close into his eyes and poked a finger into his mouth, feeling around the inside, then passed her hand over the top over his head, gently probing the soft spot. She closed her eyes for a moment before she spoke.

"How old's this young'un?"

"Nigh on to three months, I reckon," Darlin replied.

Hattie smothered a gasp. The baby was no bigger than a newborn.

"He's got rickets." Ma said. "And a bad case of thresh."

Darlin twisted the skirt of her dress between her hands, and looked at her shoes. "Miz Delaney's boy can cure the thresh. That's what my neighbor said. She said 'If'n that boy who was borned after his daddy died will blow in Levi's mouth, the thresh'll be gone in two days time.' She tol' me that."

"You gonna need more'n that, Ma snapped. You got to feed this baby good food and keep him clean and..."

Hattie laid a hand on Ma's arm. "I'm sure she's doin' the best she can, Ma. Willa," Hattie directed another of her sisters, "run in there to my chest and get one of Jackie's old gowns. We'll clean him up and send him home with a few things..."

"No, ma'am!" Darlin jumped to her feet. "We don't take charity from nobody," she stated proudly. "We just need the cure, that's all."

Hattie made sure the baby was secure on the table with Ma and turned to the young mother. *Lord, let me say this right. Help me to help her and her baby without hurtin' her pride,* she prayed silently.

"'Course, you don't take charity. None of us would. Why, the very idea! We aren't talkin' charity at all. We're talkin' helpin' a friend. I got a boy that's outgrown his clothes; you got a boy that'll fit 'em. That's all. It's as simple as that. Now, tell me, is this your first baby?"

Hattie kept the conversation going with the young mother while Ma Richards, Carrie, and Marva bathed the baby and dressed him in clean clothes. Willa would come to the bedroom door behind the woman with a little sacque or shirt and Hattie would give a slight nod, "yes" or "no". The "yesses" went into a paper bag and the "no's" were returned to the chest. Willa shook her head, but kept going until the bag was filled.

Smith came to the door with Jackie in his arms.

Hattie smiled at the plump toddler. "C'mere, honey," she

said, and took Jackie with her back to the table.

"Look at this baby, Jackie. Ain't he sweet?" Jackie poked his finger in his mouth and looked. "Now, I want you to blow in the baby's mouth, all right?" Jackie buried his face in Hattie's shoulder. Hattie jounced him up and down. "Jackie-boy, where are you?" He giggled and pushed back to look at her face.

"Be sweet, Jackie, this little baby needs you."

Jackie leaned over from her arms and looked at the baby. Darlin pried the baby's mouth open and Jackie, placing his face close to Levi's, blew hard. The baby reflexively swallowed as the breath passed over the back of his throat.

"He swallered the cure! He done it," Darlin exclaimed. "Oh, I'm obliged to you, Miz Delaney!" Tears formed in her eyes. "Just like my neighbor said! Why, it was just like he knowed what to do!"

Hattie nodded her agreement.

Ma Richards snorted at the woman's ignorance. "You got milk?" she asked bluntly.

Darlin blushed and stammered, "No, ma'am. My milk dried up. I been givin' him sugar water. An' my man, Gideon, gets milk from the man he works for when he can, but it don't happen too often."

"Listen here, that baby's got to have milk. I don't care if'n you have to steal it! He's gonna be a cripple, *if* he lives at all, if'n you don't feed him more'n sugar water. You hear me?"

The young woman's eyes grew large with fear.

"I got this here cod liver oil," Ma said, pulling a bottle from her ever-present black bag. "You give it to him *every day.* It'll he'p. You understand?"

"Yes, ma'am, but…how am I gonna explain it to Gideon? He ain't gonna be happy with me takin' things we ain't paid for…" she faltered.

"He ain't gonna be happy if'n that baby dies, neither. You tell him whatever you have to tell him to make him understand."

"Yes, ma'am." Darlin swallowed hard. "I'll make him

understand," she whispered.

Hattie sent Jackie back out to play with the children in the yard and set about wrapping up thick slices of ham in brown paper. She added four roasted potatoes and ripe tomatoes from her own garden. These she put in a sturdy paper sack, added the ham, and tied the package up with twine for the long mule ride home.

"Now, I was thinkin', Hattie said, "you must'a got up with the sun to ride all this way from Belton. You got to go back the same as you came, so there won't be much time to be fixin' supper when you get there. We got all this food for the buryin' that's just gonna go bad when all the folks are gone. We'll never be able to eat it all, so it would be a kindness if you'd take this on back with you." She placed the neatly tied bundle on the table next to the sack of baby clothes.

"Miz Delaney, I can't take that, an' the clothes, and the medicine! Why, it wouldn't be right!" Darlin said.

Hattie waved the girl's objection aside. "Just a minute. It would be wrong to let all that good food spoil. We'd have to throw it to the pigs. Wouldn't that be a worse wrong?" Hattie asked kindly.

Darlin nodded her head slowly, "I reckon I best be gettin' on my way then." She picked up the now-clean baby, and Hattie walked her out to where the mule waited patiently. Darlin stepped up onto the fender of the car where the mule was tethered and threw a leg over the animal's back. Hattie handed her the wrapped packages of clothes and food.

"You need anything, you come back, hear? Anything at all," Hattie said.

"Miz Delaney, I'm obliged to you, more'n you know," Darlin replied.

Hattie watched her turn the old mule and go down the drive and turn up the road. When the woman neared the top of the hill she turned back, waved and went on.

Smith came up behind Hattie and wrapped his arms around

her. "You got to have the biggest heart in all of Muhlenberg County, Hattie Delaney."

"Just doin' what I'd do for anyone else, honey," she replied.

Smith turned her in his arms and leaned down to press a soft kiss against her lips. "I love you an' your big heart, Hattie."

Hattie smiled up at him as they walked into the house arm in arm.

Ma Richards stomped around the kitchen gathering up the pitiful clothes Levi McBride had worn and threw them into the stove. "She's gonna bury that baby in those nice clothes you give her. You know that, don't you, Hattie?"

Hattie rubbed the small of her back with one hand and eased down into the chair at the table, her other hand on her rounded belly.

"She may, but if she does it won't be for lack of tryin' on our part. I couldn't send that baby home the way he came." Hattie rested her head on the table for a moment.

Ma fumed out loud about the ignorance that still pervaded the hills and valleys of the small communities surrounding them. The persistent belief that a knife under the pillow would cut the pain of childbirth; that an oral yeast infection could be cured by the breath of a child born after his father's death. "I tried to warn you this would happen when Jackie was borned!" she fussed, her glance coming to rest on Hattie's white face. Ma whirled on Smith and pointed back at Hattie. "You gonna be buryin' *her*, if'n she don't get more rest! Look at her. She's wore out!"

Smith's face creased with obvious concern. "I told her she was doin' too much..."

"I'm fine, Ma!" Hattie raised her head. "I'm just tired. Soon as the buryin's over, things'll go back to normal and I'll be fine."

Carrie joined the conversation. "Honey, it won't be normal at all. You got four extra children to take care of. Why don't you let us take 'em for a few days, or Forrest and Vida, or even

Eldon and Rose Ellen? Just 'til their daddy shows up again."

Hattie was bone tired. She briefly considered sending the Dunford children with any of her brothers or sisters before answering, but declined the offer. "No. I reckon Deke'll turn up today for the funeral. An' if he don't, they'll stay here. They been through enough without any more changes. They're used to us," Hattie replied firmly.

Marva walked over to Hattie and reached out to rub her shoulders for a moment. "With Mom and Dad Fenton at the United Mine Workers convention, me an' Conroy are stayin' at the house right there in Drakesboro. We'll come down and help you 'til they get back. They're sweet kids." She said.

"Marva, that would be a wonderful help," Carrie said. "I was relieved to hear Conroy was free to do the funeral today, with Preacher Fenton off to the convention."

Marva laughed. "Conroy is *Preacher Fenton*, too."

"I know, I know," Carrie smiled. "It's just that we're all used to *old* Preacher Fenton."

"Hey! Don't let my dad hear you call him that," said Conroy from the dining room door. "He still thinks he's young."

"Acts like it, too," added Forrest, standing behind Conroy. "Still mines every day and gives a good sermon on Sunday, and represents the UMW at the conventions. That man don't quit."

"Mom Fenton tells him to slow down, but he says he's got too much to do to be sittin' in the rockin' chair on the front porch," Marva said as she walked to her husband's side.

"Miz Fenton told us at the ladies' Bible study that he spends an hour in prayer every mornin' before he goes to the mine, then another every night 'fore he goes to bed," Willa said.

"I heard that, too," said Smith. "That true, Conroy?"

"Uh-huh. He's done that every day for years and years," Conroy answered.

"You spend your fair share of time in prayer, too, honey," said Marva quietly.

"Yep, can't get through the day without it."

Smith shook his head. "Man, I don't know as how you do it. I pray all right, but two hours a day?"

Hattie smiled. "You just ain't used to it yet. We all pray, honey. Maybe not for hours at a time like Conroy and Preacher Fenton, but during the day, I'll bet every one of us prays enough to fill an hour."

Smith grinned at his little wife. "I'm sure you do, come to think of it. You're always prayin' about somethin' or for someone." He paused and looked thoughtful. "Now you'll be addin' Darlin McBride and her young'un to the list, won't you?"

"Already did," she replied.

6

The congregants of Jackson Chapel and other friends and neighbors of Mamie Dunford spilled out of the front room of the old house under the hill, out through the dining room, into the bedroom and kitchen. Some gathered on the screen porch. Many more stood in the yard where they could hear the service through the open windows. The Stoneworth brothers and sisters stood just inside the front room and sang for Mamie the beautiful old hymns that were a part of their heritage. Breaking into multipart *a capella* voices; they sang the words of *Wayfaring Stranger*, so fitting somehow for the broken body of the woman lying in the simple pine coffin that sat on two sawhorses that were discreetly hidden under the draped folds of Mamie's beautiful "Sunshine and Shadow" quilt.

I am a poor wayfaring stranger,
traveling through this world of woe.
And there's no sickness, toil nor danger
in that bright land to which I go.

Seemingly impossible intricate harmonies flowed from the eight brothers and sisters there that day. High soprano lead from Hattie, alto and contralto from Carrie and Chloe, high tenor and second soprano from Willa, Marva and Lalie. Eldon and Forrest split bass and baritone between them. The harmonies blended into a confection of song that wafted through the house, lifting the congregation gathered there.

Conroy Fenton cleared his throat and rose to address the assembled body of believers who had come to say goodbye to Mamie.

"There is simply no way to express our horror at the way Mamie died. It is an appalling thing to see someone as precious and loving as she was die. Her death is somehow worse because we know she didn't have to die. By rights, she should have gone on to raise her children, to continue giving to her community, to go on touching our lives with her quiet faith and presence.

"One of you asked me why God would call Mamie home the way He did. Well, while I believe God welcomed her home, I don't believe that He called her home the day she died. I believe that what was done to her had nothing to do with God's will for Mamie's life. That was one man's decision. What I believe is that Mamie didn't suffer alone. Our Lord suffered with her. He felt every blow, and bled every drop of blood she lost. He was with her every second of the way."

Hattie slipped around the room and stood next to Becky and Dorie. She glanced around and saw Mary Claire curled up on Marva's lap. Digger sat beside them, staring up at the ceiling.

Conroy ran the fingers of his left hand through his sandy hair and glanced at the open Bible and then at the expectant faces looking at him.

"Jesus told his followers, 'I will be with you always, even unto the end of the world.' We know that our Lord was with Mamie as she walked through death's shadowy vale and into the bright sunlight of eternal life. She was not alone. He walked with her.

"Jesus said, 'I go to prepare a place for you,' echoing the assurance given so long ago by David, the shepherd. He said, 'Yea, though I walk through the valley of the shadow of death, I will fear no evil, for thou art with me.'"

A soft "Amen" came from Hattie's lips, and from several others.

"Friends, if I were to give this brief memorial message a title, I'd call it, 'Waiting in Another Room.' There is much that is wonderful and comforting in the gospel of John, Chapter

Fourteen. Jesus assures us that He has gone to prepare a place for us, and that just as surely as He has gone to prepare a place for us, He will come again, that where He is, we may be also. Listen again to the well-known words in verse two: 'In my Father's house are many mansions. If It were not so, I would have told you.' He is saying that God has room for us all. Room for Mamie, and room for you and me.

"I read an interesting article not long ago. It was by one of the people who study the language that Jesus spoke back in the first century. The scholar pointed out that when the Bible was put into English a few hundred years ago they chose to put 'mansions,' in this passage. But the word Jesus used really means rooms. In our Father's house there are many rooms. Don't you know they are magnificent rooms! How wonderful it is to know that our sweet sister, is waiting in one of those beautiful rooms—a room prepared for her by our Lord Himself."

The young minister paused and looked through the open doors leading to other rooms in the Stoneworth home. "Some of you here today aren't in the room where I'm standing. Some are around a corner from me. So I can't see you—though you are here, in another room. But you can hear my voice. Just so, Mamie is in another room. We can't hear her voice, but we know she's waiting there, and perhaps she can hear ours. Certainly we can hear our Lord's voice, even as we mourn the departure of our sister from our earthly dwelling place here. Listen to Him. Jesus says, 'Come unto me, all ye that labor and are heavy laden, and I will give you rest.' Jesus is not slack concerning his promises. What He promises, He will give."

Conroy paused again, and took a sip of water from a glass on the table that substituted for a pulpit. "We find comfort knowing that Mamie has simply gone before us. Right now she is waiting in another room, and if we accept that invitation from the Lord, and walk in the light as He is in the light, it's just a matter of time 'til we'll join Mamie. Then there will be no fear, no tears, no pain and no sorrow. Instead, we'll have the joy and love of our Lord, the Holy Spirit, and our Heavenly Father. And we'll be with the saved of all ages."

Picking up his heavy Bible, Conroy closed it and held it to his chest as he turned to the mourners. He looked down at Mamie's broken face, then at the audience. "Our tears," he said, "are tears for our temporary loss and for the senseless way our sister was taken from us. And tears for the empty place created by her leaving." He looked at the faces of Mamie's children, sitting with Marva.

He swallowed hard, tears welled up in his eyes, then he smiled and said, "We have tears, even as the Lord did at the tomb of his friend Lazarus. But our tears are not the tears of those who have no hope. We know we soon shall be where she is. By God's grace through Jesus Christ, we'll soon be in our room in the mansion he's prepared for us. Let us pray."

❧

After the graveside service at Ebenezer, the family and friends gathered back at Hattie's house. She scanned the crowd over and over again for a glimpse of Deke Dunford. Finally, Hattie cornered Smith.

"Have you seen Deke?" she asked.

"Nope. Guess he's too 'shamed to show his face," Smith replied, shaking his head.

Hattie glanced around to make sure the Dunford children weren't in sight. "He should have been here for the children, if for no other reason, Smith!"

"If you ask me, they're better off without him, Honey."

Hattie's eyes flashed and she whispered furiously, "Well, I didn't ask you. He's their father. He should be the one comfortin' them!"

Smith took Hattie by the shoulders and held her close. "Hattie, I think Deke reckons he's the wronged party. We took his young'uns and won't give 'em back. I think he's got his back up."

He held her at arm's length and gazed down into her soft

brown eyes. "You stay close to the house for the next few days. Hear me?"

Hattie nodded. "I will, but I don't think Deke'll get out of hand with me."

Smith shrugged. "Prob'ly not, but no sense givin' him the chance to do somethin' stupid."

Hattie leaned against Smith's chest again. "Surely he couldn't do anything more stupid than he's already done," she murmured.

"Sure he could, sweetheart."

He kissed the top of her head.

"He could go after *my* wife—then I'd have to step in. That would be real stupid on his part."

"Don't talk like that, Smith." Hattie shuddered. "I don't even want to think about such things."

"That's fine, Hattie," He hugged his wife. "You let me do the thinkin'. I'll take care of you, Hattie. He has to come through me before he'll get to you."

"I know. That's what worries me."

❧

The afternoon wore on, and, one by one, the crowd thinned until only Hattie and her brothers, sisters, and their families remained.

The six women cleaned up the food and set things to right in the small kitchen and began packing up their things to go home.

"Hattie," Marva said quietly, "why don't you let Conroy and me take the Dunford kids home with us. We have lots of room, and..."

Hattie glanced sharply at Marva's pretty, oval face. It was filled with longing. Even as she shook her head at Marva she could feel her sister's aching heart.

Marva and Conroy wanted children more than anything. Marva had miscarried twice and then never gotten pregnant again. She would have made a wonderful mother. Hattie knew that, but she just couldn't bring herself to let Becky, Mary Claire, and Dorie go. Even angry little Digger had worked his way into Hattie's big heart.

Hattie looked away from Marva's expectant face. She brushed crumbs off the table and replied, "Now, Marva, don't you go settin' yourself up for disappointment. Those kids have a daddy out there somewhere. He's already been down here once to get 'em. I don't know why he didn't show hisself today, but he'll be comin' back around sooner or later."

Marva exclaimed, "But Hattie, he could see 'em at our place just as easy as yours. Maybe..."

Hattie cut her off. "No. They need to stay here."

She gave the same answer she'd given Carrie earlier in the day. "They know us. They don't need any more changes. That settles it."

Carrie, Willa, Chloe and Lalie listened silently to the conversation between the other two sisters, but they exchanged looks that showed their concern over the brewing conflict between Marva and Hattie.

Carrie dried her hands on the dishtowel tied around her waist and finally interrupted the interchange. "For now, it's probably better to leave things as they are. Maybe down the road..."

Hattie's eyes flew to Carrie's. "They stay here. That's final. I mean it." She said it softly, but with such determination that none of the other sisters responded at all.

"Now," Hattie said briskly, changing the subject, "have y'all heard from Berk?" The subject of the Dunford children was dropped and the tense moment passed.

Long after the brothers and sisters had left to go to their own homes, after the children were tucked in bed and their prayers said, Hattie heard Marva's voice in her head. She heard the longing in Marva's voice, and the ache in her heart.

Hattie unbuttoned her dress and let it fall to the floor, then, standing in her slip, picked it up and slid it onto a hanger.

Smith pulled his Sunday shoes off of his feet, and wiggled

his toes. The bed creaked under his weight as he sat down on its edge.

"What you thinkin' about, Hattie?" he asked.

"What? Oh, nothin'. Just..." She turned to face him. "I keep thinkin' about Marva. She's got real attached to Mary Claire. That's all."

Smith nodded. "Yup. I noticed that. That little girl's gonna miss her mama the most, her bein' the youngest an' all."

Hattie's voice faltered a little. "Marva wants the children. I think she's fantasizin' they could be hers and Conroy's if I'd let her have 'em."

Smith unbuttoned his shirt and stood to pull the tail out of his trousers. "It ain't up to you to let them go nowhere. They ain't ours."

"I know that, but Mamie sent 'em to me. She tol' Becky if they were ever in trouble to come to me."

"Uh-huh. An' that's just what Becky did. So now, are you thinkin' they're yours?"

Hattie's head snapped up to face him. "No, of course not. Their daddy's still here. I... I mean, Deke's still out there somewhere. He's got legal claim, but..."

"But if'n he don't, you're aimin' to keep 'em." Smith said it as a fact, not a question.

She slumped down on the bed next to him. "I guess so."

Smith walked to the oak dresser next to the kitchen door and emptied the contents of his pockets onto its smooth top.

"You know, Hattie. I can see why Marva'd want them young'uns. She grieved mighty hard for them two babies she lost. I reckon she sees us with our kids and money bein' tight, an' she figures it would solve two problems at once. We wouldn't have to struggle to feed four more kids, and she an' Conroy'd finally have the family they been prayin' for."

"But Mamie sent 'em to *me*, Smith..."

"For help, Hattie." Smith pulled off his pants and laid them across the back of the chair in the corner. "She didn't give 'em to you free and clear. They ain't pups."

Hattie bristled. "I know that. It's just…"

"It's just you think God expects you to open your door and your heart to every hurtin' rabbit you see on the trail. Could be sometimes, though, that God sent that rabbit for food for the table."

"What?" exclaimed Hattie.

"Not the young'uns. I'm just sayin' maybe God intends them for Marva and Conroy. You're just the… His way for gettin' 'em there."

Hattie's heart sank. She wasn't getting the kind of support she'd hoped for in her desire to keep the Dunford children.

Smith walked back to the bed and lifted her chin so she had to look at him. "I ain't sayin' you're wrong, Hattie. I'm just suggestin' *maybe* God has a different plan than you."

She slid over to her side of the bed and pushed her feet under the covers. Smith climbed in next to her. He pulled the sheet up to his chest, then turned to her.

"All this worryin's silly anyway. Like you said, they got a daddy out there. If'n he wants 'em, he can come get 'em any time he chooses. Ain't much we can do to stop him."

She flipped onto her side away from Smith. "We'll just see about that," she said.

7

Smith strolled casually around the perimeter of the old house. Once in a while he stopped and looked up, his eyes sweeping the eaves as though looking at the overhang of the roof. Mostly, though, he kept his eyes on the ground under the windows. Already he'd seen boot prints squashed into the soft earth in the flowerbed beneath the bedroom window and the faint outline of a boot in the clay outside the dining room. Last night he'd heard a muffled scraping against the edge of the house, as though a man were sidling along the thin wooden walls to stay tucked into the shadows as deeply as possible.

More than once, in the two weeks since Mamie Dunford's death, Smith had seen a man slinking along the corn rows that ran across the back of the property. He hadn't been close enough, nor fast enough with his bad leg, to catch the man where he'd crouched in the field, but he had seen the boot prints the visitor left behind often enough to know that the prints under the windows matched those in the field. The right print, with its now-signature crack across the sole, cried out its ownership.

Not once had Deke Dunford made an appearance to claim his children since the night before Mamie's funeral. Nor had he been seen in town. Smith knew. He'd been asking around. It worried him that Deke was out there somewhere watching the house.

A huge racket came from the top of the hill. Metal on metal screamed, and blue smoke blew out behind the contraption that appeared. A young man inside the vehicle, face set in determined lines, fought his way down the hill and brought the belching pile of rejected parts to a shuddering stop.

Smith walked toward the road.

"You Mr. Delaney?" the boy asked.

"I am."

Climbing out through the empty space where a door should have hung, the lanky lad stretched to his full height.

"Name's Gideon McBride. You an' your missus sent my woman home with charity goods a few weeks ago. I been meanin' to come make it right..."

"Now, son..." Smith interrupted.

"No, sir. Ain't meanin' no disrespect, Mr. Delaney, but hear me out. We don't take nothin' we ain't paid for. I ain't got money, but I got time an' a strong back, if'n you need any he'p around the place."

Smith struggled to control the smile he could feel creeping around the edges of his mouth. There was no way he would laugh at the boy for trying to do the right thing. But there he stood in his castoff clothes, one toe poking out of a broken shoe, driving his old wreck of a car and determined to "make it right."

Smith rubbed his hand across his chin and seemed deep in thought. He cleared his throat.

"I reckon I could use some help clearing the lot across the road. My wife's been after me to clean out the brush. She's afraid of snakes, with the young'uns an' all."

A soft scratching at the seat of the vehicle caught Smith's attention. Gideon McBride motioned a sleek hound out without ever taking his eyes off Smith. The dog jumped down from the seat. Another flick of Gideon's wrist and it sat motionless at his feet.

"I could clear that mess outta there for you. I ain't afraid of hard work."

Smith knelt down to scratch the dog behind the ears. "You got a fine hound, here, son. If you're sure you want the job, I'd be glad of the help."

For the first time a smile broke over the young man's face.

"Yes, sir! I'd be obliged to you." He stuck out his hand.

Smith raised up and took the outstretched hand in his own, and they shook on the deal. "Now, you better come on in the house and tell my Hattie how that baby's doin'. She's been prayin' for 'im, you know."

"Has she now? Well, then I'm obliged twice," Gideon answered while Smith led the way to the back door.

Hattie, alerted by the noise of Gideon's car and curious about the transaction taking place between Smith and the strange young man, stood by the screen door waiting for them.

"Honey," Smith said, "this here's Gideon McBride."

Hattie's face softened into a sweet smile. "Why, Mr. McBride! Come right on in. How's Mrs. McBride and little Levi? I've thought of them often since we met." She pushed the door open and welcomed them inside.

Again, without looking at the dog that trotted along beside him, Gideon pointed his finger down, and the hound lay down next to the door, while Gideon followed Hattie inside.

"They're just fine, Miz Delaney. The boy's been pert since Darlin started giving him that tonic you sent home. I been tryin' to get milk for him, like the granny woman said. Sometimes it ain't much more'n a fruit jar, but we water it down some and he seems to be takin' to it now. Darlin 'bout worried herself sick over that young'un' 'til your boy give him the cure. We're obliged to you for what you done."

Gideon had snatched the hat off his head and wrung it between his hands as he talked to Hattie. He glanced around the house with what appeared to be awe.

"My land! Y'all got you a fine place here. Why, it's so clean and purty…You a company man, Mr. Delaney?" he asked suspiciously.

Smith threw back his head and laughed. "No, son. I'm a dirt farmer, like most folks that ain't in the mines. I done my share of minin', but I ain't never been management." He slapped his knee. "Why, they'd laugh me out of a management meetin'."

Hattie herded the men to her table and motioned them into seats. She stepped down into the kitchen and wrapped a towel around the handle of the coffeepot. Smith followed her in with a wave of his hand for Gideon to stay seated, and gathered three cups. Hattie poured each of them a cup of the coffee, then joined them at the table.

"Well, sir. You must be doin' somethin' right to have you a fine place like this!"

Hattie's heart went out to the boy. There was such a look of longing on his face.

"Mr. McBride, this house was built by my daddy. He built it for my mama when they were courtin'. It's where I was born—me and my brothers and sisters, that is. I'm the last of 'em. It actually belongs to all of us, but the rest of 'em either have homes of their own or live in company houses close to the mines where they work. There's nine of us in all. And we're all but one still right here in the county."

"An' they just give you this house?" Gideon's face reflected doubt.

"Not exactly," Smith said. "Like Hattie said, the older ones had homes of their own when Hattie's parents died. Only the three youngest ones still lived here. Once their folks were gone they went to live with Hattie's sister, Carrie, in Drakesboro. The house sat empty 'til the youngest boy, Berk, moved down here. Then he met a girl from Louisville and married her. They moved up there so she could be close to her folks. When Hattie and her first husband got married, they moved in. They fixed it up like you see it now. She's been here ever since."

Gideon's eyes moved from Smith's face to Hattie's. "An' your first man?" he asked quietly."He was killed. A mine cave-in. He lived for a few months, and then he died, " she said simply.

"I'm real sorry for your loss, ma'am." His face showed genuine compassion. "But you had your kinfolk to he'p you out?"

"Yes, I did. I don't know if I would have made it without the Lord, and the help of my brothers and sisters."

Gideon looked thoughtful. "My Darlin comes from a big family like that. I got a couple of brothers, but they still livin' at home. I'm the oldest of my family."

"Where d'you hail from, Gideon?" Smith asked. "You got that mountain twist to your words." Smith grinned his famous lop-sided Delaney smile. "Sounds close, but not exactly like us. Who's your kin?"

Gideon's face closed up like a door slammed shut. His chair scraped loudly against the board floor of the porch as he stood up to leave.

"Best I be gettin' on out to that brush across the road," he said, averting his eyes. "Thank you for the coffee, ma'am," he said to Hattie.

Smith, hampered by his bad leg, stumbled to his feet. "Wait, son. We got time. That field has been growin' for years. It ain't a-goin' nowhere this afternoon."

Gideon never looked back. He went though the screen door, snapped his fingers at the dog waiting outside, and did everything but run across the road. He bent over and grabbed the downed branch of a tree and dragged it to the edge of the lot. Tossing it down, he went for another. Next he grabbed a dead sapling and tugged at it until he wrenched it from the ground and pitched it on the heap.

Smith and Hattie watched from the house.

"That boy's got demons," Hattie murmured. "The kind of demons no tent revival preacher can pray out of you." She shook her head. "What d'you reckon he did he's so 'shamed of?"

Smith wrapped his arms around Hattie and rested his chin on the top on her dark head.

"I don't know, Honey. He's got a powerful pride, I'll tell you that much. He come here to pay his debt for all those things you sent home with his wife. She tol' you he wouldn't take charity, and she was right about that."

Hattie shook her head. "He doesn't owe us a thing,"

A worried frown marred her forehead. "You think he's in trouble with the law? You think he's hidin' out?"

"What—in plain sight, with a wife and baby? I don't think so. He seems like a good boy, just young and maybe a little scared is all."

They watched Gideon stomp over a small shrub that had sprung up from a windblown seed and jerk it out of the hard earth.

"Looks to me like he's tryin' to rid hisself of them demons."

Smith shoved the door wide and brushed a kiss across Hattie's forehead before he walked to the smokehouse. He collected a grubbing hoe and an axe and crossed the road. Not speaking a word, he leaned the axe against a tree and began grubbing out an old stump. Gideon neither acknowledged his presence nor acted as though he knew Smith had joined him. Every now and again he'd glance at the hound that lay in the shade of the oak tree close by.

Side by side the two men worked for over an hour as the silence grew between them.

A soft growl from the dog alerted Smith. He started to turn when the boy's soft voice cut through the tension. "Don't turn around, Mr. Delaney."

Gideon never raised his head. Something in his voice stilled Smith's movement on the spot. Instead of turning toward the dog, he squatted to the ground and pulled his handkerchief out of his back pocket and mopped his forehead as though he was simply taking a break in the heat of the day.

Gideon grabbed the weeds that stood between them and pulled, then moved a little closer to Smith.

"There's a man standin' behind your smokehouse. I reckon he's been there 'bout a quarter hour. Me 'n' Pride been keepin' watch on 'im. He's slender and broad-shouldered, sorta dark complected. He's wearin' overalls and a blue shirt. Keeps lookin' over his shoulder, so I know he don't b'long here. Think you can put a name on 'im?"

Smith's face hardened, but he casually reached out, plucked a piece of sweet grass and stuck it between his teeth. "Yeah. I think I know who it is—does he have a mustache?"

Gideon hesitated, "Yep—You…you want me to send Pride after 'im?"

The sleek hound raised his head at the mention of his name.

Smith thought for a moment. The idea of Gideon's dog tearing Deke Dunford to bits didn't bother him much at all. Still…

"Gideon, what's he been doin' besides lookin' over his shoulder," he asked.

The younger man stopped yanking weeds and strolled back to squat by Smith. He unbuttoned the top button of his shirt, and rocked back on his heels.

"Well, sir. Seems to me he's been listening more'n anything. He keeps glancin' around an' kinda cockin' his head to the side like he's tryin' to hear what's goin' on in the house. He got a real ugly look on his face when your missus was singin' a little while ago. Kinda like he was wantin' to shut her mouth. Gotta say I ain't seen that kinda hate on a man's face since…" Gideon didn't finish the sentence.

Smith's thoughts flew in a million directions. He could try to circle around the house, move in behind Deke. Catch him red-handed. Beat the tar out of him. He could casually stroll up the drive to the house, get his shotgun, blast Deke off the map. He could…

Gideon crooked his finger at the dog. It was at his side instantly. The boy scratched the dog's head gently and patted its side.

Smith and Gideon could have been any two men taking a rest from a hard hour's labor. The boy's quiet voice broke through Smith's murderous thoughts.

"Mr. Delaney, I hope you know I wasn't gonna just set down here and let him… I been watchin' him real close. I got my revolver under my shirt. Didn't figure to let him go after your woman after all she done for mine."

That got Smith's attention. *Where did you come from that you need to carry a gun? What are you afraid of?* Smith knew from the way Gideon had shut down communication before that he couldn't ask those questions, so instead he asked, "Son, you carry a gun under your shirt every day?"

Gideon stammered a little, "Where I come from… I mean, I… I reckon you cain't be too careful these days, what with all the tramps on the road, with the Depression an' all," he finished lamely.

Pride's head swung toward the house. From the orchard came the sound of children laughing. Little-girl squeals and giggles.

Smith's anger turned to stone-cold fear as he thought of the children coming back from their play only to be met by Deke Dunford.

"Come on, we're gonna go meet the young'uns." He stood up and turned toward the house. "You been doin' a good job of watchin' him without him seein' you do it. Think you can keep it up while we walk?" he asked softly.

Gideon nodded and pulled his brimmed hat down to just above his eyebrows. It looked as though he was watching the ground in front of him. Every few feet he'd chronicle Deke's movements. "He's looking up the hill toward them trees. He's looking back at us. Now he's cutting around the back of the building."

They strolled between the house and the smokehouse as though they didn't know Deke was there. Gideon seemed to stumble to the right, toward where the man hid. He knelt in the grass and tightened up his boot lace. He raised his eyes from under his hat, his face shadowed by its brim. Deke now stood behind the back corner of the outbuilding, and followed Smith with his eyes as Smith moved toward the sound of the children's voices. Deke's face turned an ugly, deep red. He raised his right hand, and cocking an imaginary pistol, he aimed and fired at Smith's head, then turned and melted into the woods at the edge of the property.

In just a couple of strides Gideon caught up with Smith. "He's gone. Left as quick as he come." Gideon laid his hand on Smith's arm to stop his forward movement.

"Mr. Delaney, that man's got hard feelin's against you." Gideon described what he'd seen. "If'n he'd had a real gun, I would'a dropped him where he stood. Since he was just play actin', I left him be."

Gideon blew out a breath and then finished in a rush. "Seems to me he was makin' you a promise to see you dead sooner or later."

Smith's deep blue eyes glittered. "He may be promisin', but I ain't takin' him at his word."

Relieved that the crisis was over for the moment, Smith's face broke into a grin. "Let's go get them young'uns."

He turned back toward the children and opened his arms. "C'mere, y'all. I got someone I want you to meet!"

❧

Digger fell in love with Pride at first sight. Gideon allowed the boy to play with the dog the rest of the afternoon while he and Smith worked to clear the brush out of the lot across the dirt road.

Smith quietly told Gideon the Dunfords' story. The young man stood with his head resting on the handle of the hoe for a moment, watching Digger romp with Pride, then said, "Makes me kinda 'shamed to be a man."

Smith clapped him on the shoulder. "That's what *makes* you a man, son. Knowin' the difference."

❧

After the supper dishes, the bedtime stories and the prayers, Hattie took down from the top of the Hoosier hutch the small notebook Smith had given her the day they were married. She dated the top of the page and then began to write. *Today was a beautiful summer day. The children are settling in. Digger is still so angry that it hurts my heart, but I know he's watching and seeing how things can be different. I pray we can keep them all long enough so that it is a real life lesson and not just a tiny moment in time that won't stay with them. The little girls are doing well. Becky is afraid. She watches out the windows all the time, waiting, I know, for her father. Gideon McBride came today to pay his imaginary debt for small acts of kindness. He seems a sweet boy, but again, such shadows of the heart. Must get to Radburn's tomorrow to pick up a few things. Ma Richards wants to see me later this week. I'm doing fine, and this baby's rolling like the ocean all day long.*

Hattie closed the journal and carefully replaced it on top of the hutch. She picked up the lantern and climbed the stairs to check the children one more time before going to bed herself. Each little girl slept peacefully. Soft breaths whispered past rosebud lips. Only Digger was restless, his quilt twisted and knotted by unconscious pain. Hattie knelt heavily by his side and straightened the covers. Lightly she rubbed the bony back. A soft touch on his tousled hair.

Lord, we can't do this without Your blessing, without Your hand. Give us the time, and the example to show them more—more love, more kindness, more of You. You know we're just barely scrapin' by with what we have. It would be easier on this family to throw them back to their father, or... Hattie swallowed hard...*or let Marva have 'em. But I can't. I just can't. Help us to find a way...*

8

Stars still twinkled in the early dawn when Smith felt the cold air brush against his shoulders. He rolled over on the soft featherbed and squinted down the length of his body in the dim light as the sheet slowly crept toward his feet. Jackie's cherub face peered between the bars of the iron crib that stood there. In his chubby fists he held the sheet, pulling it hand over hand toward him.

The tot grinned into Smith's astonished face.

"Uh...up!" Jackie crowed.

Smith laughed softly. "Up? You want up?"

Jackie's smile widened. "Up!" he repeated.

Pushing off the bed, Smith wrestled the sheet from the chuckling toddler, and carefully covered Hattie, trying not to wake her. He walked to the crib and plucked up the little boy. He rolled the child into a ball and scrubbed the baby-soft cheek gently with the whiskers on his chin. "How'd you like that. Got me an alarm clock with two legs."

Jackie giggled at the tickling.

"Outside?" he asked.

"Not just yet, young man. We've got work to do."

"Work?"

"Yep. Gotta find us some clothes," he said, lighting a lamp and rummaging through the dresser drawer, "and start the coffee boiling for your mama."

"Mama!" Jackie clapped his dimpled hands and then squatted, distracted by the pattern on the rug beneath his feet. "Look! Flower."

"I see that," Smith answered softly, then beckoned the boy.

He helped button Jackie into his short pants and shirt, then dressed himself. "C'mon. Let's go get some water."

"'Kay."

Jackie clasped his hands behind his back and strutted behind Smith into the kitchen. He clambered up onto the stool at the table and pounded it with his fists.

"Daddy, Daddy, Daddy, Daddy," he sing-songed.

Smith smiled as he picked up a bucket and stepped out the side door. It took only a moment to open the well cover and lower the roped bucket into the deep shaft, then draw it back up again. He poured the cold water from the well bucket into the one he'd brought out of the house, and returned to the kitchen.

Jackie had changed his song to "Mama, Mama, Mama, Mama."

"Shhhhh! Honey, Mama's still sleepin'. Let her rest a while longer."

"No, Mama's awake." Hattie said from the doorway. She yawned and pushed her long hair back, then bent and cupped Jackie's little face between her hands, and kissed his soft forehead. "Bet you're hungry this mornin.'

"Yep!" Jackie nodded.

Hattie straightened and smiled at Smith. "Give me a minute to put my hair up and I'll get breakfast on."

Smith turned from the stove where he'd placed the coffeepot. "Why don't you sleep in today, Honey. I'll feed the young'uns."

Hattie smiled. "That's a mighty sweet offer, Smith, but I can't." She yawned again. "I've got the girls comin' for the quiltin' today."

Smith rolled his eyes toward the ceiling, threw his head back and blew out a long breath. "Women-folk! I'm gonna be drownin' in women-folk!"

Hattie laughed out loud. "And you'll eat up all the attention you get. Every minute of it."

Smith wiggled his eyebrows up and down. "Every minute!" he conceded.

❧

Before Gideon McBride had left for home the night before, Hattie had asked him to extend her invitation to his wife for the quilting. She was the first to arrive. This time, though, instead of riding the mule, she rode in Gideon's car. It came thundering down the hill and careened to a nerve-shattering halt in front of the house. Darlin McBride stepped out of the car and reached back in for her baby. She carefully picked her way up the rutted drive with him in her arms. Gideon walked across the road into the lot and took up clearing brush where he'd left off the night before.

Hattie threw open the door to the screen porch and beckoned Darlin in. "C'mon in. Let me see that baby."

Darlin smiled shyly and handed the child to Hattie.

Hattie made sweet cooing noises to Levi and he smiled at her. "Well, I swan! He's lookin' so much better!"

"Yes, ma'am. He is. The cure done started him on the road to gettin' healthy," Darlin answered. "I'll thank you for the rest of my life!"

Hattie slipped her arm through the young woman's and led her into the house. "Don't be silly. We're friends. That's what friends do. I'm sure you've been tryin' to get milk for him, too."

"Sure have. I been doin' a little light cleanin' for a lady in Belton. She trades me milk for the housework. She even lets me bring Levi along."

"That's wonderful! And I'm so glad you could come today."

"Awful kind of you to ask me," Darlin responded. "I do enjoy a quiltin', an' I'm fair with a needle. I'll try not to shame you, anyway." The girl ducked her head.

Hattie laughed. "You couldn't shame me if you tried! I can make a real mess when I want to. My mama always said you have to make a few messes before you get it right."

Together they settled the baby on a blanket on the floor in the front room and turned toward the quilt frame.

Darlin's face lit up. "Look at that. You got it strung from the ceilin'."

Hattie nodded proudly. "It was my mother's. Mama was always workin' a quilt, so Daddy hung the frame where it could be lowered and raised as it was needed."

Small pulleys hung from the ceiling with ropes running down to the wooden frame.

Hattie pointed. "See, Mama could have her quilt down to work on when she had time, or raise it up if company was comin'. Mostly it came down at night after we were in bed."

"Sure makes sense to do it that way, don't it," Darlin replied. "A quilt frame takes up an awful lot of room!"

"It does, and with nine young'uns in the house..."

Darlin's eyes flew open.

"You got nine young'uns?" she gasped.

"No!" Hattie laughed. "But my mother did. So they needed every bit of floor space in this little house. That's why Daddy built the frame that way."

Darlin' ran her hand across the quilt which was already lashed to the frame with heavy cord. "Look at that. Ain't it purty! Did you do it?"

"Part of it," Hattie replied. "My sisters and I all piece the squares, then I put 'em together. They'll all be here today to help with the quilting. So will Ma Richards and Mother Crowe."

Darlin looked a little concerned. "Ma Richards? Ain't she the midwife?"

"Uh-huh."

"She kinda scares me," the girl admitted.

Hattie smiled gently. "She's one of the kindest women I've ever known. Don't be fooled by her. She's not near so hard as she tries to let on."

"Who's the other woman you mentioned?" Darlin asked, threading a needle.

The usually unflappable Hattie gulped a little. "She's my mother-in-law—or I guess I should say, she's my first husband's mother." Hattie lowered her eyes to the quilt and ran an idle hand across the squares.

"Gideon tol' me you been married before. I'm real sorry you lost your man." Darlin said softly. "Gideon says Mr. Delaney's a good one, though."

" He is. He's wonderful. I've been blessed to have had two good husbands."

"So what's wrong with Miz Crowe? Don't you like her?"

Hattie's eyes flew to Darlin's. "Of...of course I do. She's just a little...well, opinionated is the best way to describe her, I reckon. My children are her grandchildren by Jack, so she thinks she should have a say in how I'm raisin' 'em. She'd like me to do things differently, and doesn't mind tellin' me so."

Darlin snorted. "I know just what you mean! I remember the time..." Suddenly she clamped her lips together, choking off the words.

"Wha...what can I do to help you get ready for the quiltin'?" she finished lamely.

❧

Quiet chatter and laughter surrounded the old quilt frame as the five Stoneworth sisters and the three other women worked careful stitches into the brightly colored fabric.

"So, Darlin," Carrie said, trying to draw the girl into the conversation, "how'd you get such an unusual name?"

Seven pairs of eyes suddenly turned to the shy young woman. Deep color reddened her cheeks.

"It's...it's kind of silly, really," Darlin answered slowly, ducking her head. "I'm the youngest of four girls. My sisters' names are Faith, Hope and Charity..."

"Stiffen your spine and speak up!" Eunice Crowe demanded from her chair on the other side of the frame. "I cain't hear a word you're sayin'!"

Carrie shot Eunice a look and then reached over and patted Darlin's hand. "Go on," she encouraged.

"My sisters' names are Faith, Hope and Charity," Darlin

repeated a little more strongly, sitting up straight in her chair. "When I was born, Daddy was so sure I was gonna be a boy that he didn't have no names picked for a girl. So he just called me Darlin. It stuck."

"Oh, for Pete's sake! But what's your Christian name?" Eunice glared.

"Th...that's it," Darlin stammered. "It's on my birth certificate that way. The county man come to register the birth an' that's what Daddy wrote down. Said he figured they could change it later, if'n they come up with somethin' else. Reckon they never did, 'cause I'm still Darlin."

The Stoneworth sisters and Ma Richards laughed at Darlin's explanation.

But Eunice snorted. "Hmmmh! Give me a good ol'-fashioned name any day of the week. Mighty frivolous of your folks, if'n you ask me," she sneered.

Hattie's sister Lalie, sitting on Darlin's right side, whispered under her breath, "Ain't you glad nobody asked her?"

"I heard that, Lalie Stoneworth! Oh, you are the limit. Just the limit!" Eunice stabbed her needle into the edging of the quilt and scraped back her chair. "Since it's plain I ain't wanted here, I'll go see to my grandchildren."

"Oh, Lalie!" Hattie cried after Eunice sailed from the room.

"I'm sorry, Hattie." Lalie's face was beet-red.

"I... I thought she couldn't hear me with the way she was picking on Darlin to speak up. I know that's no excuse, but...I'm so sorry."

Ma Richards turned a stern eye on Lalie and shook a thimbled finger in her direction.

"You was raised better, Eulalie. I knowed your mama. She'd a been 'shamed of you."

Suddenly her eyes twinkled. "But I ain't!" The old woman cackled.

That did it. They all howled.

❧

Eunice Crowe never returned to the house after she left the quilting. Through the window, Hattie watched Eunice's brother, Ferd, arrive in his pickup truck to take the old woman home. It was obvious Eunice was still seething when she left. Hattie had just barely made it to the door before Eunice was gone. She hadn't even said goodbye.

That's not a good sign. Hattie sighed as she walked back to the front room. *She's gonna find some way to make me pay for Lalie's remark. Thank goodness Smith was outside with the children! At least she couldn't take it out on them.*

Hattie knew from experience that she couldn't trust Eunice alone with Dulcie. The woman bedeviled the little girl for information about Hattie and Smith, and generally made her miserable when given the opportunity. Once, she'd slapped Dulcie and locked her in the dark closet under the stairs. And Hattie had learned that when Dulcie had visited her grandmother a few months earlier, Eunice had shut the little girl in the root cellar. To this day, Dulcie was terrified of the dark, and what might be lurking there—particularly mice and rats. Hattie didn't allow Dulcie or Jackie to go to Eunice's home any more unless she herself was visiting. As bad as things were between Eunice and Hattie before, they had only gotten worse since Hattie married Smith.

It was late afternoon before the women rose from their chairs amid much moaning about aching backs. They gathered their needles and thread, and helped Hattie remove the cording from the almost-finished quilt. She would bind it herself during quiet moments, as she found time. They pulled the ropes that raised the frame back up to the ceiling and replaced all the chairs in the dining room.

Smith tromped onto the back porch just as the women were leaving. "Well, now. Don't I feel like one of them fish, swimming upstream!" he called as they passed him on their way out.

Carrie patted his cheek as she went by. "Ladies first, Smith."

"Age before beauty," he retorted.

Carrie whirled around. "You are an awful, awful man!" she teased. "Don't know what I was thinkin' when I let you marry into this family."

"Carrie, you never stood a chance before my charmin' ways." Smith swept an imaginary hat off his head and bowed low to see her out the door. "Once you heard my smooth tongue speakin' those beautiful French phrases, you knowed I was just the man of class for your youngest sister."

"Ha!" Carrie exclaimed. "I figured you out! You knew how to order ham and eggs. For certain, not much more!"

She laughed all the way to her car.

❧

Late that night, while Smith and Hattie were lying in bed, they talked about the day's events. Hattie sighed over Dulcie's naughty behavior at the supper table.

"I hate fussin' at her, and it's just so unlike her," she lamented.

Smith yawned and adjusted the pillow under his head. "There's an awful lot goin' on right now, Hattie. We got four extra kids in the house, an' you've got a new baby comin'. 'Sides, you cain't expect her to be good all the time. Young'uns gotta try their folks every now and again. Otherwise they wouldn't be young'uns."

"I s'pose. I reckon I'm being silly. It's just that with her actin' up so bad right after what Lalie said to Mother Crowe..."

"What did she say?" Smith asked.

Hattie told him about Lalie's smart remark.

"I'm prob'ly makin' too much of it, but you know how Eunice is when she gets her back up."

Hattie sighed again. "That's why I was so thankful you were outside with the children," she said.

Smith slowly turned toward her. "But, honey, I wasn't. I was over in the lot with Gideon most of the afternoon."

9

Sunday morning dawned bright and clear. Hattie got up early and dressed with special care, fixed breakfast and made sure the children were ready for Sunday school and church.

Smith swept out the bed of the pickup truck, then turned the crank to start the engine. He helped load Dulcie and the older children into the back, then lifted Mary Claire and put her on Digger's lap.

"You hang on to this little treasure. We don't want her bouncin' out, now do we?"

Digger wrapped his gangly arms tightly around the roly-poly little girl.

Smith chucked the little girl under her chin, then picked up Jackie and plunked him down beside his mother on the front seat and slid in next to the youngster.

"You gonna be a good boy in church today, son?" he asked the toddler.

Jackie nodded solemnly, then, at the top of his lungs, lisped his way, word for word, through the Twenty-third Psalm. When he was finished, he proudly looked from one parent's astonished face to the other.

"Jackie, that was wonderful!" Hattie exclaimed. "When...? How...?"

Smith wrestled the old truck into reverse and turned it around.

"He must have heard it when Dulcie was learning it for her memory verse."

"But he's only two. I never heard such a thing from a two-year-old!" Hattie protested.

Smith tousled the little boy's dark hair and grinned. "I got a feelin' this little feller don't miss much of what's goin' on in this house. He may not say a lot, but he's thinkin' all the time, ain't you, boy?"

Jackie turned huge brown eyes toward Smith and nodded vigorously.

Smith threw back his head and laughed out loud. "See, Hattie, his wheels are turnin' all the time. He'll be runnin' the county one of these days."

Again the baby nodded, then turned his attention to his shoelaces.

Smith glanced through the window behind his head and made sure the five older children were sitting safely along the walls of the truck bed, then eased down the drive and pulled out into the lane. At Mrs. Collier's house, they made the sharp right toward Jacksontown and then a left up and over the hill to Jackson Chapel.

"Hold on back there," he called out the window, as the truck bounced up the rutted road.

Hattie turned and looked back at the children. They clutched the rails and laughed with each bounce of the truck.

Jackson Chapel stood on a hillside on the right side of the road. Trucks and cars already surrounded the white clapboard building. Behind the church a lone mule was tied next to a horse and wagon.

Smith parked the truck next to Gene and Carrie's sedan and climbed out. He walked around and, opening Hattie's door, helped her out.

Jackie hopped across the seat and stood expectantly waiting. He bounced up and down and held his arms out.

"Jump!" Smith said.

The little boy's face dimpled into a huge grin and his eyes danced. He leaped squealing into the air. Smith caught him and swung him up in his arms.

"Smith, don't be gettin' him all wound up," Hattie warned.

"He's gonna have to sit still for the next two hours. Now's not the time for rough-housing."

Smith winked at the little boy, then hung his head. "Yes, ma'am," he said meekly.

Hattie laughed at his antics. "Honest to Pete! You're worse than the children!"

Digger jumped over the side of the truck onto the ground, and stuck his hands in his pockets.

Hattie looked him over. The last month had seen a dramatic change in the little boy. He was still wary, but the haunted look in his eyes had faded. He no longer constantly looked over his shoulder. And, with Smith's gentle example, Digger didn't order the little girls around as often, or as harshly. His temper was still there, though. It lay under the surface and exploded in unexpected moments. Hattie had learned the warning signs and usually could head off an eruption. She was amazed at the child's capacity for patience when it came to animals. He loved feeding the chickens and gathering the eggs. And when Gideon brought his dogs to the house, Digger was enraptured.

"Look there, Digger." Hattie pointed toward the McBrides' car. In the rumble seat lay two of Gideon's hounds. "I bet if you're good durin' the service, Mr. McBride'll let you spend some time with the dogs before we go home."

Hattie hesitated, then lightly put her arm around the boy. "How 'bout we ask 'em home with us for lunch. Would you like that?"

For the first time, Digger didn't pull away from Hattie. He glanced away from the dogs and directly up at her. "You mean it, Miz Hattie?"

At her nod, he whooped, then stilled. "Can I ask 'em?"

Hattie's face crinkled into a sweet smile. "The dogs, or the McBrides?" she teased gently.

"Both!" he responded with an answering smile.

"Of course you can."

Smith lifted the girls down from the tailgate of the truck

and began herding them toward the building. They walked up the five steps into the church and down the aisle.

The one-room building was broken into "rooms" by hanging curtains strung on wire. During the worship service the hangings were pushed against the wall. Hattie left Digger and Becky in the small enclosure for their Sunday school group. Dorie and Dulcie went to another corner of the building, and Hattie gathered Jackie, Mary Claire, and the smallest children in the back where she taught the toddlers.

The adults met in the front of the building for their class. Some of the men waited outside for the worship service to begin. They talked about the mines, and though they would never have admitted to it, they quietly gossiped about the happenings in the community.

Smith returned to the truck for his Bible and headed back inside for the adult class. He waved at his friend Clarence Hunt, who stood out in the yard with two other men.

Clarence called out, "Hey, what's the word on Dunford?"

Smith glanced toward the building, hesitated, then walked over to the group of men.

"Haven't heard from him. He's around, though. I been keepin' a lookout. How 'bout you? Heard anything?"

"Just that he's been drinkin' hard over in Mannington," Clarence replied.

Mannington was a small town in the next county to the southwest and was not far from Hopkinsville, which had its share of taverns and houses of ill repute.

Smith frowned. "That don't surprise me. But it does concern me. Deke ain't right in the head when he's drinking. If he's hittin' the booze..." He left the statement hanging.

Bud O'Neil pushed his fedora back on his head and joined the conversation. "Ever since he grew that mustache, an' Annie Radburn tol' him he looks just like Clark Gable in *It Happened One Night*, he's had his nose in the air, a-lookin' down at us regular folks like he was right out of Hollywood hisself!"

The heavy-set man leaned over and spat into the weeds. "He ain't never been right, you ask me," he continued. "I ain't had nothin' to do with Deke Dunford since we was kids. Always had a mean streak."

Ed Tompkins rolled his eyes. "Who you tryin' to kid, Bud. We was *all* rooked by Deke. We even voted him deacon a few years back. All we knew of Deke was what he done in public. What he done in private was never common knowledge."

Smith shook his head. "That ain't exactly true, Ed. The ladies knew. I heard Hattie and Carrie talkin' about Deke when I was workin' for Hattie. Long before I ever seen a bruise on Mamie, I knew what Deke was doin' to her."

Smith looked toward his feet, then squared his shoulders and looked at the other men. "Every single one of us is partly to blame for what happened to Mamie. The way I see it, we stood by without a word and let Deke kill her."

Ed rocked back on his heels, while red color crept up his neck. "Now wait just a minute, Delaney. I ain't takin' no blame for that! That was between Deke and Mamie. You got no call to put the blame on us."

Smith held up his hands, palms out. "Settle down, Ed. I'm just sayin' our wives knew what was happenin' to Mamie, and most of us heard about it. We should have called Deke on it. Instead..."

Bud clenched his fists. "I'm with Ed on this. We didn't have no right to interfere with Deke and his woman. What a man does with his wife is between him and her and God."

Smith looked from one man to the other. "You go on tellin' yourselves that. Maybe it salves your consciences." His blue eyes bored into theirs. "It don't salve mine."

Clarence Hunt was the only man who met Smith's gaze. He nodded his agreement. Smith turned on his heel and walked into the church building.

❧

"Fine sermon today, Brother Fenton!" Smith pumped Eli

Fenton's callused hand. "You got a way of preaching that always seems aimed right in my direction."

Smith looked over both his shoulders, winked, and stage-whispered, "Just between you an' me, Eli, I'd prefer it if you'd aim at some of the other folks once in a while."

Preacher Fenton glanced around too, then answered in the same way. "Sounds like you got a guilty conscience, Smith. Anything you want to confess?"

Both men, good friends and former co-workers at Coaltown Mine, shared a laugh at Smith's expense.

Hattie touched Smith's arm.

"Honey, the McBrides are coming for lunch. We better head home. I wouldn't want them to beat us there."

Smith nodded and said goodbye to the minister. He held Jackie's hand as they walked down the steps and into the sunshine. Hattie called the children and soon they were on their way.

Jackie hummed a slightly off-tune *Jesus Loves Me* on the seat between his parents.

They'd been home only a few minutes when loud backfires sounded from the lane.

Digger raced down the stairs from changing into his play clothes. "They're here! Pride and Princess are here!"

Smith reached out and grabbed the boy. "And Gideon, and Darlin and Levi! They're here, too!" he exclaimed in exactly the same tone the boy had used.

Digger laughed and squirmed in Smith's embrace, but not very convincingly. Smith rubbed the top of the boy's head with his knuckles, then let him go.

"Well? You gonna let 'em stand out there in the sun, or invite 'em in?"

Hattie called after the racing boy, "Just the McBrides, Digger! The dogs stay outside!"

❧

The adults sat around the dining room table long after the

older children had gone outside to play.

Jackie piled up his blocks and knocked them down, and Levi slept on a folded quilt on the floor next to Darlin.

"Mighty fine meal, Miz Delaney, mighty fine!" exclaimed Gideon, rubbing his stomach with satisfaction.

"Sure was!" agreed Darlin. "I'd sure like your recipe for jam cake. That was the best I've ever tasted."

"I cain't quite say she's the best cook I've met on four continents, but she's in the top hundred or so," Smith grinned at his beaming wife.

"Aw, Mr. Delaney," replied Gideon, "she'd have to be amongst the top ten...." He paused abruptly. "Did you say *four continents?* You been on four continents?" He looked at Smith with awe.

"Yep: North America, Europe, Asia, and Australia."

"Wow!" said Gideon. "And I ain't even been out of Kentucky, except over the Tug Fork of the Big Sandy River into West Virginia."

"You musta seen some wondrous sights, Mr. Delaney," said Darlin.

"I reckon so. I've seen the Eiffel Tower in Paris, Tower of London, an' the Silver Pavilion in Japan. Lots of man-made stuff—but nothin' to equal the Statue of Liberty in New York Harbor. And scenes of nature that'd boggle your minds. The Grand Canyon in Arizona, giant redwoods in California, jungles of the Philippines, Mount Fuji in Japan—things that sure make a feller think about God's mighty hand."

"Were you ever scared?" asked Gideon. "Ever get in a scrape where you wondered if you'd come out alive?"

"Many a time in fightin' in the World War. But before that, one time in the jungles of Borneo, I was runnin' from headhunters and thought for sure I was a goner!"

"You mean real, sure 'nuff headhunters? You're not spoofin' us, are you Mr. Delaney?" asked Darlin.

"Not kiddin', Darlin'. If they'd a caught me, they'd a

beheaded me and shrunk my head and right now it would be hangin' by the hair in some hut in the jungles of Borneo. And it wouldn't be any bigger than this." He held up his clenched right fist and with his left forefinger made a motion as if cutting the fist off at the wrist.

"Smith, that's just awful!" said Hattie. "Don't talk about such things right after we've eaten."

"Aw, Hattie, don't be so skittish!" Smith winked at his wife. "Reckon I could change the subject a little."

He leaned toward the younger man. "Gideon, something you might be interested in is how the Japanese fight. When I was in the Philippines, an American soldier boy I knew got into a row with our Japanese houseboy, Hiroshi Natsahara. He was a real nice fellow."

"Hiroshi—what?" Gideon gasped.

Smith grinned. "It's a mouthful, ain't it? I just called him Hiro. Anyway, our soldier boy was drinkin' a bit. He got riled about something, an' just 'cause he was drunk and spoilin' for a fight, he took a swing at the little fellow. Hiro ducked and tried to back away. The American boy started laughin' and callin' him a coward. He took another swing. The next thirty seconds beat anything I ever saw."

"What happened?" asked Darlin, her blue eyes wide.

"Hiro kicked out of his sandals, crouched for a split second with his arms bent at the elbows out in front of 'im, and in a instant he was a blur, a whirlin', leapin' in the air, and kickin'. One barefooted kick to that soldier's head and the American went down like a truck tire punctured by a railroad spike."

"Did he kill 'im?" asked Gideon.

"Nope, but the soldier spent a day or two in the infirmary. Anyway, I decided right there an' then I had to know something 'bout that kind of fightin'. Next time I was off duty, I asked my buddy, 'Hiro, you know how you fought Buck Jones?'

"He bows to me and says, 'Smith-san, I have black belt to prove knowledge of *kuh-rot-tee.'*

Well, I could see he had on a black belt but couldn't figure what that had to do with fightin'. '*Kuh-rot-tee,*' he said, 'is system for *defense* of self, not for fighting.' So I asked him if he'd teach me. And he did."

"And you really learned it?" Darlin asked.

"I learned a little. Not much—it ain't easy. But I can still hear him sayin,' 'Focus, Smith-san, spin, leap, kick! Focus, spin, leap, kick.' He learned me a bunch of drills, but that's the one I remember best. Prob'ly 'cause that's what leveled the soldier boy I told you about."

"You ever use—whatever it was you called it—in a fight?" asked Gideon.

"*Kuh-rot-tee,*" said Smith. "Never have. Figured it wouldn't be fair. Not with me bein' the only one knowin' how to do it."

He paused and took a sip of his coffee. "Now, if a bunch ganged up on me, I might. Or if I was in a one-on-one with a feller and he was armed and I wasn't. But I ain't practiced in ages, and with a bum leg, probably wouldn't be much good."

"And..." said Hattie, with an expectant look on her face.

"And, besides, Hattie's been workin' on me." He grinned. "Helpin' me see I need to love the fight out of folks instead of thinkin' I can beat it out of 'em."

"He's doing lots better, too. Why don't we talk about something more pleasant? Smith, why not tell Darlin and Gideon about how you caught monkeys in the Philippines?"

For the next hour Smith relived catching monkeys, chasing wild boars and being chased by them, looking into the maw of active volcanoes, and other tales of his travels. Finally the conversation turned to the Depression and hard times.

"Gideon, didn't you tell me you have a litter of pups out of Princess?" Smith asked.

"Yessir! Got eight of the purtiest little hounds you ever did see. Purebred, too. You needin' a dog, Mr. Delaney?"

Smith shook his head. "No, we got enough mouths to feed. I don't need another one. But I might know some folks who'd be interested. What'd you want for one of them pups?"

Gideon leaned forward on his elbows. "Well, sir, I reckon a couple of dollars would be fair, don't you?"

Smith's eyebrows shot up. "Son, you're undersellin' your dogs! I been watchin' you with Pride and Princess. I ain't never seen a man could train a dog like you do. If'n you train them pups, you oughta be able to get a lot more'n two dollars. Might even be able to get fifteen or twenty."

Gideon scooted himself back from the table so fast that Hattie thought he was going to tip the chair over.

"Twenty dollars! Why...Oh, you're funnin' with me. Who ever heard tell of that kind of price for a dog!" The young man shook his finger at Smith. "You must think I'm some kind of dunce."

"No, I don't," Smith answered firmly. "And I ain't funnin' you neither. I'm tellin' you true, you can get good money for those dogs."

Darlin counted on her fingers, "Twenty times eight... My gracious! Gideon, that's a hundred and sixty dollars!"

Gideon looked skeptical. "Mr. Delaney..."

"Let me think a minute." Smith rubbed his chin. "Look here. Let's you an' me take Pride and Princess up to Jockey Day in Greenville on Tuesday. I'll bet you anything we can sell them dogs."

"Pride and Princess ain't for sale," Gideon stammered.

"How 'bout Bart and Caesar, then," asked Darlin. "They're ready to sell. An' the pups..."

"But...but the pups ain't trained yet," Gideon protested.

Smith snapped his fingers. "You say you got two more dogs like Pride and Princess, already trained for game?"

At Gideon's slow nod, Smith went on. "We'll use them for a demonstration—and get top dollar for 'em. Then we'll sell the pups for half the money down up front, and the rest when the dogs are trained like the buyer wants 'em. How'd that be?"

Gideon looked as though the crown jewels had landed in

his lap.

"That would be fine, Mr. Delaney. *Real* fine!"

❧

Late that afternoon, the McBrides got ready to go home.

"Miz Hattie, we sure do thank y'all for your hospitality," said Gideon as the couple started to leave.

"And we appreciate you tellin' us those stories, too, Mr. Delaney," said Darlin, as she bundled up the baby. "I learned more about the world this afternoon than I ever did in a whole year at the schoolhouse."

"We're mighty proud you came," said Hattie.

"That's for sure," said Smith. "See you Tuesday, Gideon, for our trip to Greenville."

Soon the rumbling, rattling, roadster topped the hill and was out of hearing.

❧

That night, Hattie wrote in her journal. *Gideon and Darlin are such a sweet couple. He sure thinks the world of her. I watched him today. Every little thing she does is a treasure to him. And that baby! He's coming along just fine. I believe he's getting a little chubby. Darlin's so proud of him. Maybe whatever it is that they are afraid of is done. They seem to be more comfortable with us now, though other than knowing how Darlin got her name, we still don't have any idea of their backgrounds.*

Hattie straightened up to listen to the crickets for a moment then bent over the journal again:

Yesterday, Marva came down for a while to see the kids. I have to admit, they loved the time they spent with her. And she longs for them. I can see it in her eyes. We don't seem to be able to talk about it, though. And I don't know what to do about it. There's never been any kind of strain between us before. I only want what's best for the children. Why can't she see that?

I suppose it's silly to worry over it when they have a daddy. We still haven't seen Deke since the night before Mamie's funeral. I think I'll just die if he comes for them.

10

Marva came early the next morning and took the four Dunford children to shop for new school shoes. She'd promised to take them to Cotton's Corner in Greenville for ice cream after their shopping was done. Dulcie stayed home. Her mama and daddy would buy her shoes when they could.

Feeling left out, and a not just a little jealous, Dulcie wandered down to the swing that Smith had hung on the huge oak tree that stood at the front of the yard. She clambered up on the board seat, and swung her feet slowly back and forth.

As much as she loved Dorie, and enjoyed the company of the other children, it hadn't been easy sharing her room and her toys—and now they were even taking Aunt Marva!

Dulcie hung her head. She knew that wasn't fair. Aunt Marva would always be there for her, but it was still hard. She bit her lip and blinked to chase away the angry tears that threatened to spill over and roll down her cheeks.

None of it would be so hard if she hadn't learned the truth about *him*!

Grandma Crowe had explained it to her on the day of the quilting. They'd sat together on the porch swing, and she'd told Dulcie how *he* wasn't her real father. She already knew that, but she'd thought—she'd really thought—that *he* loved her like her real daddy would have.

She didn't remember her real dad any more. Not really. When she thought of "Daddy" now, it was always Smith. Jack Crowe had slowly faded into a shadowy presence in her memory.

Grandma Crowe had told her *he* had planned it that way. *He* had wanted Dulcie to forget her real daddy. *He* knew her mama wouldn't have had anything to do with marrying a man who didn't act like he loved Dulcie and Jackie. So *he'd* fooled them all, and *he'd* made her forget the daddy that God had given her.

Dulcie was so upset by what her grandmother told her that now she refused to call Smith Daddy. In fact, she didn't refer to him at all except in pronouns. Oh, she answered him when he called her name, and she wasn't disrespectful to him—she'd been raised better than that. But she wasn't going to call *him* Daddy any more, ever!

Grandma Crowe had explained it all. How *he* had cozied up to her mama, and her mama was so weak she let him. *He'd* married up, Grandma said. *He'd* had to accept Dulcie and Jackie to get their mother, but when *his* baby came...the truth was going to come out!

Dulcie remembered the conversation almost word for word:

"He ain't gonna even bother to act like your daddy no more. He'll stop pretending. You mark my words, Dulcie. Grandma knows all about the likes of Smith Delaney!"

"But, Grandma, he loves me!"

Grandma Crowe had waved away Dulcie's protest with a wrinkled hand.

"He don't know what love is, sugar. A man like that—he's only after one thing. An' what that is you ain't old enough to know, but it ain't a sweet little girl like you."

Grandma had been so nice to her that day. Much nicer than she usually was. She'd pulled Dulcie up on her lap, and with a comb from her black purse she'd fixed Dulcie's hair into pretty plaits.

It had felt so nice to know that Grandma really loved her. She'd even told Dulcie why she didn't come around much any more—*he* wouldn't let her.

"Why, I have to get permission to come down here now. Did you ever hear such a thing? Do you think your mama has to ask permission to see your aunts and uncles?"

Dulcie had shaken her head "no." Mama and her brothers and sisters wandered back and forth between their houses all the time. No one ever asked. They just went.

"Course she don't. It's HIM! He laid down the law. Your mama's not strong enough to stand against him. An' when that new baby comes, it'll just get worse!" the old woman had whispered. *"I hate to think how bad it's gonna be. Grandma just weeps for you, sugar..."*

Grandma Crowe had plucked her crumpled handkerchief from her bosom and swiped at her eyes. *"I just don't know what'll become of you and Jackie!"*

A thrill of fear had shivered its way down Dulcie's spine.

Grandma had rubbed her bony hands up and down Dulcie's arms.

"Ain't it already started, child? Ain't he already ignoring you? He got all them other young'uns in here, an' don't take near the time for you he used to. Ain't that right?"

It was true. Smith *was* spending a lot of time with the other kids. He took Digger to town with him, when he always used to take her. Seemed like he was either doing something with all of them, or alone with Digger, or else he was over in the lot with Mr. McBride.

"Bet you ain't done one thing—just you and him—since them kids got here."

Dulcie had sat still as stone on Grandma's lap.

"Bet he ain't been tellin' you none of his stories, neither—not just to you alone."

No, he'd told all of them his stories.

"Ain't read nothin' out of a book just to you neither, has he?"

He read to all of them.

"He ain't give you the time of day."

"Treated you like a step-child."

"Don't love you enough to adopt you."

"Didn't give you his name."

Grandma had kept talking and talking. Dulcie finally covered her ears. It was too much! The old woman had gathered her in her arms and crooned softly to her while Dulcie cried. She felt so sad. And stupid! She'd been stupid to think that *he* had loved her.

Dulcie kicked her feet harder and sent the swing flying higher and higher.

I won't be stupid any more, she vowed to herself. *I'll stop loving him, too. He can't make me love him. No matter what he says.*

Dulcie let go of one of the chains to knuckle the white-hot tears away. Her insides felt all mushy and queasy. She just wanted to wrap up in her quilt like a little baby, and not come out ever again.

Baby—there was still the problem of the new baby.

Dulcie jumped off the swing and started back toward the house. On the way, she made her six-year-old self another promise.

I ain't lovin' *his* baby, neither!

11

Smith said, "C'mon, Dulcie. Climb up here on the swing with the rest of the young'uns!"

"No, thank you." Dulcie pressed her back against the outside wall of the house.

Smith shrugged and turned to the porch swing where the rest of the children were piled. He glanced back over his shoulder toward Dulcie.

"Last chance. You sure, honey?"

"Yessir," Dulcie mumbled.

Smith waited a moment longer for Dulcie to change her mind. When she lowered her eyes to look at her shoes, he turned back to the children on the swing.

"Becky, you hold on tight to Jackie. Digger, put your arms around Dorie and Mary Claire," he directed.

"Now, everybody, close your eyes tight, and hold 'em shut for a minute and I'll show you what the earthquake in Japan felt like when I was there."

It was only 7:30, but they had already had breakfast, and Smith was awaiting the arrival of Gideon McBride. Smith walked around behind the swing, leaned down and gave it a bit of a sideways push.

"Whoa!" Digger exclaimed. His eyes popped open. "I didn't 'spect it to go sideways!"

"Yep," said Smith, "and that's just what it feels like sittin' in a swing. Imagine what it would feel like if you were walking along, or sittin' in a straight chair, when things started to move like that. Why, sometimes an earthquake'll knock people off their feet. Buildings come tumblin' down and fires break out."

"Weren't you scared, Mr. Delaney?" Dorie asked.

"Sure was! I'd never been around an earthquake before."

Dulcie marched to the swing. "Me and Jackie talked it over. We decided we want to go with you an' Mr. McBride to Jockey Day," she said.

Smith regretted his answer the moment he gave it. "Honey, that won't work out this time. Me and Mr. McBride have serious business to take care..."

Dulcie's face set into stubborn lines. "An' you ain't gonna be bothered takin' us two young'uns. I understand."

She turned and flounced into the house. The screen door banged against its frame.

"Wha..." said Smith.

The Dunford children cleared off the swing and stood expectantly, eyes huge in their faces. Becky clutched Jackie to her chest. All eyes were on Smith.

Smith stared at the spot where Dulcie had stood only a moment before. Confusion mixed with mild irritation. Dulcie had never spoken to him like that before, and she'd certainly never slammed a door! He replayed the conversation in his head. He hadn't intended to give her the impression that he thought she was a bother. He rubbed his hand across his chin, then caught sight of the Dunford children, frozen like deer in headlights.

"Down!" Jackie demanded, squirming against Becky's arms.

Smith walked around the back of the swing, and taking the little boy from Becky, threw him up in the air and caught him.

"Well, somebody woke up on the wrong side of the bed, this mornin'. Sure wasn't you, was it, son?" Smith asked the chuckling tot.

Becky, Digger, Mary Claire and Dorie still looked as though they were waiting for an explosion, and all four visibly jumped when a sound like two gunshots rang out, then a third.

"There comes Mr. McBride!" announced Smith, "C'mon, y'all. Let's go meet 'im."

Gideon's ancient jalopy backfired once more as it reached the bottom of the hill and turned up the drive. It came to a quivering, rattling halt. There was no door on the driver's side, so the lanky youth slipped out of the seat, reached into the rumble seat and pulled out a chunk of wood. He jammed it under the tire to keep the car from rolling backward down the hill.

Smith's greeting of "Mornin, Gideon," was followed by near echoes of "Mornin' Mr. McBride" from the children."

"Hidy, Mr. Delaney, children."

Hattie pushed open the screen door and called a hello.

"Mornin', Miz Hattie."

"Hi, Gideon. Smith tells me you're gonna parlay that ol' car for a brand new pickup truck today," she teased.

Gideon rolled his eyes, "Yes ma'am, an' a diamond ring for Darlin, an' a pony for Levi."

Smith carefully controlled his face. "Now, I don't know about the pony, Gideon—seems to me Levi's a little young."

Gideon's look of surprise at Smith's tongue-in-cheek remark sent Hattie and Smith into peals of laughter.

"Y'all are too much," the youth finally said. "Always pickin' on me." He said it with an embarrassed smile.

Smith leaned over and kissed Hattie goodbye. She leaned into him for a moment, then straightened.

"You sure you're gonna be all right by yourself with this herd of young'uns?" he asked.

Hattie patted his arm with one hand, and pressed against her back again with the other.

"I'll be just fine."

Smith let his eyes drop to her rounded belly.

"You sure?" he asked again.

Hattie flapped her hands at him.

"Go on," she urged. "Have a good time."

❧

The creaking old roadster was barely moving when it finally crept over the crest of Ebenezer Hill.

"Sure glad we didn't have to go by Central City," Smith said, looking at the slowly passing countryside. "Doubt we coulda made it up Coon Hollow Hill." He grinned and looked at Gideon. "Only if'n we'd backed it up."

Gideon smiled. “Must be a steep one. Mr. Delaney, you reckon we can sure enough trade this thing for a truck?”

“I cain’t give you no guarantee, but if we play our cards right—and the right folks are there—with this old car and them dogs, no tellin’ what might happen. Rumor has it that Mr. L.B. Knight, who runs the big car dealership in Greenville, got his start at Jockey Day. Mind you, I ain’t sayin’ it’s true—He was postmaster at Cleaton, and the story is that he come to Jockey Day with nothin’ but a pretty fair pocket knife and a two-dollar bill. All day he traded up, and at sunset he drove off in a year-old Cadillac!”

“Did not!” exclaimed the youth. “Don’t mean to be disrespectful, sir, but that don’t seem possible.”

“Like I said, I don’t know if’n it’s true or not, but I ’magine there’s at least a dab of truth in it. I’ve seen plenty a man better his lot at Jockey Day. ’Course, you got to know what you’re doin’. An’ if we’re gonna set you up as the top huntin’ dog man in these parts, you’re gonna have to learn how to horse trade.”

The radiator spewed steam and the car backfired a couple of times as they went down the slope toward Pond Creek. Gideon pulled to the side of the road, grabbed a bucket from the rumble seat, and ran down to the creek for water. By the time he got back, Smith had carefully removed the radiator cap and allowed the steam to escape. Gideon filled the radiator and they chugged on their way.

“So what’s the secret to bein’ a good trader?” Gideon asked.

Smith shrugged. “There’s lots of things. I reckon the biggest is knowin’ the customer. What’s he like? What does he want?” He paused, then continued. “Not what does he *say*, but down inside, what’s he got a deep hankerin’ for? Does he want something to show, or something to use, or both? Is he the kind of feller who’ll stretch a little? Will he take a risk, or play it safe? If you get close and then back off, will he follow you or drop the matter?”

Gideon blew out a breath. “Well, how in the world am *I* gonna know them things?”

Smith laughed at the comical look of desperation on Gideon’s face.

"You ain't. Those are the kinda things you get to know by experience, by bein' around folks. That's why I'm goin' with you. You want me to do the talkin' this first time?"

"That would relieve my mind! I ain't much for talkin to strangers anyhow," said the youngster. "But even you won't know everyone there. How you gonna deal with a stranger? One you ain't never laid eyes on."

"Well, I won't be tryin' to take advantage of 'em. Christians just ortn't do that."

Smith pulled his handkerchief out of his back pocket and mopped at his face, then continued. "I'll just try to find out what you have that they want, and make it possible for them to have it. But only if'n we can get what you need at the same time."

Gideon glanced over at Smith. "I didn't figure you'd try to take no one, Mr. Delaney, but that still don't explain how you know if'n you're gettin' a good deal or not. Or even if the folks are interested in what you got to sell."

Smith concentrated on his words. "They'll tell you true with their bodies a lot more than with their words. Most folks have learned to play games with their words. But their bodies will tell you true if, like the Bible says, you have eyes to see."

"Like how?"

"'Spose a feller says, 'Let me see that there pocket knife, Delaney.' I'll hand it to him respectful-like, not just shove it at 'em. I'll treat it like it's a treasure—and watch what happens. See if he checks the spring on each blade to make sure they have good tension. If he looks careful at the brand, then tries it to see if it'll shave the hair on the back of his arm. If he does all that, I'll figure he knows something about knives."

Gideon nodded. "That makes sense," he said.

Smith continued. "If'n he makes a sensible comment about the brand or the metal in the blades, I'll know for sure. But, most important, I'll watch his eyes—an' this counts in all deal-makin', not just knives—if the pupils of his eyes get big, I'll know he's likin' what he sees."

"Is that right? I wouldn't a thoughta that," said Gideon. He wrestled the gears to climb the hill past the cemetery and into Greenville.

"An' you gotta watch his hands. How does he handle the knife? Does he run his fingers over it, like he's enjoyin' the feel? Remember, Gideon, folks generally go for what they're yearnin' for deep in their hearts—but not 'til their heads give 'em a nod to go ahead. So, if you're gonna be good at tradin' or sellin', learn what their hearts want, and figure a way to get their heads to o.k. it."

Smith stared through the windshield. "So questions are important. I'd ask, 'What do you need the knife for, Ed?' Then I'd respond to whatever he answers. I'd point out how the big blade is ideal for skinning game, or how the little one is just perfect for whittlin,' or whatever."

Gideon said, "I b'lieve I'd like to buy me that knife."

Smith laughed. "Main thing is to make sure whatever you trade him for will bring you something that you can keep tradin' up."

Suddenly realizing where they were, Smith said, "Oh, turn left just before you get to the courthouse. We're almost there."

Gideon's apprehension was obvious. "You're right about tradin' up. I sure cain't afford to lose this car. 'Sides the fact it's the onliest one I got, my Uncle Anse give it to me. I'd feel real bad..."

Smith recoiled. "Anse? You got an Uncle Anse? Only Anse I ever heard of was Anse Hatfield."

"Th... that's right," Gideon stammered, glancing anxiously at Smith

"You're a Hatfield?" Smith asked incredulously. "Pull the car over, son. We gotta talk!"

When the jalopy hit the curb, an old revolver hidden under the seat slid forward. Gideon lunged for it.

12

Hattie organized the children for their morning chores, then climbed the stairs to make the beds. She was bending over to straighten the sheet on Dulcie's bed when the cramping started. She patted her belly and smiled, then suddenly gasped and grabbed at the iron bed frame. She gripped the cool metal tightly with her left hand while circling her belly with her right hand, and waited for the pain to pass. She wasn't worried. She'd had a few false labor pains when she was pregnant with Dulcie and Jackie. She'd just wait a minute and it would go away. Slowly the pain faded. Hattie straightened up carefully. The aching in her back intensified.

I just gotta slow down a little bit. That's all there is to it. Smith's right, I been tryin' to do too much.

She sat down on the edge of the bed and closed her eyes for a moment. She'd been awfully tired when she woke up this morning. Seemed like she was tired all the time these days.

Through the open window she could hear the children laughing as they did their assigned tasks. Digger's voice was loudest. He complained about "woman's work," but Hattie could tell by the heaviness of his steps on the back porch that his arms were loaded with wood for the stove. She smiled. *Good boy, Digger,* she thought. *You're comin' along. 'Course, I know it helps to see Smith doin' things around here. I'm sure your daddy would never have hauled in wood. But Smith does it all the time. Kind of hard for you to stand against that kind of example. And speakin' of examples, reckon I need to be settin' one myself, 'stead of sittin' here...*

Hattie finished making Dulcie's bed, then crossed the narrow space to Becky's. She pulled the covers up, fluffed the pillows and smoothed them flat.

Turning to Digger's pallet, she leaned forward, grabbed the ends of the bedclothes, shook them out, folded them in half, then quarters, and laid them across the bow-topped chest that sat at the top of the stairs. Bending to pick up one small sock, she started to stand, gasped, and doubled over again. A low moan escaped before she could clamp her lips together.

The pain was so crushing that she threw a hand behind her to feel for a bed, eased backward until she could sit down, and then curled into a ball, cradling her belly in her arms. She held her breath against the pressure in her lower abdomen. *Breathe, Hattie, breathe.*

She forced herself to take tiny breaths and blow them out slowly. *I'm fine, the baby's fine. I'm fine, the baby's fine. I'm fine, the baby's fine,* she told herself over and over again.

Hattie's thoughts rushed and collided into a jumble of pain and panic. *It's just false labor. That's all. This baby ain't comin' 'til the middle of September. That's what Ma Richards said. It's nothin' to worry over. Right, Lord? You're watchin', right?*

The pain overrode her ability to think. All she could hear was the rushing in her ears and a high-pitched keening.

Digger tripped over the doorsill with the second load of wood, and swore softly under his breath. He heard her from the porch. The little boy turned toward the sound and stepped into the kitchen, tumbling the wood into the box. He leaped the stairs two at a time and then turned and raced back to the yard. He dashed up the rise, through the orchard, and to the garden. Becky, carrying a half-filled basket of tomatoes, stood at one end of the plot. Dorie and Dulcie chased after each other at the other end. Mary Claire and Jackie squatted a few rows away from Becky, examining a bug.

Digger skidded to a halt in the soft earth, and whispered frantically, "You gotta come quick, Becky! It's Miz Hattie. There's...there's somethin' wrong with 'er."

The ten-year-old girl's eyes swept her brother's face. His eyes were huge.

"Stay here with the young'uns," she said softly. "Take 'em to play on the flat rock. Just don't let 'em come to the house."

"But, I want to..."

Becky did something she'd never done in her life. She grabbed Digger by the arms and shook him. "You stand right here, then. Don't you say nothin' to the little ones. An' don't you move off this spot 'til I find out what's goin' on."

Digger's mouth dropped open. He blinked his eyes rapidly to fight the tears that stung his lids. Mary Claire tugged at his overalls. He picked her up and set her on his hip while Becky hurried toward the house. Finally he sat down in the dirt and stumbled his way through his first attempt at telling the children a story.

Becky walked as fast as she could until she was out of sight of the children. Then she ran down the hill, across the yard, and into the house. It was deadly silent. Hattie wasn't in the kitchen. She wasn't in the bedroom. Becky whirled around in a circle. Where could she be?

"Miz Hattie? You here?" she called softly.

Overhead, the bed creaked. Carefully, placing one foot in front of the other, Becky climbed the stairs, searching for the source of the sound.

"Miz Hattie?"

Hattie lay on the small bed, rocking herself. Her eyes stared sightlessly, glazed with pain. Becky ran to her, and knelt at her side. "Miz Hattie, what is it?"

Hattie fought the pain, and tried to focus on the little girl's anxious face. "Becky..." she murmured, "Smith...I need Smith."

Her eyes fluttered closed.

Becky pushed up from the floor and took one of Hattie's clammy hands between her own. She rubbed briskly. Then, only then, did the little girl's eyes see the crimson stain spreading slowly from beneath Hattie, across the sheets and creeping toward the floor.

She dropped Hattie's hand. Her fingers flew to her mouth as she backed away. Bumping into the other bed, she sat down hard, then jumped up and ran for the stairs.

Back through the house, back through the orchard, and on she ran until she found the children.

Doubled over to catch her breath, she gasped softly, "Digger, run for Radburn's store. Run hard as you can. Tell Miz Radburn somethin's bad wrong with Miz Hattie. She'll know what to do."

❧

Digger didn't hesitate. He sprinted off at an angle behind the house. He cut across Mr. Hammer's pasture and jumped the fence at the other end. Landing hard in the dirt on the other side, he stumbled, then righted himself and ran on. The rough road punished his bare feet with each step, but he ran on.

❧

Becky snatched Jackie up and grabbed Mary Claire by the hand. "Come on, children," she said, jerking her head toward the house. She directed Dorie and Dulcie, "We got to go home now."

Dulcie's short legs pumped to keep up with Becky's fast-paced walk. "What's the matter with my mama?"

Becky bit her lip and looked down at the little girl with the mop of black curls. "She's...she's restin' upstairs," she answered. "You know, she's been workin' awful hard takin' care of all us kids. She's just restin'. That's all."

Dulcie's eyes narrowed. "Then how come you sent Digger to fetch Miz Annie?"

Becky slowed and then stopped. She dropped Mary Claire's hand and knelt beside Dulcie. "Why, so she can come he'p your mama out when she wakes up. That's why. An' you an' me, and the rest of us, we got to be real quiet when we go in the house, too. Can you do that?"

Dulcie rolled her eyes. "'Course I can. I'm not a baby!"

Becky smiled. "That's right. Tell you what we'll do. We'll get the butcher paper and the colors out, an' you and Dorie can draw out on the back porch where the breeze is blowin' so nice. Want to?"

Dulcie and Dorie clapped their hands and jumped up and down.

"All right. That's what we'll do then. You two can color." Becky nodded at Jackie and Mary Claire. "And these two can have a little rest along with your mama. We'll build 'em a nest in the front room."

"Mama won't like it if we make a mess while she's sleepin'," Dulcie said. "She won't like it at all."

Becky swallowed hard. "I'll make sure we pick it up. We'll put everything away before she even knows we did it. Now come on. We need to hurry."

The children made their way to the house and Becky carried four dining room chairs into the front room. She draped the chairs with a sheet and made a pallet inside.

"No, giggling, or comin' out," she told the toddlers. "You close your eyes. After a while, when you wake up, I'll make you something to eat."

Jackie and Mary Claire obediently lay down and closed their eyes.

Becky walked back to the kitchen and glanced out onto the porch. Dorie and Dulcie were each coloring bright pictures.

Slowly she turned toward the stairs and forced herself back up into the room where Hattie lay bleeding.

❧

The front door to Radburn's store banged open so hard it smashed back against the wall. Annie Radburn dropped a five-pound bag of flour. It burst and blew out into the room.

"Digger Dunford, what do you mean comin' in here like that! You pert' near scared the wits out of me. Why, the very idea. Just look at this mess!"

"Miz Radburn...help...Miz Hattie..." Digger gasped.

Annie had bent over to retrieve the flour sack, but at Digger's halting words she dropped it again, and jerked back upright. She came around from behind the counter and took the little boy by the shoulders.

"What's wrong with her? What's happened, boy?"

"I...I don't know. She was just lyin' there. Becky said you'd know what to do."

Annie's flour-covered hands fluttered in the air. "Me? Why, I don't even know what's wrong with her. She was just lyin' there, you say?"

Her eyes narrowed. "Are you sure she wasn't just sleepin'?

Maybe takin' a little nap?"

Digger shook his head. "No, ma'am! Weren't like no nap. She was kind of rockin' and cryin', only not like any cryin' I ever heard before. More like a...like a rabbit that's caught its foot in a trap. Real high and frantic-like."

Annie Radburn turned toward the phone. "I'll call Carrie. She'll know what to do."

With one hand she picked up the receiver and held it to her ear, and with the other she turned the crank on the side of the wooden wall-mounted phone. Standing on her tiptoes to speak into the mouthpiece, she said, "Exchange?...How're you, Ruth?...Fine...Uh-huh, he's fine, too...Would you get me Carrie Beckwith, please?"

❧

Carrie's car careened to a screeching halt in front of Ma Richards' small, neat cabin. She left the engine running and ran to the door. It opened before she got there. Ma Richards hurried down the porch steps as fast as age and arthritis would allow. In her right hand she carried her black bag.

Carrie took her by the arm and rushed the old woman toward the car. "Hurry, Ma. She's bleedin' somethin' awful. The children said Smith is at Jockey Day. I'll send one of the men after 'im if you think I need to."

"Let's just wait 'til I can look at her. A little bit of blood goes a long way. It may not be as bad as you're thinkin' it is."

Carrie threw the car into reverse, then shot out onto the main road. "It's bad, all right. You wait. You'll see." Carrie swiped at her eyes. "I cain't hardly see the road for cryin'. I couldn't cry in front of the children, but I've been cryin' ever since I pulled out of her driveway to come get you! Cain't seem to stop...OW!"

Ma Richards withdrew the gnarled hand with which she'd pinched Carrie's thigh.

"Quit that! Straighten up. You're gonna get us both killed, an' that won't do Hattie no good. Now, quit your snivelin' and drive this car like you was sane, or put me out an' I'll walk down to Hattie's."

Carrie dragged the sleeve of one arm across her face, then gripped the steering wheel with both hands.

"Digger said Hattie was cryin' when he found her and went to get Becky. But she didn't make a sound while I was there. I wanted to move her downstairs to her bed, but thought I'd wait until I brought you back so I can send Becky outside to keep an eye on the children. I don't want Dulcie to see all the blood..."

Carrie choked up again, took a deep breath, then continued. "Anyway, I didn't know what to do. She was lyin' there, lookin' like she was dead, an' Becky was standin' there, an' Digger, and they was expectin' me to *do* somethin'. An' I...Well, I didn't know *what* to do!" She repeated.

Carrie glanced over at Ma. "You know how when there's children in the room, you got to be strong? Cain't go lettin' on that you're scared outta your wits, less'n you scare them, too?"

Ma nodded.

"I remembered seein' a movie," continued Carrie "There was a man and he was sick or wounded—I don't remember which—but they raised his feet. Said he was bleedin' and that raisin' up his legs would slow it down, so that's what I did. I raised her feet up and put pillows underneath her legs."

This time when Ma reached for Carrie, it was to pat her leg. "You done fine. That was a good idee."

"Then I sent Digger down to watch the little 'uns, and left Becky with Hattie. And I come after you. I didn't want to leave her, but..."

"You do what you have to when the time comes," Ma said firmly. "You didn't have no choice."

"I s'pose." Carrie let go of the steering wheel with one hand and again wiped at her eyes. "She looks real bad, Ma."

"We'll see. We'll see."

❧

Seven decades of midwifery had taught Ma Richards well. She didn't blanch at the sight of Hattie's body lying still and white on the upstairs bed. Instead, she efficiently moved around the room, opening her bag, retrieving the items she needed and ministering to the unconscious Hattie.

Together, she and Carrie moved Hattie downstairs to her own bed. While Carrie cleaned up the bloody mess upstairs, Ma examined Hattie. Her contractions were coming regularly now, but the loss of blood and excruciating pain had sent Hattie far away—into a place where she no longer heard or saw the commotion around her. A blessing, Ma told Carrie later.

Ma prepared the birthing bed. She folded towels and placed them under Hattie. She set Carrie to boiling water and finding baby clothes and blankets. As she had done at the bedside of hundreds of women, she waited. Her deeply creased, placid face belied the fear that coursed through her veins with every beat of her anxious heart—and she prayed.

Annie Radburn had done what she did best. After she'd called Carrie, she'd sent Digger back home with a pocketful of candy for the children. As soon as he was gone, she'd called Marva and passed on the news that Hattie was in trouble. All morning, she told the horrible news to customers who came into the store to buy tins of baking powder, a box of raisins for baking, or shotgun shells. She sadly reminded each one that she and Smith Delaney were cousins. The buyers went home and told their husbands or wives, or stopped on the way to tell their neighbors. Ruth, at the phone exchange, tangled her lines trying to keep up with the phone calls that flew between the small houses.

As quickly as news travels in small towns, clustered knots of people gathered, and with lowered voices, they spoke of Hattie and the baby that was coming too soon. They clucked and tsked and wondered where the burials would be. They speculated that the shock of loss would send Smith back to drink, and what a crying shame that would be after all this time. They supposed Dulcie and Jackie would go to Carrie and Gene, since Smith wasn't their legal father, though surely Eunice Crowe would fight them for custody. And a few unkind souls wondered if it wasn't about time the Stoneworths had a come-down.

Marva called, or sent messages to, the rest of the Stoneworth brothers and sisters. Soon heaven rang with the prayers of family and friends who begged God for Hattie's life and the life of her baby. It was too hard to say, "Thy will be done." Instead, they pleaded and bargained and beseeched.

Forrest Stoneworth, coming off working extra time after his night shift at the Black Diamond mine, raced the narrow roads to the little house under the hill. He fishtailed his truck up the drive and thundered into the house, still coated with coal dust.

Marva arrived, red-eyed and shaky, and shepherded the six children into her own car and drove them home with her.

With the children gone, and the preparations made, time seemed to stop. Outside the house, birds sang and cicadas buzzed. Up the hill in Mr. Hammer's pasture a cow lowed, and somewhere a dog barked. But inside, the house was silent. No childish laughter pealed, no silly songs were sung. Whispers echoed off the walls and around the simple rooms.

Forrest paced and Carrie prayed—then she cried. And prayed some more.

She wept for this youngest sister of the clan of nine children—the "Least'un," they'd called her. She remembered when Hattie was born—so small and fine. How proud she'd been of her baby sister. Of course she'd been proud of all her brothers and sisters, but none more than Hattie, who'd come into the world sweet and gentle, always with the most thoughtful listening ear, the most open heart. The rest of them were fine, too, but Hattie was different. Where the men were tall and deeply muscled, and the women were tall and willowy, Hattie had started small—and she'd stayed that way.

A throwback, they said, to some many-times-great-grandmother high up in the family tree. She was fairy-like. Small hands and feet, tiny waist—and strikingly beautiful, with her black hair and eyes.

On the day of her birth, Jeb Stoneworth had sat at the edge of his wife's birthing bed holding his tiny daughter in his arms. He'd breathed softly, *"She may not be long of this Earth. Don't know that God lets His angels wander far."* Lettie Stoneworth had leaned out and taken the baby from him. She placed the baby on her breast and hushed him. *"Don't mark her with your words, Jeb.*

Leave well enough alone." And God had let them keep her.

The memory of Hattie's long-dead father's words clashed and bounced through the house. Ma Richards had attended all the Stoneworth births. She remembered Jeb Stoneworth's words. Forrest remembered, Carrie remembered, and wherever they were, the rest of the clan remembered, too.

The wooden clock on the living room mantel slowly ticked the hours by, and still all was silent.

Forrest sat on the couch, his sleep-deprived head bowed down between weary shoulders. Carrie busied herself with mindless tasks, then stood at the window fingering her mother's age-mellowed white lace curtains, wide-eyed, gazing out—seeing nothing.

Sometime after midday, Ma called out.

"Baby's comin'".

13

When Gideon's car hit the curb, Smith's eyes flew to the revolver on the floorboard. He quickly pinned the gun to the floor with his left foot, and clamped the boy's reaching right arm in the steel grip of his left hand. He held the boy against the seat of the old jalopy.

"Whoa there, Gideon! I got Hatfield blood, too! Me and you are kin, son! We're kinfolks! My mama was a Hatfield—second cousin of Devil Anse Hatfield."

The boy's panic subsided a bit, but his face was still furrowed with fear.

"How do I know you ain't a McCoy out to get me?"

Smith relaxed his grip, but kept his foot on the revolver.

"To tell you the truth, Gideon, my great-grandma *was* a McCoy. But my folks were already out here when all the fightin' started back in Pike County and across in West Virginia."

Gideon's eyes narrowed. His face still reflected suspicion. "You mean it, Mr. Delaney? You mean you got both Hatfield and McCoy blood?"

At Smith's nod, tears welled up in the lad's eyes. His words began to overflow and run together.

"Darlin is a McCoy. Our kin back home wouldn't let us be. An' the feud's been over for 'most forty years! We had to get outta there. After my uncle, Little Anse, was murdered, we come here. Then Levi got the thresh. We didn't have no one to turn to 'til Darlin heard about Miz Hattie and Jackie, and y'all treated us like kin, an' I felt so indebted to you, an'..."

"Gideon," Smith interrupted, "the Bible says we're all beholden to each other. God made us in His image. If'n any of us are hurtin' we ort to pitch in and help out. My Hattie's made it her mission in life! But when we're kinfolks, we got a double responsibility to each other."

"That ain't the way it was back home!" said Gideon. "If'n one side was mad at the other, we was all s'posed to take up for our own. 'Bout split me an' Darlin right up the middle."

Gideon hung his head. "I'm sorry 'bout bein' so skittish, Mr. Delaney."

"That's all right. I didn't mean to spook you. Knowin' how bad things were over in Harlan County when Little Anse was killed, I understand—An' since we're kinfolk, don't you think you should start callin' me 'Smith?'"

Gideon cocked his head to one side. "Don't seem quit fittin', with you older an all, but I'll try."

At Gideon's shy nod, Smith leaned over, took the gun from under his heel and handed it to the lad.

"Still think you're gonna need this?"

Gideon sheepishly accepted the revolver and slid it back under the worn seat.

"Look, Gideon, you're wise to stay on your toes. There's people who'll take advantage of you, if you let 'em, but I don't think anyone around here is out for blood 'cause of that ol' feud back east. If any of 'em *do* show up, my brother, Colt, or me will be 'bout the first to hear. We'll let you know."

He reached over and touched Gideon's shoulder.

"If'n we have to, we'll face 'em down together. You, me, Colt, and the rest of the clan. Don't forget, Hattie's folks are our folks, too. She's got an army of brothers and sisters to take up for us if we need it."

The worry lines smoothed from Gideon's face. "I reckon you're right. Me an' Darlin ain't alone any more!"

Smith gave the boy a playful shove. "Nope. Now, if we're gonna get any tradin' done, let's get on down to Jockey Alley—which ain't actually an alley—it's a street that becomes a lane.

Gideon backed the car away from the curb, made a left turn and drove past the courthouse.

The number of cars parked around the beautiful domed

building suggested that the circuit court had a full agenda for the day. The old vehicle made its way past the jail and turned left on a narrow street that led out to the edge of town.

"Man, look at all the stuff, Mr. Delaney! There's things all over the place!"

Sure enough, lining both sides of the lane were trucks, cars, wagons, even a buggy here and there. Merchandise was spread on blankets and tarpaulins stretched over the ground. Coops and cages of animals, boxes, baskets, jugs and jars were scattered helter-skelter.

"Better pull in the first place that looks big enough, son." Smith pointed. "If you can get in there by the edge of that tree, the shade will be comin' this way in an hour or so. That'll make it easier on the dogs—not that we'll leave 'em in the cages long."

Gideon did as told. The two men clambered out of the rattletrap car and stretched. The lad got the bucket of water—what was left of it—from beside the dogs' cage and gave them a drink. He patted each, scratched behind their ears and spoke to them. They wagged their tails and smiled at him with their eyes.

"Let's get the lay of the land, then we'll come back for the dogs," said Smith.

"Fine by me."

The Lincolnesque youth shortened his stride to match the limping gait of the older man. Smith used his cane more to point at items of interest than to aid his walking. As they made their way down the right side of the street, greetings and banter came from person after person.

"Delaney, you been down any airshafts lately?"

"Nary a one."

"Smith, when's the last time you took a shot at the sheriff?"

"Been a while, now, Boyd."

"You and ol' Sawyer gettin' along these days?"

Fire flashed in Smith's eyes.

"None of your business, but we're stayin' outta each other's hair. And I'd advise you not to ask that question again."

"No offense meant!"

"None taken."

"Hey, Delaney, you still got that brown three-bladed Tree Brand pocket knife?" asked a big, red-faced man with an Irish accent.

"Sure do, Paddy. That Solingen is right here in my pocket—and a purty good Barlow, too."

"Wanta make a trade?"

"Mebbe. Depends on what happens down at the track at ten o'clock."

The large man cocked his head and rocked back on his heels. "What's happenin' at ten? Ain't no races 'til two."

Smith clapped Paddy on the shoulder. "Come on down an' see. It'll beat any race you've ever seen, less'n Man o' War comes to town—but I ain't tellin' no more now." Smith greeted farmers with baskets and boxes of fruit and vegetables of every type.

"Hey, Smith, how's Eldon doin'?" asked a man leaning against the fender of a pickup. "Is that brother-in-law of yours gonna make it?"

"Don't know, Rager. If prayer and hope have anything to do with it, he will. But the mines mighty nigh got 'im. His lungs are about done in."

"That's too bad. He's a good man."

"That he is." Smith let his eyes wander over the three guitars lying on a folded quilt in the back of the man's pickup truck. "You ain't got a good guitar you'd let go cheap, do you, Rager?" he asked casually.

"Might have. And I got a fine old banjo for five dollars."

"Hattie would sure like to have a guitar, but she can't play a banjo."

Mr. Rager smiled. "If it's for Miz Hattie, the price automatically drops to four dollars, Smith."

"Thanks. I ain't got that kind of money right now. Let's see how the day goes."

Smith started to turn away, but saw that Gideon had picked up the banjo. He cradled it gently near his left ear, and softly plucked the strings.

"You play that thing, son?"

"Yessir."

"Got one?"

"Used to."

"Mebbe you'll have another, if all goes well."

"Mebbe."

They walked past coops with guinea fowl, banty roosters, ducks, Rhode Island Reds, Barred Rock and Plymouth Rock chickens. When they came to a boy with a cage of three wild rabbits, Smith stopped.

"How much for the rabbits, Stevie?"

"Dime apiece, Mr. Delaney."

"How about a quarter for all three?"

The boy narrowed his eyes and made a triangle in the dirt with his bare toe as he contemplated the offer. "Nope. Cain't do that yet. Day's too young. 'Fore sundown I ort to be able to get full price for each. If I don't, you come back by and I'll make ye a deal then."

"How about a deal now where you get thirty cents for just two?"

"Huh? Howzzat?"

"I'll give you a nickel down right now on each of two. At ten o'clock you bring one down to the track and I'll give a dime for that one. At noon, bring the other down and I'll give you a dime for it, too. How's that for a deal?"

"Yeah, Buddy, I'll take it!" the boy shouted.

A number of people had gathered around, and from the crowd a freckle-faced, red-headed youngster sidled up to Smith.

"I got a cage of squirrels, Mr. Delaney. Wanta make me a deal like that?"

"Why, sure, Albert, we might be able to cook something up. Your squirrels healthy?"

"Yessir! Just caught 'em yesterday in a safe trap. They're in fine shape."

"Okay. Same deal."

Smith reached into his pocket and dropped two coins into the boy's outstretched hand. "Dime apiece with a nickel down for each, an' ten cents for each on delivery at ten o'clock and noon. Deal?"

"Deal!" said the boy, as he shook Smith's hand and took his two nickels.

"What's goin' on at ten, Delaney, and who's your friend?" asked a raw-boned middle-aged man.

"Howdy, Walt. You'll have to come on down to see. You'll be mighty sorry if'n you cain't go home and tell your family 'bout it first hand! My friend here..."

Smith paused, gestured to the crowd and raised his voice. "This here's my kinsman, Gideon McBride. He's originally from Pike County, and lately from Harlan."

A murmur swept through the crowd. "I'll tell you more about 'im at ten o'clock at the track. An' you need to hear what I have to say."

With Gideon at his side, Smith made his way through the crowd and down the lane with the banter continuing. Finally Gideon stopped and put his hand on Smith's shoulder.

"Everybody seems to know you, Smith. How come?"

Smith shrugged. "I was born and raised here. I've hung around Jockey Day regular-like for years—except short periods when I was off workin' somewhere else. Or away in the Army on two tours of duty."

He paused. "And I was tried for murder last year. Most of the folks who didn't know me before got to know who I was then."

"Oh."

When they reached a flat area at the end of Jockey Alley, Smith waved at the expanse and said, "There's the track where the horse races will be run later today. Used to be a sure-enough racetrack further out of town. Now this is just a place where informal races take place. And it's where you an' your dogs'll do your demonstrations at ten and noon."

"The whole idea makes me a mite nervous, Smith," said Gideon, as he ran his left hand through his black hair and wiped his sweaty right hand on his overall leg. "I ain't used to standin' in front of people."

Smith clapped him on the back. "Aw, you'll be fine. You know your dogs and they know you. They'll come through just fine, and you will, too. I'll do the talkin' and the deal-makin', but you'll have the final say."

Smith pointed back up the road. "Let's head back up the other side of the street and see what's here that might be worth dealin' for."

The two men had gone most of the way back up the lane when they saw a crowd gathered around a commotion ahead. They could hear the snarls and guttural growls of a dog—and over the sounds of the dog, the high-pitched voice of a man.

"Meanest dog I ever laid eyes on. That makes 'im the best guard dog I ever seen, too," boasted the man. "Name's Satan."

"That's Jeb Sawyer," Smith murmured to Gideon, as they maneuvered to where they had a better view.

The crowd kept a respectful distance between themselves, Sawyer, and the caged, menacing animal.

Smith elbowed Gideon and whispered, "Watch out for that man. He's meaner than the dog. And a liar."

"I hate to let this fine dog go," said Sawyer. He jutted a huge walking stick at the cage on the back of the pickup truck. The dog growled low in his throat.

"But I need a little cash-money, and I'm willin' to part with the finest guard dog in Muhlenberg County for just seven dollars."

"He's a ugly critter, Jeb! What kinda dog is he?" someone called to the huge man.

"Half pit bull and half mastiff. You tie 'im to your porch with a strong chain—a rope won't hold 'im—and I guarantee nobody'll get to your front door. He respects this club in my hand, or I wouldn't get within ten feet of 'im myself."

He smirked at the crowd, then menaced the dog with a vicious swing of the cudgel toward the top of the cage. The dog went wild, snarling, and lunging at the bars.

"Now, y'all think," Sawyer continued, "he's acting up on account of me." The man cut his eyes toward the crowd. "But I think it's 'cause he seen Smith Delaney over there—or likely smelled 'im."

The slovenly man slapped his leg and guffawed. A few joined in with snickers, but most of the watching men went deathly still.

Smith stepped out of the crowd. Gideon followed on his heels.

"Another poor critter you've mistreated, Sawyer? Shame, too. Looks like he was once a fine animal," said Smith. "Look at 'im now." He shook his head, disgusted.

"Shut up, Delaney, or I'll turn 'im loose an' let 'im make short work of you."

Smith took a step forward. The dog went wild.

Gideon put his hand on Smith's shoulder and shook his head almost imperceptibly.

"Hold on a minute," he whispered.

Gideon took one step past Smith.

"Mr. Sawyer, you say that dog don't like strangers. You ever seen me before?"

Sawyer narrowed his eyes. "I ain't. But seein' the kinda company you keep, I cain't say I much care for ye. Satan don't likely, neither."

"What d'you say I walk over there and pet your guard dog?"

Jeb Sawyer's face twisted into a sly grin. He turned his attention to Smith. "Where'd you get this boy, Delaney? Pick him up on the road? What'd he do? Escape from Western State over at Hopkinsville?"

Sawyer swung his weight back toward Gideon. "Boy, you put a hand in that cage and you'll do well to pull back a bloody stump—less'n he smells Delaney on you, then he'll take your whole arm!"

The big man laughed again, but this time no one joined him.

Gideon slowly walked back and forth at a distance from the cage, eyeing the huge animal.

Gideon turned away from the dog to Sawyer. "You ain't got nothin' to lose, then," he said. "Give me ten minutes. You don't sic 'im, or talk to 'im or make any move toward 'im—an' see what happens. I won't hurt 'im. You game?"

Sawyer's eyes rolled back in his head. "*You* won't hurt *him!*

That's rich! Take your chances, boy. But don't blame me when you end up mangled. I'll bet five dollars to a dime you never get a hand in that cage!"

Smith spoke up. "Stop your yammerin,' Jeb. Everybody knows you ain't got five dollars to bet."

Smith turned and faced the crowd. "Y'all heard the terms. Sawyer is to hold his ground and keep his peace. If'n he don't and causes the boy any trouble, I'm gonna whip Jeb's tail from here to Elkton and back."

His glare in Sawyer's direction left no doubt as to his meaning. The big man bristled, but said nothing. Smith nodded at Gideon. "Go ahead."

The lanky youth slowly moved to within fifteen feet of the dog. Satan ran from side to side in the cage, snarling and growling. Gideon said, "Easy, boy, easy."

He held his hands just in front of him, elbows against his side and palms down. He crept another five feet forward in this position.

Smith slipped along beside Gideon at the edge of the crowd. He watched Gideon, yet kept an eye on Sawyer, directly across from him.

Gideon paused, keeping his open hands parallel to the ground. The dog stopped running, but continued to growl and bark. Gideon pursed his lips as though to whistle, but the sound he made was more of a hum with just a trace of a whistle.

Smith noticed that the boy looked in the direction of the dog but did not threaten him by looking directly into his eyes. The dog stopped barking and cocked his head to the side to listen, but he still growled low in his throat.

The young man eased forward to within five feet of the cage, continuing the hum-whistle. Then he went silent. The dog started barking and snarling. Gideon began making the sound again. The dog quieted, except for a low growl. "Easy, Satan, easy. Easy, boy. I ain't a-gonna hurt you."

Smith watched Gideon's features soften and heard the compassion in his voice.

Taking another step forward, Gideon was within easy reach

of the cage. The dog bristled and lunged against the bars, growling and snarling. Again, Gideon hummed/whistled for ten seconds or so. He spoke quietly to the dog.

Satan dropped to the floor of the cage with his jaw on the floor and his nose against the bars, the low guttural growl less threatening now.

Near stone-still silence fell over the crowd. Smith saw Sawyer take a step forward, and stopped him with a look.

"Don't you move," he breathed.

Gideon didn't even glance over his shoulder toward the other two men. He slipped a half-step closer to the dog, alternately speaking softly and making the unusual hum/whistle sound. Finally he placed the back of his right hand within reach of the massive head.

Smith's heart pounded in his chest. His stomach tightened into a knot.

The dog flicked his tongue out and licked the back of Gideon's wrist!

Not moving a muscle on his body, Gideon turned his hand over and the dog licked his palm, then his fingers. He continued to talk to the dog, while slowly easing his hand under the animal's huge chin, then up behind its left ear. He scratched gently. The dog leaned his head against the caressing hand. Gideon patted the dog.

"You're a good boy, Satan."

He pulled his hand out of the cage and turned away.

14

Applause erupted from the gathered crowd. They whistled and cheered. Satan savagely lunged at the bars, growling and barking.

Gideon's face appeared set in stone. He stalked toward Sawyer.

"Mister, anybody who'd treat a dog like you've treated that one don't deserve to be called a man!"

He jutted a finger toward the newly-enraged animal. "You're more of an animal than he is. You're nothin' but a cur!"

With one hand, Sawyer grabbed the boy by the shoulder, jerked him close and shook him hard.

"Don't you call me no cur!" He raised his cudgel to strike. "An' don't you tell me how to treat my own dog. I'll..."

Smith's clipped words shot toward Sawyer like bullets from a rifle.

"Hands off 'im, Jeb! Now!"

Smith neither raised his voice, nor took his eyes off of Sawyer's enraged face as he approached.

"Now, Jeb, or I'll break that club over your head."

"Leave 'im be, Sawyer!" A man shouted.

"Drop it Jeb! You called his hand and he beat you fair an' square," yelled another.

Others joined in.

Sawyer dropped his hand to his side. His face twisted with fury.

"Y'all seen it!" he shouted. "He 'witched my dog! That boy cast a spell on 'im. Y'all seen it. That boy's a witch!"

Most of the men in the crowd laughed. A few shook their heads. They all turned and walked away. None offered to buy Satan.

Smith said, "You all right, son?"

At Gideon's tight-lipped nod, Smith gestured down the lane. "Let's go, Gideon."

They walked a few paces before Smith spoke again.

"That was somethin' to see! Man, oh man! How'd you do it? How'd you get that dog to settle down so quick?"

Gideon shrugged. "I don't 'zactly know how I did it. It just comes natural to me. I reckon animals know I ain't gonna hurt 'em."

He kicked at the grass on the edge of the road. "I know the first thing I gotta do with a dog like Satan is get his attention—get his mind off the kinda treatment he's had before. My whistle/hum did that. Then I had to make sure I didn't threaten 'im none. An' he didn't smell nor sense no fear nor anger in me. Just respect. Down deep, dogs know that they an' us are s'posed to be friends. Somehow I'm gifted to be able to reach that knowin' place in them."

By this time they were back at the truck where Gideon's hounds waited.

Gideon opened the door of the cage that held his dogs. They stood at the ready, but didn't leave the cage. He reached behind the front seat of the car and pulled out a .22-caliber rifle. Then, at his command, the two hounds jumped from the rumble seat to the ground. They frisked around his heels until he petted them both.

"Let's go, Bart. C'mon, Caesar," he said, as he and Smith started back down Jockey Alley. "Heel."

Smith watched the darker dog slip along to the rear of Gideon at his right side, the other at the left. They were lean but healthy, with alert eyes and glossy hair.

When they reached the place where Stevie had his cage of rabbits, Bart, the larger of the dogs, began to whine and fidget.

"Steady, Bart. Steady," Gideon commanded.

The dog whined softly, but with an eager gaze toward the cage, stayed at his master's side. The other dog seemed not to notice the rabbits at all.

"See you at the track at ten," Smith called to the boy by the cage.

"Yes, sir, Mr. Delaney. I'm gonna bring you my biggest buck rabbit."

A few steps further down the way a well-dressed man called out, "Well, if it ain't Smith Delaney."

Behind him a small group of spectators surrounded several men down on their knees. "C'mon, Smith, get in on the action. Craps over here—c'mon and join in."

Smith laughed. "Ezra, you know I ain't gambled for the last two years. How come you keep askin'?"

The man named Ezra grinned. "Why, 'cause I know what a good Christian you've become." He wheedled, "Think how big your contribution to the church could be if you win!"

Smith chuckled again. "Yup! An' I'd have to go to church worse than naked, 'cause my sweet Hattie would skin me alive."

"Boxcars! Yeah!—Seven, come eleven, now..." called one of the participants, as he rolled the dice.

"Heard you married Hattie Stoneworth Crowe, but didn't figure you'd let a woman keep you from havin' a little fun."

Smith grinned his lopsided grin. "I'd prob'ly take your stake, Ned. That wouldn't be real Christian of me, now would it? Just don't think the Lord would want me to take advantage of y'all."

They walked on.

A short time later a short, red-faced man called out, "Delaney, come over here! Got somethin' I want to show you."

He held a gun upright at his side.

Smith and Gideon turned aside and joined the fellow under the shade of a spreading oak.

"Grayson, this is Gideon McBride—Gideon, Lem Grayson."

The men nodded at each other

"What you got, Lem?"

Lem handed Smith an old rifle. "Clarence Hunt's daddy brought this back from the Civil War. He give it to Clarence. A while back I traded that old white mule of mine for it. Clarence couldn't get no ammunition for it—nowadays, they don't make the special bullet tubes it takes. I figgered I'd convert it, but I just ain't got around to it. You're pretty good at fixin' things. How about takin' it off my hands for five dollars?"

Smith looked the rifle over. He sighted down the barrel and hefted the weight.

"This is a Spencer seven-shooter. You got yourself a purty good old gun, Lem. It ort to be worth more than five dollars."

"Would be if I could shoot it. I don't have time to mess with fixin' it. You got the five dollars, Smith?"

"Yep, and here it is, if'n you're sure." He reached into his billfold, pulled out a five-dollar bill and handed it to Grayson. "It's a deal."

The two men shook hands.

Smith held the rifle barrel-down. "I got the better of you on this deal, Lem." He rubbed his jaw. "Tell you what I'll do, you be down at the track at ten, an' I'll give you fifteen dollars credit as a down payment toward a twenty-dollar McBride hunting dog." He pointed at Caesar, then at Bart.

"Are you outta your ever-lovin' mind?" gasped Grayson. He burst out laughing. "Them's pretty fine dogs, thank you, but I think I'll be keepin' my five bucks. Ain't no dog worth twenty dollars. But thanks for the laugh, Smith."

He nodded to Gideon. "Mr. McBride, good to 'ave met you."

After they walked out of earshot, Smith stopped and turned to Gideon. He held out the gun. "Son, there's the down payment on your truck."

"What?" exclaimed the youth. "What—this old gun?"

"Yep. You wait an' see. Oh, yeah, and from the lips of Lem Grayson, the word about the demonstration at ten will spread faster than it would if Annie Radburn had five phones and could talk on 'em all at once."

"Who's Annie Radburn?"

"She's my cousin. She an' her husband run the store close to the school in Drakesboro. She's the talkin'est woman I've met on four continents."

A bit later a rawboned man in worn overalls held a bottle in a paper sack toward Smith. "You and the lad like a bottle of...er...ah...'sassyfrass tea'? Got a special goin'."

"Nope, but, Eb, have you seen Jordan Pickens from Owensboro? He here today?"

"Ain't seen 'im."

"I did," interrupted one of the bystanders. "As I was comin' from Livermore, I seen him on the side of the road at Island Station fixin' a flat on his truck. I reckon he'll be here directly."

"If he comes along, would you tell 'im I want to see him down at the track?"

"Sure will."

As the pair continued toward the track, both dogs began to whine softly. Just then a familiar high-pitched voice called out, "Them dogs got to be caged or on leash, Delaney! You know the rules."

Jeb Sawyer had walked away from his own caged dog, and stood legs planted, hands on his hips, and glaring across the lane at Smith, Gideon and the hounds.

"Why, Jeb, these dogs are on leashes. It's just that you can't see them. Show 'im, Gideon."

Gideon patted the dog on his right. "Go, Caesar." He pointed straight ahead. The dog loped down the lane about twenty feet.

"Stop."

The dog stopped.

"Turn—Wait." The dog turned and faced his master, then sat and watched with an expectant look. The other dog waited at Gideon's side until his name was called. He followed the same instructions, and waited beside Caesar until he heard, "Come, Bart." He returned to his master's side, as the other dog did when called. A crowd had gathered and applauded.

Smith turned to the big mine foreman glaring across at them. "Sawyer, let's see you train a dog to do that with that club of yours."

The big man shook his fist and screamed, "Y'all better watch out for that skinny feller! He's got them dogs 'witched! I tell you, he's a witch!"

"Aw, shut up, Sawyer!" yelled one of the onlookers.

"Yeah, let's head to the track. It's almost ten o'clock. Let's go!"

When they arrived at the track a large group had already gathered. By the time the group tagging along got there, about one hundred and fifty men were on hand.

"I got my rabbit right over yonder, Mr. Delaney," said the youngster whom Smith had made the deal with. "Let me know when you want 'im."

"Sure will. I got your money. Albert here with the squirrel?"

"He's comin' down the hill right now."

"Have 'im wait back 'til I call for 'im."

"Yes, sir!" he responded, and hurried off with an air of importance to relay the word to the boy with the squirrel.

Smith started to step out onto the track when he heard a voice call, "Smith, I hear you want to see me."

He turned to see Jordan Pickens making his way toward him.

"Yeah, Jordan, I thought you might want to trade your old truck for this gun." He held it up where Jordan got a good look, but carefully kept his hand over most of the name inscribed on the plate. "I'll talk to you later. Right now I gotta take care of the business at hand first."

"Why, that old gun ain't..."

Smith held up his hand. "Sorry, Jordan, I gotta get this demonstration under way. I think you'll enjoy it. Let's go, Gideon."

Leaving Pickens standing with his arms crossed in front of his chest, Smith limped out onto the track, with Gideon and the dogs following right behind. When they reached the middle they turned and faced the crowd.

Smith placed the old gun on the ground beside him, leaned on his cane, and began to speak.

"We got a little demonstration I think y'all will enjoy. Specially you hunters and others who appreciate a good dog. Name's Smith Delaney, for any of you that don't know. I'd like to introduce you to one of Muhlenberg County's newest citizens. After today, he'll likely become one of the better known and respected ones."

Gideon, obviously embarrassed, shifted his weight from side

to side. Bart and Caesar sat at attention on either side.

"This here is Gideon McBride. He lives beyond Belton, near Dead Man's Curve. Mark that in your heads if you're a hunter. You're gonna want to know." Smith paused to let that thought soak in. "Gideon moved here recently from Harlan County—'Bloody Harlan.' Up until three years ago he lived in Pike County."

A murmur swept through the crowd.

"Gideon's mama was a Hatfield—a niece of Devil Anse Hatfield—sister of Little Anse."

The murmur became a muffled roar.

Smith raised his hand for quiet. "Y'all know that mine management shot down Little Anse on the streets of Harlan. Y'all know what the McCoys did to Devil Anse, an' what the Hatfields did to Ol' Randell McCoy and his clan."

Smith paused dramatically.

"Gideon is married to Darlin McCoy."

Now the crowd erupted.

"Listen to me, y'all. Hear me out!" Smith took a step away from Gideon and pointed his cane at him.

"In that young man, Muhlenberg County now has perhaps the best dog breeder and trainer in the state of Kentucky, maybe in all the South."

"Aw, c'mon, Delaney!" yelled a miner, still black with coal dust from a night shift underground.

Smith ignored him. "Most of y'all know me. You know I'm a straight shooter, and I ain't particularly talkin' about with a gun..."

"Sheriff Westerfield knows all about that," someone shouted.

The crowd erupted in laughter.

Smith held up his hand. "Me and him let bygones be bygones. We're on fine terms. But I want you to understand something—then we'll have a demonstration you won't forget. You need to know my grandma was a Hatfield. An' on my daddy's side, my great-grandma was a McCoy. I'm kin to both this young man and his wife. I aim to see they get a fair shake. Anybody takes advantage of them will have to answer to me."

"We got it, Smith. Welcome, Mr. McBride," shouted Lem

Grayson. "Let's give 'em a hand, and get on with the show!"

Applause broke out.

Smith again raised his hand for silence. "Now, let's talk huntin' dogs. I've seen y'all eyeing these fine hounds. Well you might. You probly ain't seen anything like 'em. They're purebred and from a fine line. You'll learn about their pedigree later. You can see they're healthy and well groomed. But looks ain't what huntin' dogs are about. Huntin' is. Now, for the demonstration.

"Would y'all in the front sit down on the ground, so those in the back can see better?" He paused and waited until the crowd shifted.

"Thank you. Gideon, tell 'em about the dogs."

Gideon pointed to the dog on his right. In a clear bass voice, shaking from nervousness, he said, "This here dog is called Bart. He is purebred out of Empress Julia Augustus the third and his sire is Anthony Napoleon Bonaparte the fourth. Both his parents and all four grandparents have won state championships or placed second. Main thing is, he can hunt. He's a rabbit hound. I got American Kennel Club certified papers on all the dogs."

He looked at Smith, who called out, "Stevie, would you hurry out with that buck rabbit?"

When the boy, holding the rabbit by his ears and back feet, made his way out on the track, Bart became agitated and began whining.

"Sit," said Gideon. The dog sat, but his alert eyes and shifting posture showed that he was much interested in the approaching youth and his prey.

"In a minute, Stevie will turn the rabbit loose. I'll give him a head start, then send Bart after 'im. The rabbit might get down a hole or otherwise get away, but odds are good Bart'll get 'im."

He pointed to a spot ten feet away. "Right there, Stevie. Set 'im down."

The boy did as he was told and the rabbit headed toward the crowd, then made a quick turn to the right and scampered down the track. The dog jumped to his feet, but waited.

Gideon raised his hand. "Now, Bart!"

The dog lunged away as though loosed from physical restraints. He sped after the rapidly disappearing rabbit. The crowd broke into applause when the dog began to rumble a deep bellow.

"Listen to that boy sing!" someone shouted.

"Listen to him yodel!"

"Hey, what about that other dog, McBride?" asked Jordan Pickens. "He ain't moved. Is he just for decoration?"

"Nope, he's a *squirrel* dog," Gideon answered loudly. "That weren't a squirrel. Before you get a dog from me, you tell me what you're gonna hunt, and I train him to hunt just for what you want. Most of us has been huntin rabbits, only to have the dog chase a field mouse, or flush a covey of partridge an' take off after 'em. To me, that's as frustratin' as frustratin' gets."

"Yer right about that," yelled someone in the back of the crowd."

"From me," Gideon said, "a squirrel hunter gets a squirrel dog, a coon hunter gets a coon dog, and so on. Now, since Caesar is a squirrel dog, he ain't gonna bother with rabbits. He's had rabbit huntin' trained out of 'im."

Gideon looked at Smith and nodded.

"Albert, bring us that squirrel," Smith called.

The freckled-faced youngster ran out toward them, carrying a small cage. Gideon's dog jumped to his feet and barked.

"Quiet, Caesar. Sit," said Gideon, and the dog sat, but pawed and whined softly.

"Close enough, Albert," Gideon said when the boy was fifteen feet or so away. "Open the cage and let 'im out."

The boy opened the cage, the squirrel jumped out, spun around and raced toward a big sycamore tree down the track. When he was almost there, Gideon bent over, patted the dog and said, "Go, Caesar!" The dog darted after the squirrel. It reached the tree well ahead of him. It dashed up the tree and around to the backside. The dog ran at the tree, leaping up as high as he could.

Gideon lifted his rifle to his shoulder. "Around, Caesar," he called. The dog circled the tree and the squirrel came into sight. Gideon squeezed the trigger, the rifle fired, and the squirrel dropped into the weeds. Instantly the dog grabbed him and ran toward the men in the middle of the track. The crowd applauded.

"Good shot, McBride!" came a call from the crowd.

"Good dog, Caesar!" yelled another.

"Yeah!"

The dog brought the squirrel up to Gideon and dropped it at his feet. The lad patted Caesar's head and said, "Take 'im to Smith." The dog picked up the squirrel and dropped it at Smith's feet.

Smith picked up the squirrel. "Folks," he said, "Gideon dropped that squirrel from fifty-sixty yards with a head shot. Didn't mangle the game. An' the dog didn't damage 'im in the least. It looks to me like..."

"Look yonder!" A fellow squatting in the front row leaped to his feet. "Look yonder!" he repeated, pointing down the track to his left.

The crowd turned in the direction he pointed. There, hurrying toward Gideon, was the proudest-looking dog a person could imagine. Bart, holding his head as high as possible to keep from dragging the rabbit on the ground, seemed to prance toward his master with the trophy. The audience again broke into applause.

Smith joined in, then held up his hand for silence.

"You just seen a rare spectacle. It's uncommon you'll meet a man who can communicate with dogs like Gideon McBride does. You seen that he's trained each of these dogs to hunt a particular animal. This morning, many of you watched him walk up to the cage of Jeb Sawyer's pitiful deranged dog. With your own eyes you seen him put his hand right in the cage and scratch old Satan's chin and ears.

"Now, here comes the best part. A couple of you fellers are gonna go home today with these two dogs trained by Gideon McBride. Eight more of you can sign a paper that will make you owners of the litter of pups he's got ready to train. All of 'em are registered purebreds with championship bloodlines."

"How much, Smith?" yelled one of the men.

"Ain't gonna be cheap, cause you ain't gettin' a cheap dog—

but that ain't the most important part. McBride will have you write on a piece of paper what animals you want your dog to hunt. That's what Gideon'll teach 'em to do. Nothin' else. You can write down as many as three game animals for each dog.

"If'n I was you, I'd choose two, and make one of those choices be for day huntin' such as rabbits, or squirrels, and the other for night huntin' such as coons or possums. That way, no matter what shift you work, you'll have a good dog ready when you are. By choosin' to have 'im hunt what your family likes to eat, you can help out with table meat durin' this time when most of us are a little short on cash.

"There's another matter. Write down the name you want your dog to be called. He'll have a high-falutin' name on his papers, since he's a registered purebred, but you can choose something short to call 'im. Nobody wants to be hollerin' for Anthony Napoleon Alexander the Great Ulysses Sherman Beauregard Forrest the Third!" Smith laughed, and the crowd did, too.

He shifted his weight on the cane and continued, "One other thing. You'll notice Gideon treasures these dogs. On your paperwork you'll agree to treat the dogs with respect. An' if it can ever be proved that you mistreat a dog you've bought from Gideon McBride, you agree for him to take 'im back for half price."

"Yeah, Smith, we agree. Quit your stallin'! How much?"

"Gideon is gonna make Bart available this mornin', but reserves the right to have him for the demonstration at noon. The cash goin' price is twenty dollars for this amazin' rabbit hound."

"What? Twenty dollars for a dog? You start drinkin' again, Smith?"

"Yeah, Delaney! Who you kiddin'?"

Smith held up his hands to the crowd. "Now wait just a minute. We're talkin value. Why, accordin' this week's *Greenville Leader*, it'll take around fifteen dollars to get a man's new wool suit. Everybody knows a good hound is worth more than a fancy suit of clothes."

"Yeah, but I ain't about to buy no suit, neither," yelled the unwashed miner.

"Fellers," said Smith, "we ain't talkin' about you taking home *a dog*. We're talkin' about years of you havin' a purebred hound leadin' the hunt day after day, night after night. We're talkin' about listenin' to him sing as he chases game up an' down the hills an' hollows around here. We're talking about puttin' good wild meat on the supper table durin' lean times. We're talking about *you, personally,* ownin' a *McBride hound.*

"Like I said, Gideon will let these two dogs go today. One this mornin', one this afternoon. To take home Caesar or Bart will cost you twenty dollars. Or for five dollars down toward your purchase of one from his present litter or the next, you can be on your way to ownin' a Gideon McBride hound."

Several of the watching men turned and walked away. But more stayed.

"Let's head back up the hill. Y'all think it over without pressure. We'll have the dogs up yonder by the old roadster under the shade of the big oak."

As Smith and Gideon walked back up the way, one man joined them. "Smith, this is way too much, and you know I'm one of your strongest allies."

"I know it's a lot, Rager. 'Specially when you just came to Jockey Day to sell or trade a guitar or two. But you've seen what the boy here can do. He's honest as the day is long. Goes out of his way to do right by ever'body. Those dogs are worth every bit of the money."

"Smith," said Lem Grayson, as he slipped in alongside the limping ex-miner. "I wanta take you up on that offer you made me earlier. I got my five dollars right here, an' you said you'd credit me fifteen dollars for that gun swap we made. That makes twenty dollars—right? So I get Bart. A deal's a deal, and you set the terms. Shake?"

"Gideon, I guess there goes your dog. I made the offer, and you didn't question it. Now he's called our hand." He winked at the boy and nodded. "You willin' to shake on it?"

Gideon looked regretful. "Yessir, I guess so. We did make the offer. Would you bring 'im by once in a while, Mr. Grayson? Or let me stop and see 'im now an' again?"

"Why, sure. That'd be fine. Shake on it?"

Grayson shook Gideon's hand, then pumped Smith's up and down.

"You can pick'im up after the demonstration this afternoon, Lem," said Smith.

"Yahoooooo!" yelled Grayson, rushing into the crowd. "I got Bart! I got the first 'un!"

"Watch," Smith whispered. "He'll be back in two minutes."

Sure enough, when they were almost back to the car, there came the happy man.

"Smith," he said, "your mind musta wandered! I sure 'nuff got the best of that deal."

Smith raised his eyebrows. "You did?"

Grayson cackled. "You paid me five dollars for that old gun, and give me fifteen dollars credit toward a dog. So to the credit I added the five dollars you paid me for the gun. I really got myself ol' Bart for nothin' but that old gun! That's a far cry from the twenty dollars cash money the others will be payin'!"

Grayson snatched his old felt hat off his head and slapped himself on the leg with it. "I hope you don't mind me crowin' a bit. Looks like I got myself a mighty good deal!"

"Sure looks like it, Lem. It sure does," admitted Smith.

15

In the next half hour two men approached Gideon with five-dollar down payments on next-litter pups. Buck Vincent wanted a female. "Me an' Braddy been talkin'. I'm gonna start breedin' dogs myself," he announced.

Braddy Bowman wanted a male. "An' my dog can provide stud service—I'll get the first of every litter he sires. 'Fore you know it, I'll have a whole pack of good ones, too!"

Dewitt DeArmond handed Gideon twenty dollars, cash, for Caesar. "Why, there's not a squirrel dog like this'un in south Muhlenberg, nor north Todd and Logan counties." He chuckled. "We just might wipe out the entire squirrel population amongst the bluffs and hollows around Sulphur Springs."

Walking up in time to hear the close of the transaction for Caesar was Jordan Pickens. When DeArmond left, Pickens said, "I'm a little curious about that old gun— even if it's not worth much. Lem Grayson told me he couldn't get ammunition for it."

Smith retrieved the Spencer rifle from Gideon's old roadster. He stroked the gun gently and cradled it as he might if walking across a field on a hunt. His left hand supported the barrel and his right hand was on the trigger mechanism.

He shook his head. "Lem's right—so far as it bein' a hunting gun. You'd have to do some work on it—wouldn't be worth it, cheap as common huntin' guns are. But as a showpiece—an' a piece of history..."

He held the gun at arm's length and looked at it admiringly, then ran his fingers over the engraving on the side. "This here rifle is somethin' special."

Shaking his head, he slowly passed the gun to Pickens, as if reluctant to do so.

Gideon watched the transaction, and Smith wondered if the boy saw how the man's eyes flashed to the nameplate and then quickly away.

"Seems in pretty good shape," said Pickens casually, examining the firing mechanism and checking the barrel for rust. "But so what, if it won't shoot?"

He shrugged his shoulders. "Guess I could give a few dollars for it. Just as a souvenir of the War Between the States." He made as if to hand the gun back.

Smith didn't take it. "Jordan, look at that nameplate again. That name mean anything to you?"

He pointed at the engraving, but peered intently at the older man's eyes. The pupils widened perceptibly and Smith heard a slight intake of breath as Pickens stared at the fancy scrolled engraving: "Colonel John Wilder."

"You are holdin' in your hands the personal rifle of one of the heroes of the Civil War. That's a Spencer seven-shooter—see that bullet tube in the stock? First repeatin' weapon ever used in warfare. It's the weapon that was responsible, more than any other, for opening the South to the Feds. You know, at Hoover's Gap after the Battle of Stones River. The gun that held back the Rebs at Chickamauga long enough for the Yanks to escape back to Chattanooga. The gun that…"

"Are you joshin' Mr. Delaney?" gasped Gideon. "All that really true?" Suddenly he clapped his mouth shut and looked very embarrassed that he had interrupted the transaction—and had questioned the integrity of his friend.

Smith barely glanced at the boy. "Tellin' it like it is, son." He nodded at the man with the Spencer rifle. "An' Mr. Pickens knows it. He knows guns and he knows the Civil War.

"Jordan, you've known me since the Big War. Many's the time me and you've talked about that fine gun club you're part of in Owensboro. When I looked at this gun of Gideon's, I thought of you right away. 'This gun ort to belong to Jordan Pickens,' I thought. Made me smile to think about what'll happen the next time that club meets at your house."

Smith grinned and winked conspiratorially at the prospective buyer. "Cain't you just imagine their jaws droppin' when they see that Spencer seven-shooter hangin' over your mantel? And when they walk up close and see the nameplate, that it's the very one owned by Colonel John Wilder, hisself—why every single one of them buddies of yours will be kickin' hisself that he warn't here to get a chance at it!"

Jordan Pickens rocked back on his heels and ran his fingertips over the nameplate. "I see what you mean, but trade my truck for it? That truck is just a year old—only has 1,700 miles on it. It's worth a lot. I sure couldn't trade it for one old gun..."

Smith reached for the gun. "Well, we got another dog demonstration coming up, Jordan. Better head that way."

He tucked the rifle under his arm, barrel to the ground. "Just think about the deal."

He directed that comment to Jordan, then turned to Gideon. "We'll need to leave right after we finish the demonstration. I'd like to stop and see Mayor Knight on the way home."

"The mayor?" gasped Gideon. "We're gonna go see the mayor?"

"Yep," said Smith firmly. "Mayors put on their britches just like we do, one leg at a time. Only Mayor Lucian B. Knight happens to own the big car dealership there on Courthouse Square. He likely has a good used truck—or maybe a new one—he'd be willing to trade for this historic weapon."

"Mebbe," said Gideon. "Oh, he's the postmaster who came to Jockey Day and...."

"The one," interrupted Smith. "And if he's not in, we'll run by and see Mr. Duncan, of the Duncan Coal Company. He has a mighty fine home, an' this gun sure would look good above his mantel."

Smith turned back to the older man. "Jordan, what do you suppose the folks up in Greensburg, Indiana, would give for this gun?"

He looked back to his young friend. "That's where Colonel Wilder put together his brigade. When the army wouldn't supply 'im with the Spencers, the bank there financed a rifle for every one of his men. In June 1863, carryin' these guns, they swept through Hoover's Gap in a day and became known around the world as 'Wilder's Lightning Brigade.' Yessir! I bet that bank would be proud a-plenty to have Col. Wilder's own gun hangin' in their lobby with a big nameplate under it."

"Yeah," said Pickens, softly. He pulled at his left ear lobe as he gazed at the gun cradled in Smith's arms.

"On the other hand..." said Smith, pausing briefly—"Gideon needs a truck *now.* Wouldn't wanna take the time to go all the way to Indiana—unless he had to." He paused again. "What do you think, Jordan? There are lots of trucks out there, but this gun—there's not another one anywhere, and there won't never be another one."

"Wish you weren't asking so much..."

Smith looked thoughtful. "Tell you what I'll do, we'll let you have the gun *and* give you a dollar to boot. That way, when people ask you what you paid, you can say, 'Well, for my old truck, I got this unique historic gun and cash. You don't have to say how much cash."

Just before the noon demonstration at the track, Jordan Pickens handed Gideon the keys to the truck, took the rifle and walked up the hill to Knight's Motor Company to buy a car to drive back to Owensboro—with his Spencer rifle on board.

Following the demonstration, six more people put five dollars down on a dog to be delivered from future litters. Gideon had filled an empty Old North State Tobacco sack, which substituted for a billfold, with money and papers with names of customers who were buying the dogs—and dog names and wild game preferences for each.

As the pair went up Jockey Alley, Gideon practically danced. It was obvious he could hardly contain himself. "Smith, I'm sheer flabbergasted! I got more money than I've ever had in my life—more than fifty dollars! And a new truck! And more money to come!"

Smith smiled at the young man's exuberance.

Gideon continued, "An' I got a way to make a livin' doin' what I love—workin' with my dogs! Ain't life grand? Ain't Darlin gonna be thrilled when I come drivin' up? She won't believe what she's seein'. I'm gonna miss Bart and Caesar, but..."

When they reached Gideon's old roadster, Mr. Rager was sitting on the running board in the shade.

"Jordan Pickens came by, and he told me about your trade. Seemed to think he got some kind a fine deal." Rager laughed with gusto. "Son, if you ain't gonna need this old roadster, I'd give you eight dollars for it. It ain't worth much, but I got one just like it and could trade parts and keep one or the other of 'em runnin'."

"Well," Gideon replied, putting his hand on the top of the ancient vehicle, "it's been a mighty good old car. My uncle give it to me.... Say, I see you ain't been able to get rid of your banjo or that flat-topped Gibson guitar you were trying to sell this mornin'."

"Nope. Fer some reason it seems like everybody was mostly talkin' dogs today" He laughed a hearty laugh and winked at Smith.

"How about me tradin' you the roadster for the banjo and the guitar?"

"One or the other," said Rager, shaking his head, "but not both."

Gideon flashed his eyes toward Smith, then back at Rager. "Tell you what I'll do," he said, rubbing his jaw in a pretty good imitation of Smith. "I'll let you have this automobile and give you a dollar to boot."

Smith watched his pupil at work and grinned.

The boy continued, "You can tell folks you got the car, plus cash, for the musical instruments, and you don't have to say how much cash—but I can't let the dog crates be a part of the package."

"Make it a dollar and a half" said Rager, thrusting out his hand, "and we got us a deal!"

A few minutes later Gideon drove the almost-new 1935 Chevy pickup along the road to Drakesboro. Smith held the guitar in his lap and had the banjo on the floorboard with its neck sticking up between his knees.

"How'd you know all that stuff about the rifle, Mr. Delaney? I mean, I know it was true, or you wouldn't have said it, but..."

"Gideon, listenin' an' payin' attention will give a feller all kinds of knowledge an' a real edge in life. And it don't cost nothin'. I didn't get much schoolhouse learnin', but my mama and daddy taught me to listen, pay attention, and remember, and I got purty good at all three."

"Yeah, my folks tried tellin' me the same."

Smith rubbed his right hand down the length of his bad thigh. "I guess I learned pretty early that you can do a whole lot more with a full bucket than you can with an empty."

He shifted in the seat to find a more comfortable position for his aching leg. "One time, when I was a boy, I sat a-whittlin' on the porch at the Rosewood store. Old Mr. Fletcher Carver and some other old timers were sittin' there talking about the war. As a part of the Kentucky 11th Infantry, Mr. Carver fought at Shiloh, Perryville, Stones River, Knoxville, and even Atlanta."

"Wow, it's a wonder he came back alive!"

"Sure is. Anyway, Mr. Carver told how, in the spring followin' the Battle of Stones River, the 11th Infantry was a part of the army under General Tom Crittenden that tried to get around to McMinnville, Tennessee. They were gonna attack the Rebel army at Manchester from its right flank. But while Crittenden's boys got bogged down in the muck durin' a rainstorm, Colonel Wilder's 'Lightning Brigade' swept through Hoover's Gap on horseback and flung open the gates to the rest of Tennessee. Mr. Carver said that Wilder's troops took the hills at the end of the gap and used those Spencer seven-shooters to hold off the whole Confederate army 'til the Yankee main forces got there."

"Ain't that somethin'!" said Gideon, as he shifted gears to climb the hill toward Ebenezer from the Pond Creek bottoms.

He flashed Smith a broad grin." Ain't this smooth? An' feel that power! We hardly slowed down at all climbin' that hill!"

"Sure enough!" Smith tried to match the boy's enthusiasm. "Anyway, Jordan Pickens has mighty deep pockets and he loves guns. So when I saw we had Wilder's personal Spencer rifle, I knew the Lord had given us a mighty strong hand. I'm sure glad I heard those old-timers talkin' at Rosewood that time, and I'm likewise glad I paid attention—and remembered."

"Me too!" exclaimed Gideon. He stroked the dashboard with his right hand. "Sure is nice."

They rode in silence until they passed the school in Drakesboro.

"Mr. Delaney, if you don't mind, I'd like to give that guitar to Miz Hattie."

"Son, you don't need to do that," Smith said. Then he caught himself, and remembered, 'It is more blessed to give than to receive.' He repeated, "Don't need to—but if you want to, that would be mighty fine of you. And you sure would make my Hattie a happy lady."

They topped the hill by the Sumner place and Gideon geared down for the descent. It was early dusk when he guided the pickup truck down the hill and started up the drive beside the house. Carrie's car was parked right at the back door. Forrest's truck was pulled up at a wild angle next to hers. The door on the driver's side of the truck was standing wide open.

"Something's wrong!" Smith said. "Bad wrong!"

16

Smith's heart hammered wildly when he saw Forrest step out the back door. Gene Beckwith, Carrie's husband, was at his side. Both men wore grim expressions. No welcoming smile greeted Smith as he climbed from the truck and hobbled across the coal-waste surface of the driveway.

"Smith..." Forrest began.

"What is it?" Smith interrupted. "Is it Hattie? Is she...?"

"Whoa, Smith." Gene put a hand on Smith's shoulder. "Hattie's had the baby. It's a little boy."

A rush of blood pounded in Smith's brain. He brushed past Gene, but Forrest stepped into his path, the larger man blocking his way.

"Wait, Smith. You need to know things didn't go too good."

Forrest turned Smith away from the door.

"She lost a lot of blood, Smith. An'...the baby's small. Real small."

Forrest gulped hard. "Ma Richards ain't sure...She says he might not...he's awful small..." His voice trailed off.

This time when Smith pushed past, they let him go. He opened the screen door and eased across the porch and into the house. Chloe stood at the stove, quietly stirring a pot of beans. Her downcast eyes did not meet his.

He moved past her into the bedroom.

Hattie lay on a nest of pillows, her white face framed by her dark hair. Deep black circles haloed her closed eyes.

Ma Richards sat in the rocker next to the bed, holding a tiny bundle wrapped in flannel. It took Smith a moment to realize that his new son lay inside the wrapping.

Ma raised a finger to her lips. "She's quiet now," she whispered.

"Let her be, son. She had a real hard time."

Smith bent over the midwife's shoulder, and with one finger moved the blanket aside. Inside, a tiny, wrinkled face appeared. The eyelids were so thin that that he could plainly see the web of blue blood vessels through the skin. The little head, the size of an orange, seemed too impossibly small to be real. The baby's lips were tinged with blue. His open mouth gasped for air.

Ma raised her eyes to Smith's face. "He's strugglin', son. He weren't ready yet, so he's havin' to fight mighty hard."

"Hattie..." Smith began.

Ma shook her head. "I think she'll live, but she's awful weak."

The hammering in Smith's head became a roar. "You think? You mean you ain't sure?" he whispered.

Ma Richard's wrinkled face settled into deeper creases. "Cain't tell yet, son. She's in the Lord's hands now."

She reached up with one hand and patted his cheek. "I ain't never gonna lie to you, Smith. She's bad, but she's got a mighty will to live. Now's the time for you to pray. Pray for her..." she nodded toward the baby, "...an'for this here little boy."

Questions danced through Smith's brain like a swarm of gnats.

"When...? How...?" he stammered.

"Shhhh!" Again, Ma Richards held a finger to her lips. "Best I can tell, she musta started laborin' right after you left this mornin'. By the time Digger found her, she was unconscious. He ran for Becky, and she sent him to get help."

Ma glanced down at the baby, then continued. "I b'lieve if Digger hadn't come in the house when he did, she would have bled to death. It's...it's just a miracle she didn't."

Smith's eyes darted back and forth between the still figure of his wife and the baby on Ma Richards' lap.

"Can I hold him?" he asked.

Ma carefully placed the baby in his arms.

"Support his head. An' hold his neck straight. He's havin' a hard time breathin'. Sometimes, when they're this early, their lungs ain't right yet." She brushed a gnarled finger down the baby's cheek. "He's a fighter, though. Just like his pa."

Some of Smith's stark terror faded away as he gazed at his son. "Ain't he a wonder! Look how tiny he is...How much you reckon he weighs?"

"Mebbe four—four and a quarter pounds."

"Ain't like holdin' a baby, Ma. It's more like holdin' a warm feelin'," Smith breathed.

Carrie peered around the doorframe. "Can I come in?" she whispered.

Smith nodded.

"Gideon's in the kitchen. He's fixin' to leave, but he wants to talk to you before he goes."

Smith kissed the baby on the forehead, then handed him to Carrie. "I'll be right back," he said.

Gideon stood in the kitchen nervously turning his hat around and around in his hands.

"Don't mean to butt in, Smith. I just wanted to thank you for everything you done today."

"You did it, Gideon. Them dogs sold themselves. I just helped a little."

Gideon held up one hand. "That ain't so. You done a lot more'n that. If'n it weren't for you, I wouldn't have known what to do or how to get the word out. I didn't know the folks or nothin'. You vouched for me. I reckon that was worth a lot. And you come up with that gun and you sure learned me a lot about tradin'." He shook his head. "I still can't believe I got a fine truck like that."

Smith glanced behind him toward the bedroom door. He ran his fingers through his hair. "Like I said on the way to Greenville, that's what families do. We help each other."

"It sure is good to have family again." Gideon shifted his weight from foot to foot. "Miz Hattie...is she doin' all right?"

All the air seemed to suck out of Smith's body. His shoulders slumped.

"Don't know yet. Ma Richards says she's in a bad way. The baby...The baby is, too. Y'all be prayin' for 'em. That'd be a help."

"You know we will, sir. Please give her the guitar for me when she's up to it—I left it on the back porch. Tell her, maybe we can pick a duet together sometime."

"Sure will, son."

Gideon pushed his hat down on his head and turned toward the door. "Thanks again."

Smith raised a hand in response. Gene and Forrest walked with the boy to his truck.

Chloe hadn't moved from her quiet vigil by the stove. Now she went to Smith and put her arm around him.

"It's gonna be all right. We're all prayin'. I reckon we got all of Jackson Chapel and half the folks in Drakesboro on their knees by now."

Smith sank down into a chair at the kitchen table. "You reckon somebody could call Colt for me? I'd kinda like to see my brother."

"Why, 'course you would. It helps havin' family around at a time like this. I'll ask Gene to run up to Radburn's to call. Is there anyone else you want us to get a hold of?"

Smith shook his head. "Colt'll let 'em all know. He'll round up our kin."

The silence of the house began to close in on him. It was so quiet. Even the birds seemed afraid to sing. Smith pushed back in the chair and gazed at the ceiling, then cocked his head to listen up the stairs.

"Where's the young'uns? I ain't seen hide nor hair of 'em since I got home."

Carrie answered from behind him. "Marva came and got them."

"All of 'em?" Smith asked.

Carrie nodded. "Every one of 'em. Marva figured they didn't need to be down here if..." she stumbled over her words. "Well, I reckon she figured if Hattie could handle six young'uns every day, Marva could do it for one afternoon."

She placed a hand on Smith's shoulder. "They're fine. Don't fret yourself about the children."

"What happened, Carrie? When I left this morning..."

"We don't really know. She just started laboring early, I guess. That happens sometimes."

"I know, but..."

"Listen here. One of mine come early an' she's just fine. Ornery as the dickens. You'll see."

Carrie didn't mention the grave that lay in Ebenezer cemetery where a tiny baby girl was buried. She didn't tell of the early birth that had cost the life of her third daughter.

"You'd have sure been proud of Digger this mornin', Smith. He ran every step of the way to Annie's store to call us. Annie said he was so winded he could hardly talk, but he wouldn't sit down 'til she got the message. Said she'd never seen him so worked up. 'Bout cried, he was so worried over Hattie."

"She's been reachin' him, slow but sure," Smith replied wearily. "She's just like Gideon with his dogs. Only she works her magic on children. I ain't never seen nothin' like it."

He buried his face in his hands. "I cain't lose her, Carrie. I just cain't. I don't think I could go on without her."

Carrie's eyes filled with tears. "That's how we all feel, Smith. None of us can imagine life without Hattie."

She snatched the hem of her apron up and wiped her tears. "An' we ain't gonna have to. She's gonna be all right. Remember when she had the influenza?"

Smith nodded. He'd almost lost her back then, too. It had been touch and go for a while, but she'd come through it.

"It's just like then. She'll fight to live, Smith. Why, she's got more reason than ever to live now. She's got Dulcie and Jackie, an' you, and that new baby in there."

"What if *he* dies, though, Carrie? I don't know if Hattie could deal with buryin' one of her own."

Carrie sighed deeply. "'Course she could. She'd just *have* to. Sometimes, we don't get a choice, an' we have to go on. That's when our faith comes in. We live through the dark days, just like the light ones. 'Cause we have to," she said firmly.

"An' as bad as it gets, we ain't alone. Remember what Conroy said at Mamie's funeral? The Lord walks with us. He feels our pain, and stands with us. We ain't never alone, no matter how lonely we feel."

Again Smith raked his fingers through his hair.

Carrie poured a cup of coffee from the pot on the back of the stove and set it in front of him, then sat down at the table.

"Listen, we got to talk about what's gonna happen in the next few days. Forrest says he'll come down to help you see to things around here when he gets done at the mine. An' Marva will keep the children as long as you need her to."

She reached across the table and patted his hand. "But maybe you should let her keep the Dunford kids with her. They're gonna be too much for Hattie now."

Smith took a gulp of the coffee. He felt the scald on the back of his throat. It almost felt good to be distracted by the burn.

He raised his eyes. "Hattie would hate that. She'd feel like I betrayed her trust. I told her she could keep 'em 'til we figure out what the legal ins and outs are. I can't betray her like that."

Smith shook his head. "An' she'd feel like Marva took 'em when she couldn't fight back."

Carrie nodded. "I know. I've thought about that, too. But she's too weak to take care of 'em, Smith. She can't make this decision. It's gotta be yours. You think on it, all right?"

Smith blew out a breath. "All right. I'll think on it."

"That's all I'm asking."

❧

All through the early nightfall cars made a slow procession down the hill to the house. Kind men and women dropped off platters of ham, chicken, fresh vegetables, and deep dishes of hot food. No one stayed more than a few minutes—just long enough to let the family know they cared.

Colt and Virginia Delaney, Smith's brother and sister-in-law, arrived after dark. They brought with them Smith's sister, Zonie, and his grandmother. Granny Delaney still practiced midwifery in the communities around Gus and Old Hebron. She and Ma Richards had a nodding acquaintance.

The family was greeted quietly at the door. Smith hugged his grandmother and introduced her to Carrie and the rest of Hattie's family.

"Zonie," said Carrie, "it's so good to see you again."

Zonie Delaney had lived with Hattie for a while after the influenza outbreak in 1933. They had become close friends.

"I know Hattie will be grateful you came," Carrie said warmly. "And Granny Delaney, your fine reputation precedes you."

"Kind words, Miz Beckwith. I'm obliged." The old woman looked toward the back of the house. "Is Hattie awake?"

Ma Richards answered softly from the bedroom door. "She ain't woke up, since the baby come." She shuffled through the door with the baby in her arms and turned to Granny Delaney. "Leticia, I'm glad you're here. You have any blackstrap molasses in your bag?"

"Sure do. When Colt come to get me an' tol' me 'bout Hattie, I packed it up. But now I don't want to intrude."

"No intrusion. I need your he'p." She handed the baby to his great-grandmother, and reached for the coffeepot. "Carrie, pour this out and fill it full of clean water. I need it boiled. When you're done, bank the coals in the oven. Smith, find me a box, just a mite bigger than the baby."

Smith found a suitable box and Carrie boiled the water. When it was done, Ma took the small ash shovel and pushed the coals to the back of the firebox next to the oven.

She explained what she was doing. "The baby ain't holdin' his temperature. We got to keep him warm or he's gonna die. I'm fixin' to take care o' that right now."

She folded three receiving blankets to fit the bottom of the box, then draped a fourth blanket over it. She took the baby and placed him into the box, rolled a small dishtowel into a cylinder and gently tucked it under the baby's neck to help keep his airway open, and set the box on the oven door.

In the meantime, Granny Delaney made strong tea with herbs from her bag and the water that Carrie had heated. She laced it generously with the blackstrap molasses.

"Nothin' like blackstrap molasses," said Ma Richards, "to put back the iron Hattie lost with all that blood."

Granny Delaney nodded her agreement.

Smith stood in the doorway between the bedroom and the kitchen. "Why didn't y'all call for Doc Wilson?" he asked suddenly. "Why didn't y'all call him? Maybe if..."

Ma Richards raised up from where she leaned over the baby. "I sent Forrest for the doctor as soon as we got Hattie settled. Miz Wilson said Doc's out of town at some medical convention. As soon as Forrest found out Doc was gone, he tried to get one of the other doctors, but they were at Graham—a boiler blew up and scalded several miners."

She pushed a loose strand of steel gray hair back into the tight knot on top of her head. "Listen here, son, I know my limits an'..." Her voice broke. "This was one of 'em."

Frustration and bone-weary exhaustion weighted Smith's feet to the floor.

"I know you done the best you could," he said.

"Smith, what you gonna call this little boy?" asked Colt, peering over the edge of the box at the tiny body within.

Granny looked up from the teacup. "Now, don't you even *think* of namin' him after a gunsmith, like your daddy done you an' Colt. I ain't callin' no great-grandchild o' mine Winchester, or Remington." She grinned a toothless grin at her grandson.

Smith reached down to smooth the fuzz on the baby's head. "No, ma'am. This here's Dalton. Dalton Lucas Delaney."

As if hearing his name had somehow registered with the baby, he opened his mouth in a huge yawn, took a shuddery breath and settled deeper into the blankets.

17

Granny Delaney and Ma Richards took turns watching the baby and sitting with Hattie. Around eight o'clock that night, the infant Dalton began squirming in the box. He opened his eyes and then crumpled his face into a howl. It wasn't much of a howl—just a thin reedy cry, but it was still evidence that he lived. The grown-ups laughed at his sad little face. Smith carefully wrapped the blankets around him and lifted him out of the box. He cradled him against his body and talked to the baby.

"It's all right, son. You're all right. Hush now."

Very gently, he rocked his son. Dalton's face turned bright red, and tiny fists, the size of a kitten's paws, beat the air. He cried on and on.

"Land's sake!" exclaimed Forrest. "I believe his lungs are just fine! Listen to 'im. He's tunin' up for a singin'!"

Granny Delaney hovered in front of Smith. She gently poked the tip of her little finger into the baby's mouth. He latched on and sucked greedily.

"He's hungry. We're gonna have to feed 'im, if Hattie don't wake up."

Ma Richards popped her head around the door frame. "She's awake. Heard him hollerin' and come awake like it was Sunday mornin'. Bring him in here, an' we'll see what he can do."

Smith carried the baby into the bedroom and sat down on the edge of the bed next to his wife. "Hi there. Lookee what I found under a stump in the yard. Can I keep 'im?"

Hattie smiled weakly. "Hi, yourself." She raised her head to peek at her tiny son. "Is he all right? I...I don't remember much...Just hurtin', then..." She slumped back against the pillows. "Cain't seem to hold my head up," she whispered.

"I'm not a bit surprised!" Ma said firmly. "You mighty nigh scared us to death, Hattie Stoneworth Delaney. Next time you have labor pains, you need to be lettin' someone know!"

Without Granny's finger in his mouth, the baby started to cry again. Smith quickly touched Dalton's mouth. He rooted for the offered fingertip and sucked hard.

"He's so small! Is he..." Hattie's voice broke. "Is he gonna make it, Ma?"

"Not if you don't feed him, he won't. You think you can?"

Hattie reached to unbutton the bodice of her nightgown. "I'll sure try."

Granny reached for the pillows on the other side of the bed and gently raised Hattie up to a more upright position.

When she was ready, Smith handed Hattie the baby. The tiny mouth immediately grabbed on and began to suck lustily.

Ma Richards and Granny Delaney shared a look that spoke volumes. This was a very good sign for both the baby and the mother.

Ma reached down and adjusted the baby's blanket more snugly around him. "He needs his head covered to stay warm. I couldn't find a bonnet for this boy. Where'd you put 'em?"

"Well, he was kind of in a hurry, wasn't he?" Hattie answered, never taking her eyes off the baby. "Most of the baby things are still in the chest upstairs—in the bottom drawer. I thought I had a while to go yet before I needed to get them out."

"An' you did. About six weeks, if I remember right," said Ma.

It only took a couple of minutes of nursing before Dalton's eyes drooped shut and his mouth went slack against Hattie's breast.

Smith's brow furrowed. "That ain't all he's gonna eat, is it? I mean shouldn't he still..."

Granny Delaney laughed gently. "He done fine, son. Newborns do that. It's just the way things are at first. He'll probably need to nurse every couple of hours, but for now he's full. Let's put him back in his warm nest."

She reached for the baby, but Hattie wasn't ready to let him go. She cradled him against her and crooned to him for a moment before handing him back to his great-grandmother. "Will he be all right?" she asked cautiously.

"Cain't say yet, Hattie," Ma answered. "We're keepin' 'im warm, an' he's eatin'. That's a real good sign. But these little ones...well, they can fool you. We'll just have to wait an' see."

Hattie's big brown eyes filled with tears. Smith moved to the head of the bed and wrapped his arms around her. "We're doin' everything we can, Hattie. Now you rest. You need to get strong so you can take care of him."

At her slow nod, Smith hugged her close. "Granny's gonna take the baby in the kitchen, then she's gonna bring you some tea she made. You drink it all. Hear me?"

Hattie's exhausted body rested against his chest. When she took the offered teacup between her shaking hands, Smith steadied it for her. After she had finished it, he laid her against the white pillows and pulled the sheet up around her shoulders.

"Sleep now, Hattie. Won't be long 'til he's howlin' again. Rest while you can."

Hattie's eyes had already closed when he slipped quietly back into the kitchen.

❧

Ma Richards sat at the dining room table with Granny Delaney. Each of the old women held a small piece of flannel and a needle and thread. Scissors and a length of ribbon lay on the table in front of them. On the top of the dark brown oak buffet lay several baby bonnets. All of them were far too big for the premature baby sleeping in the box on the oven door.

"Won't take any time at all to fix a couple of these for our little boy in there," Granny said to Ma. "We'll just sew 'em up quick, an' be all set."

"My eyes ain't what they used to be," commented Ma Richards, "but I reckon I can still fix a runnin' stitch 'bout as well as anyone else."

"I'm sure you can," replied Granny.

The two old midwives chatted as they sewed. They shared

their cures for milk fever, and clucked over the horrors of polio. They companionably whispered gentle gossip about mutual acquaintances. And with each jab of the needle they both knew the other silently prayed for Hattie and the baby.

"You know, I b'lieve I brought some of your kin," said Ma. "Ain't you related to the McPhersons at Ebenezer?"

Granny nodded. "Sure am—by marriage. Cain't say I'm a bit surprised. Is there a body this side of the county you ain't brought?"

Ma laughed. "More'n more all the time. Some of these young gals don't see fit to have their babies at home. Want to go to the hospital in Madisonville!" She shook her head disdainfully. "Filthy places, if'n you ask me. Give me good clean sheets, the family bed, an' a hot stove for boilin' water. I just don't hold with all these newfangled ideas. And do you know what it costs to have a baby in a hospital?"

"Ain't it the truth!"

Granny tied a knot and snipped the thread. "There now. That ort to do him. What do you think?"

She held up the tiny bit of flannel and turned it this way and that. Little white ribbons fell from the front to tie the bonnet on. She'd even fashioned rosettes with the ribbon where it attached to the bonnet.

"Ain't that the sweetest thing! You are a wonder with that needle." Ma looked at her own bonnet. "Reckon mine'll be for everyday—yours'll be for church."

Granny's piercing blue eyes suddenly blinked hard. "I just pray he gets to go to church," she murmured.

Ma blinked hard, too.

❧

Carrie and Gene left around eight-thirty. Forrest followed them down the drive. Everything seemed to be under control. Colt and Virginia decided to stay with Zonie and the two old women. Virginia and Zonie went upstairs to change the beds, then to the extra room in the smokehouse. Ma and Granny sat with Smith in the kitchen. The quiet was broken by the sound of an engine, and the slamming of doors.

Eunice Crowe marched through the door like Sherman charging through Georgia.

"Where is she?" she demanded. "Where's Hattie?"

Smith rose from his chair at the table and held up his hands. "You cain't see her right now, Miz Crowe. She's restin'..."

"I'll see about that..."

Eunice started across the kitchen, then came to an abrupt halt when Colt Delaney stepped in front of the old woman and stood his ground.

"I b'lieve Smith mentioned that Hattie is sleepin'," he said softly.

"Well..." Eunice sputtered. "I wasn't gonna wake her up. I got more sense'n that." She backed up a step and flicked her eyes back and forth between Smith and Colt. "An' you are...?"

"Colt Delaney, ma'am."

Eunice narrowed her eyes. "An' cut from the same cloth, I see."

Colt squared his shoulders. "I'd like to think so."

Eunice's jaw dropped a little, but any response she might have made was interrupted by the sound of a new arrival.

Smith started for the back door just as it burst open. Dulcie raced into the kitchen. He caught the little girl around the waist as she tried to push past him into the bedroom.

"Whoa, Dulcie! You cain't go runnin' in there. Mama's asleep. She needs to rest."

Dulcie looked defiant, but stopped struggling against him. "I want to see her. I'll be real quiet, I promise."

Marva appeared in the door, on her face a look of apology.

Smith turned from his sister-in-law back to the little girl, and smiled. "I know you would, honey, but we cain't risk disturbin' her right now. She..." Smith looked around for help. "It's late and she's awful tired," he finished.

Marva stepped down into the kitchen. "I'm sorry Smith. She just wouldn't stop cryin' to come home. She 'bout made herself sick over Hattie."

Smith squatted down in front of Dulcie and took her by the

shoulders. "Listen, honey, I know you're worried about your mama, but she's gonna be fine. I need you to help me, though. I want you to let Aunt Marva take you back home with her. You'll get to spend the night, and..."

"I don't *want* to go with Aunt Marva! I want to see my mama!" Dulcie stamped her foot.

Colt looked embarrassed. "Reckon I'll go get a load of wood for the stove." He stepped out the back door.

Smith took a firmer grip on the little girl. "Now listen here! That's not the way you get what you want. We don't have fits! You understand?"

"Y...yes, sir," Dulcie mumbled. "Cain't I see her, just for a minute? Please?" she begged.

Ma Richards and Granny Delaney both rose from the table.

"What's all this, Dulcie? Why you plaguing your daddy? You're a big enough girl to know better," Ma declared firmly. "What do you think your mama would say 'bout you carryin' on like that?"

Dulcie hung her head and huge tears rolled down her round cheeks. She sniffed pitifully and took a deep breath. "I just want to see my mama," she whined.

Marva put her hands on Dulcie's shoulders from behind and steered her toward the stove. "Why don't we look at your baby brother instead?" She lifted the blanket away from the baby. "Would you look at him! Isn't he sweet?"

Dulcie glanced at the baby, then turned back to Smith. She took another deep breath, and calmly asked, "If I'm quiet, and don't make a peep, may I *please* see my mama?"

Smith's resolve wavered. She was asking nicely now, and not so bent on running into the bedroom.

"How 'bout we just look through the door," he said. "You can see her from there. All right?"

Dulcie bit her lip, then nodded. Smith took her hand and led her to the doorway of the bedroom. He put a finger to his lips and let the little girl take a look into the dimly lit room. Hattie lay on her side, sound asleep against the pillows.

Dulcie watched her for a long moment, then turned back to Smith. "What did you *do* to her?" she asked, her lip stuck out.

Shock registered in Smith's brain. "Why, honey...I didn't do anything to her. She...she just had a baby, that's all."

Dulcie marched over to the oven door and thrust a finger at her new baby brother. "Then what did *he* do to her?" she demanded.

Smith was at a loss for what to say. How could he explain childbirth hemorrhage to a six-year-old? It just wasn't done!

Marva came to the rescue. "The baby did just what he was supposed to do, honey. He just came a little early, that's all. Surprised us all. That's why your mama's so tired. She wasn't expectin' him today."

Dulcie didn't look convinced, but with the other adults nodding their agreement, there wasn't much she could do to argue.

Marva reached down and took her hand. "C'mon, Honey. Let's go back to my house now. You've seen your mama, and your new baby brother. We'll come back tomorrow after your mama's had a good night's rest. Then you can talk to her yourself, all right?"

"I...I guess." Dulcie answered.

Eunice stepped forward with determination written all over her face. "That's all right. I'll take her with me. She'd prob'ly rather be with me than all crowded with them other young'uns at your house."

She reached for Dulcie's other hand, and started pulling her toward the door. It looked for a moment like Eunice and Marva would end up in a tug-of-war with Dulcie in the middle.

"Wait just a minute," snapped Smith. "Dulcie's goin' with Marva. Her brother's there, and she's goin', too." Immediately he regretted his tone of voice, but by then it was too late.

Eunice dropped Dulcie's hand like she'd been scalded, and narrowed her eyes at Smith. "You ain't got no say, Smith Delaney. Dulcie ain't yourn. She's my blood kin. An' with Hattie near to dyin' I reckon, I'm her *next* o' kin."

Dulcie's eyes flew open at Eunice's words.

Smith hastened to comfort the frightened child. "Your mama's just sleepin', sugar. You know I ain't never tol' you a lie. She was awake earlier and fed your brother. She was talkin' to me and Ma, and Granny, and Aunt Carrie. When she got tired, she went to sleep. That's all."

Eunice's face turned deep red at his contradiction. "Then why you got two midwives down here? Hmmmm? If'n she ain't knockin' on death's door, why you got two of 'em?"

Ma Richards marched forward and started backing Eunice toward the wall. "Listen here, Eunice!" She pointed her finger toward Dulcie. "You may not care that you are scarin' the liver outta that little girl, but *I* do! Now, I'm a-tellin' you, Hattie is doin' as well as can be expected after what she went through today. Just so happens Leticia Delaney is Smith's grandmother. I'd have thought you was smart enough to figure that out, since she's got the same last name. She's got a right to be here, just as much as *you* do!"

She shook her finger in Eunice's face. "You stop this foolishness right now. I expect better'n that from a growed woman."

Eunice deflated almost as quickly as she'd puffed up.

"Now, now, I didn't mean no harm," she cried, snatching her handkerchief out of the bosom of her black dress and swiping dramatically at dry eyes. "I'm just so overcome with worry..."

Ma's eyes bored into Eunice's as though searching her soul for more evil. Finally she stepped back.

Eunice's eyes darted from one angry adult to another and finally lit on the child. "Dulcie, Grandma didn't mean to scare you. It's just...why, I just wish you could come home with me, that's all. Annie Radburn tol' me what a full house your Aunt Marva's got with all them young'uns, an' I just thought..."

She carefully stepped toward the little girl, knelt down and opened her arms. "Come give Grandma some sugar," she coaxed.

Dulcie obediently hugged the old woman.

At just that moment Colt returned with the wood, and over its clatter into the woodbox, no one heard what Eunice whispered into Dulcie's ear, "I tol' you he wouldn't want you no more. He's already sending you off. Grandma's watching. You'll see..."

A moment later, Marva bundled the unhappy little girl out the door.

Eunice stood nervously twisting her handkerchief in her hands and watched them go, then straightened her spine and walked over to the baby. She flicked the blanket back and stared into the box.

"Ain't much to 'im, is there?" She snorted. "Hmmmph!"

Granny Delaney answered politely, "He's small, but..."

"Eunice, ain't you needed at home?" Ma Richards asked pointedly.

Eunice curled her lip. She spat a parting shot as she flounced out the door. "Good thing it don't cost much to buy a buryin' plot for a baby. I b'lieve you'll be needin' one 'fore sunup."

18

Hours blurred into days. Days and nights mingled and merged. Hattie awoke only to nurse the baby. Smith coaxed her to sip strengthening broth made by Granny Delaney.

He forced her to drink steaming cups of pot likker from the ever-present stew pot Granny kept bubbling on the back of the stove. He gently bullied her into taking a few small bites of fresh vegetables from the garden.

Dalton slept in fits and starts. At times his breathing became ragged and labored. Smith willed the tiny boy to take one more breath, to blow it out one more time, and then to do it again. He made himself a pallet on the kitchen floor and slept next to the little box on the oven door. He awoke and lightly placed one large hand on the tiny chest, feeling for its answering rise and fall. He changed the miniature diapers that Granny fashioned from soft dishtowels.

Under Granny's watchful eye, Smith hauled water and filled the washing cauldron in the yard. He built a fire under it, and scrubbed the diapers clean on the rough washboard. He hung them on the clothesline to dry, and when they were crisp and sweet from the summer air he folded and stacked them. He split and carried countless loads of wood to keep the oven warm twenty-four hours a day, so that Dalton never chilled.

In the cool of the evenings, he sat with Dalton tucked snugly in the crook of his arm, and read to Hattie from her beloved Gene Stratton-Porter books: *Her Father's Daughter, Laddie,* and her favorite, *A Girl of the Limberlost.* Not the whole books, just a passage here and there. And always, he ended with a chapter from the Bible. Most nights, Smith would look up from the heavy black book and see that Hattie's head had slipped sideways, her breathing deep and regular. He didn't know how much she heard, but it made him feel better, just being there beside her.

Early Friday morning a young boy pounded on the front door. A few minutes later Ma Richards hurriedly left with him to deliver another baby in another small house.

On Sunday afternoon Doc Wilson hurried into the house.

"Just got back from Louisville 'bout twenty minutes ago," he said. "The wife stuffed my hat back on my head and sent me on down here. How is Hattie?" he asked.

Smith pushed himself to his feet and reached out to pump the doctor's hand. "She's holdin' on." His face broke into a grin. "Man! Am I glad to see you!"

He escorted the older man to Hattie's bedside and hovered at the end of the bed. Doc Wilson sat down in the rocking chair and quietly asked Hattie a few questions.

"Do you remember what happened?"

Hattie shook her head. "Not really. I remember sendin' the young'uns out to do their chores, and going upstairs to make the beds...and I remember the pains startin'. After that it sort of runs together in my mind, like it was happenin' to someone else, then...my mind just goes blank."

"Do you remember delivering the baby?"

"No, sir. I woke up and Smith was holdin' him."

Doc Wilson patted her hand. "I'd like to examine you, Hattie."

Hattie bit her lip, then nodded. "Smith...?"

Smith grimaced. "I'm goin'. But, I'll be right out in the kitchen if you need me. All right?"

At her slow nod, he left the room. He could hear their quiet voices, but could not make out the words they spoke. It seemed like a long time passed, then he heard Hattie cry out and begin to sob as though her heart would break.

Smith forgot about modesty. He rushed into the room. Doc Wilson sat on the edge of the bed, cradling the young mother against his chest. Her body racked over and over with deep sobs.

"What is it? Is she...is she all right?"

Doctor Wilson looked him straight in the eye. "She won't likely be having any more children, Smith. I'm sorry."

"But she's gonna make it—gonna live?"

The doctor nodded. "She should live as long as she doesn't contract an infection. Considering all she's been through, I'm amazed at how well she doing."

Smith threw his head back and gave a prayer of thanksgiving.

"Oh, thank you, Doc!" He grabbed the doctor's free hand and pumped it up and down again. Then he looked at Hattie's crushed face. Smith dropped to his knees on the floor beside the bed and wrapped his arms around her. "Hattie, it's all right! It's all right, sugar," he crooned.

Hattie threw her arms around his neck and buried her face in his shoulder. "I'm sorry. I'm so sorry!"

Smith smiled gently into her hair. "What do you have to be sorry for, darlin'?

Hattie raised her head a little. "But you…you wanted a big family..."

"An' I got me one." Smith set Hattie back against the pillows and counted on his fingers. "We got Dulcie, and Jackie, and Dalton. We got eight Stoneworth brothers and sisters, an' Colt and Zonie. We got enough nieces an' nephews to sink the ark...And for the time bein', we got Becky, Digger, Dorie and Mary Claire. How many more do you think we need?"

Hattie gave a strangled laugh through her tears. "I reckon that's plenty." Her face crumpled again. "Are you sure, Smith? You sure you're not disappointed in me?"

Smith leaned over and kissed her soundly on the mouth, right in front of the doctor.

"I couldn't be disappointed in you if your head sprouted kudzu and you had eight toes on each foot. Don't you know that? I love *you*, Hattie. Not what you can give me."

Drained by the examination, and the emotional shock, Hattie's eyes slid closed and she slept.

Doctor Wilson grasped Smith by the elbow and walked him back to the kitchen.

"Let me tell you something, Smith. That was about the finest thing I've ever seen between a man and his wife."

Smith shrugged. "I love her, Doc. She wiggled her way under my skin the first time I laid eyes on her," he answered simply.

The doctor's gaze dropped to the small box on the oven door. "Reckon that's my next patient. He fanned himself and said, "My, it's warm in here!"

Smith proudly lifted the baby from his warm bed and handed him to the doctor. "Tryin' to keep it 'bout ninety-eight degrees."

Dr. Wilson carried the baby to the table and laid him down. He unwrapped the blankets and pulled the little gown up, pressing his stethoscope to the baby's chest. He listened, lifted the stethoscope, and listened again. With Smith leaning over his shoulder the whole time, he examined the baby thoroughly, then wrapped him back up and gently placed him back in the box.

Dalton squirmed under the blanket and finally found his fist. He fumbled it into his mouth and sucked.

Doctor Wilson laughed. "That's quite a boy you've got there. I believe he's gonna beat the odds. His lungs sound a little wet, but all in all, other than the fact that he's so small, he looks fine."

Smith released the breath he'd been holding. "You think he's gonna make it?"

"I think so."

The country doctor shook his head. "Next time you see Ma Richards, I'd say you should get down on your knees and kiss her feet for all she's done."

Smith laughed. "I'll do that. She'll prob'ly kick me in the head, but she earned the right, I reckon."

"She sure did," the doctor answered. "She did a fine job—don't know as I could have done as well. You just keep on doing what you're doing. And I think they'll both make it."

Smith's heart beat a rapid tattoo. "That's the best news I think I ever heard!"

The doctor held up his hands. "Don't get too excited, Smith. Hattie's still mighty weak and at risk for infection, so you'll have to keep an eye on her. Don't let her get too overly tired. Try to get her to eat small amounts of food several times a day. And anybody who's even had a cold, don't let 'em get near her. Wash your hands every time you go in the room, and after you come out, too."

Smith's happy smile began to fade a little.

"And the little one there," Doc Wilson continued, "he's still gonna be touch and go for a while before he's completely out of the woods. Sometimes these little ones forget to breathe."

Smith nodded. "That's what Ma Richards and Granny Delaney said. Said to watch him real close, especially at night."

"That's right."

Doctor Wilson's eyes steadily gazed at Smith's face. "Now, the next question is, how are *you* holding up, my friend?"

"Oh, you know me, Doc. I do what I think needs doin'." Smith wearily dropped into a kitchen chair, and with his foot he shoved another one out for the doctor.

The older man eased down onto the chair and leaned toward Smith.

"I don't know how she does it, Doc. Hattie cooks, and cleans and washes clothes. She keeps this house neat as a pin, an' teaches Sunday school, and quilts. She generally runs circles around all of us. She never complains, an' she's hardly ever tired."

A slow smile began to spread across the doctor's face.

Smith went on. "I'm breaking my back tryin' to keep up with one wife, and one baby. An' I've had help from Ma Richards *and* my grandmother. Hattie's sisters all bring food down, so I haven't had to do any real cookin' to speak of, just dishin' up. I tell you what—It would be easier to put in a double shift at Coaltown Mine than do this every day for the rest of my life. I...I just ain't good at this!"

Doc Wilson reached over and clasped Smith's shoulder.

"Son, you are looking at one of the great mysteries of life! My wife had to have emergency surgery when our kids were youngsters. She was laid up for a month or so, and I thought I'd lose my mind trying to keep up with just a few of the things that seemed to come so natural to her. I discovered that in one day I could only do a fraction of what she could accomplish in a single morning. Gave me a newfound respect for my wife."

"Ain't it the truth!"

"Now, listen. I know you're worried sick over this situation, but you've got to take care of yourself, too. If you get sick, who's gonna take care of Hattie and the baby?"

Smith nodded wearily. "I know that, but with sleepin' only a couple hours at a time, then runnin' the baby in to Hattie to nurse, stayin' up to make sure he's back in his box, then tryin' to catch another hour or so of sleep before the next round..." He shrugged. "But it's gotta be done."

"Sure does, and you're doing it. How 'bout those big ol' Stoneworth men. They helping any?"

"Yes, sir. Forrest comes down every night before he goes to work and takes care of the heavy chores. He takes the list to Radburn's, and whatever I order he brings the next day. I'd be hard pressed to keep up without all their help."

"That's fine, Smith. Real fine. You're lucky to have so many good folks that care about you and Hattie."

"Beggin' your pardon, Doctor," Smith stated firmly, "that ain't luck. It's a genuine, bona fide God-given blessing!"

19

Another week went by. Slowly, Hattie began to stay awake for longer than a few minutes at a time. Soon she had rallied enough to sit in the rocking chair and hold Dalton.

Early one morning Darlin and Gideon McBride shyly poked their heads through the opened kitchen door.

"Anybody home?" Darlin called softly, balancing Levi on her arm.

Smith beckoned them in. "Have a seat. How are you? "

"Question is, how's Miz Hattie?" Gideon answered.

"Better every day. She's still mighty weak, but she's able to sit up in a chair for a couple of hours every day now."

Darlin leaned across the table. "An' the boy? How's he comin'?"

Smith's face relaxed into softness. "Let me show you."

He rose from his chair and walked to the box on the oven door. Reaching in, he lifted the baby out and pointed. "Would you look at that! That is the beginnin's of a double chin, as sure as I'm standin' here," he announced proudly.

"I do b'lieve you're right!" Darlin answered.

Gideon peered over Darlin's shoulder. "He's still mighty small."

"Yup, but he's fattenin' up a little more every day. And howl! This boy can raise the roof when he's a mind to," Smith responded.

"Look at the size of them feet and hands," said Gideon. "He's gonna be a big man."

"You really think so?" questioned Smith.

"Yep. If I have me a pup with big feet, I know he's gonna be a big 'un. Always works out."

Smith grinned. He wasn't sure he liked to have his son

compared to a pup, but he liked the promise of Gideon's words. "Sounds good to me. I'd sorta like to see him a little taller than us Smiths tend to run!"

He smoothed the blankets in the bottom of the box and laid the baby down again.

"We still have to keep him warm. He struggles to keep his temperature up, but Doc Wilson says he'll regulate sooner or later."

Smith reached for a dishtowel and wrapped it around the handle of the coffeepot. He poured them each a cup, then joined them back at the table.

"Mr. Delaney," Darlin began, "I asked Gideon to bring me down here today to see Hattie and the baby, but I also wanted to tell you thanks for what you done for us at Jockey Day. We sure feel mighty fine ridin' around in that nifty truck! Never dreamed in all my borned days we'd ever have a truck like that. An Gideon's got that banjo..."

Smith started to answer, but Darlin rushed on.

"An' them men that ordered the pups? They been comin' around to see 'em. We got four more orders for the next litter. Can you believe it?"

"I'm not a bit surprised," Smith answered.

"Well, I was! Who'd a ever thought you could make a livin' off dogs?"

Smith's answer came quickly. "It's not the dogs, Darlin. It's what Gideon does with the dogs that makes them valuable. Any dirt farmer can buy a purebred dog, an' it'll be dumb as a post. But Gideon teaches them dogs to *think*. That's why you get good money for 'em. Never credit the dogs. It's Gideon who gives 'em value."

Darlin glanced at her young husband, then back at Smith. "I do believe you're right," she declared.

Gideon shifted uncomfortably in his chair. "I don't know 'bout all that, but the sheriff come to see me 'bout trainin' one of the pups like a bloodhound. He wants it for trackin' fugitives. I tol' him the onliest one I ever trained to hunt men is Pride, an' he ain't for sale. I spent a little time with Princess, too, but she didn't take to it like he did."

"But you're gonna train him a pup?"

"Reckon so. Cain't turn away the money. An' I kind of like the idea of bein' on the right side of the law."

"You ever been on the wrong side?" Smith teased.

Gideon gave an answering grin. "No, sir. An' I don't plan on startin' now. I just meant that it felt kinda good to think of doin' somethin' so important—training up a dog to work for the county."

Smith nodded.

Gideon went on, "Where we come from, workin' for the government's sorta looked down on, but I always thought, if'n you was the right kind of man, it would be...honorable, I reckon."

"You hit the nail on the head, son. It takes an honorable man to take on the big jobs and do 'em right. That's what we got in Sheriff Westerfield."

The younger man crossed his leg over the other, propping one ankle on the other knee. "I got kinfolk that would spit on the law 'fore they'd look at 'em. My daddy bein' one of 'em."

Darlin jostled Levi in her arms, then looked at Smith. "Mine, too."

"Fact is, her Pap and mine are so much alike, it's a wonder they don't start a sewin' circle together 'stead of keepin' the turmoil goin'," Gideon said ruefully.

Smith threw back his head and laughed. "That's the nature of folks. Most of 'em don't stop to look at what they got in common. They're too busy pickin' at the differences to see the sameness."

Darlin's face went tight. "I remember goin' to a dinner-on-the-ground at church one time. My mama said we couldn't eat nothin' we didn't bring, 'cause it mighta been made by a Hatfield. There was this big ol' chocolate cake, an' it looked so good. One of the church ladies was cuttin' it into huge slabs, an' I sure wanted one! Had to walk on by, though," she said sadly.

Gideon said, "An' I remember one time in school, a cousin of my dad's come chargin' in. He marched right down the aisle between the desks and yanked his boy outta his seat. Took him to the teacher and announced that no child of his was gonna spend every day sharing a desk with a McCoy."

Smith shook his head. "That ain't no way to live."

Gideon looked thoughtful for a moment. "I reckon it sounds worse than it really was. The killin' was over. The last feud killin' was twenty years ago, an' the last one afore that was twenty years earlier. 'Course, things was bad in Harlan County, but that was 'cause of the mine uprisin', not the feud."

Gideon shot Smith a wry look. "Mostly what we saw growin' up was just a lot of mouthin' and scowling' and dancin' around each other. When the government sent in the Guard to put down the feud, it sorta fizzled . But some folks sure got long memories."

"How in the world did you two find each other?" Smith asked.

The young couple looked at each other and giggled.

"Reckon we did a lot of sneakin'! That's how," Gideon replied.

The conversation turned to Smith's ties to their family trees. He racked his brain to remember who married whom and exactly how the family lines ran. They found themselves laughing at the way the branches tangled and merged, then separated again.

"Sounds like we're all double cousins somewhere up the way," Darlin finally concluded.

"That's about right," Smith answered.

"Oh," Darlin cried, "I almost forgot! I wanted to tell you what my granny always said to do for colic. She said it was the onliest thing that works every single time."

"Dalton's not colicky," Smith responded.

"Not yet. But he might get that way," Darlin responded.

She leaned forward and continued earnestly, "Here's what you do. You take nine healthy pillbugs, an' tie 'em in a cloth. You boil a pot of fresh spring water—got to be spring water, not well water—then drop the cloth with the pillbugs into the water to make a tea. After it cools, you dribble the tea into the baby's mouth. Then you bury the bugs under the floor." She dusted her hands together. "Works like charm."

Smith's face was a comedy of expression. Revulsion danced with an effort not to laugh out loud. "Only have one question, Darlin."

"What's that?"

"How do you know if the pillbugs is healthy?"

❧

Marva brought the children down to see Hattie for a few minutes every afternoon. Dulcie always lingered with Hattie after the rest had gone to play. Hattie knew that something was eating at the little girl. She was restless and clingy, never wanting to leave Hattie's side.

"Honey, is there anything you want to tell me?" Hattie gently probed.

"No, ma'am." Dulcie replied.

"You sure?"

"Yes, ma'am. Just want to be with you, that's all."

Hattie hugged the little girl. She rested her chin on Dulcie's dark curls and prayed that whatever was pulling at the child's heart would ease.

She knew that Dulcie was jealous of Dalton. That was apparent by the child's total indifference to the baby. Becky and Dorie begged to hold the infant, and Mary Claire gazed at him with longing eyes and touched his soft head with one pudgy finger. But Dulcie walked past him every time. It was as though he didn't exist in her eyes. Her total focus was on Hattie. Hattie and Jackie. When she wasn't curled next to her mother on the big bed, she smothered the two-year-old with kisses and led him around by the hand as if he were her own child. Finally, he bit her hand to make her let go. Instead of being angry, it seemed to redouble her resolve. She coaxed and wheedled him into staying with her right next to Hattie, in the bedroom.

It came to a head one afternoon when Dulcie tried to physically restrain Jackie from leaving the room.

"Leave me 'lone!" Jackie fussed. He slapped Dulcie's arm.

"Jackie, no!" Hattie cried.

Smith picked up the little boy and carried him into the kitchen.

Dulcie threw herself onto Hattie's bed and sobbed.

Hattie rubbed the little girl's back and waited until the storm passed. Then she sat her up and cupped her face between her hands.

"Honey, you need to let Jackie be. He shouldn't have hit you, but I don't expect him to stay in here with me, and you shouldn't either. There's nothin' for him to do. An' he's just a little boy. He needs to romp and play."

"But...you're his mama. He should want to be with you."

"No, he should want to be a little boy. He should want to play with his trucks and roll in the grass with Mary Claire. Don't you think that sounds better than sittin' here? Sure sounds like more fun to me."

"But..."

"No buts, Dulcie. You're expectin' him to understand things he's not ready to understand."

She tipped Dulcie's chin up "And you don't need to spend every minute with me, either. Don't you want to play with your friends?"

"No, I just want to be with you."

"Why, Dulcie? You've always played outside before, or looked at your picture books. Now, you scarcely let me be. Are you scared? Has someone hurt you?"

"No! I...I..." Dulcie pouted. "Don't you want me, Mama? Don't you want to see me?"

Hattie gathered her in a hug. "Of course I do, but, honey, it's all right to play with your friends. I'll understand."

"No, thank you, Mama," Dulcie murmured. She wrapped her arms tightly around Hattie's neck. "I'd rather be with you."

20

Hattie waited until she heard the outside door bump closed, then swung her legs over the side of the bed. Just a little dizzy, she held onto the bedpost for a moment and waited for her head to clear, then crossed the house and looked out the dining room window. Smith's back was disappearing around the end of the smokehouse. She smiled to herself and deliberately walked through the dining room and into the kitchen. She paused to peek at Dalton in his box, then plucked her apron off the hook by the side door. Tying it behind her, she went to the Hoosier hutch. Reaching up onto the top shelf, she took down the heavy earthenware bowl, then bent to scoop flour into it from the built-in flour bin below.

"What do you think you're doin', Hattie?" Smith's voice thundered from the back door.

Startled, Hattie whirled to face him, the quick movement making her head spin again. She stumbled.

Smith grabbed her by the shoulders and steadied her. "Honey, what are you doin' outta bed?" he asked.

Hattie pressed one hand against her cheek and took a deep breath. "Thought I was stronger than I am, I reckon."

She let Smith guide her to a chair and push her head down between her knees.

"Take deep breaths. It'll pass," he said.

Finally the buzzing in her ears stopped. Carefully she raised up. Smith knelt beside her.

"Reckon I'm ever gonna feel better?" she smiled wanly.

"I 'magine." He smiled, but his eyes roamed the planes of her face. "You are mighty pale yet. You still need to stay in bed."

"Oh, Smith! I'm sick to death of bein' in bed. 'Sides, it's too hot in this house. Maybe I could sit out on the porch for a while?"

she wheedled.

Smith's lips flattened into a thin line. "Allriiiiiiight. But only while I'm out there with you. Soon as you get tired, I'm puttin' you back to bed."

He helped her to the table and fussed around her like a mother hen. "Are you comfortable in that chair? Let me tuck this pillow behind you."

Hattie leaned her head back and lifted her heavy hair off her neck. She piled it up on top of her head and held it there with one small hand. "Feel that breeze. Ain't it wonderful!"

She closed her eyes and breathed deeply. The rich smells of summer floated in through the screened walls—mown grass mixed with summer flowers.

"Now, how 'bout explainin' what you were doin' in the kitchen," Smith said.

Hattie opened one eye. "Shhhhh! Listen to the birds. They're singin' so pretty. I can't hardly hear 'em in the house."

"Hattie..."

She sighed deeply. She dropped her hair and leaned forward, resting her elbows on the table. "I thought it was about time I started doin' around here myself. I been in that bed nigh onto three weeks!"

"An' you just decided you'd hop right up an' start in where you left off before the baby come?" Smith asked incredulously.

Hattie looked sheepish. "Well, no. I thought I'd start with breakfast an' see how that went. If it went all right, I thought maybe..."

"You'd fall on your face and sleep on the kitchen floor 'til it was time to make lunch," he said.

Hattie laughed. "Surely I'm not *that* bad."

Smith reached over and squeezed her hand. "Honey, you almost died."

Her face quickly sobered. "I...I know. But I'm *not* dead. I'm alive and...I need to act like it."

She quickly put one finger to Smith's lips to silence his retort. "I can't stay in bed much longer. I need to be *doin'* something.

I need to be takin' care of you and the young'uns. Dulcie and Jackie, I...I miss 'em. I miss 'em so much I can't hardly stand it. I want 'em to come home. An' Digger and Becky, and Dorie and Mary Claire. I miss the children, Smith."

"Now, Hattie..."

She held up one hand and rushed on. "Please don't *'now, Hattie'* me. I mean it. There's something goin' on with Dulcie. I just got the awfulest feelin' she needs to be home with us. An' Jackie! He's talkin' up a storm all of a sudden, like somebody flipped a switch. An' I'm missin' all his new words! I want the young'uns to come home! All of 'em."

Smith pushed his chair back and paced back and forth the length of the porch.

Hattie breathed a silent prayer. *Please, please, please!*

After what seemed a long moment he finally turned back toward her. "How 'bout we wait 'til the weekend. You take things slow just a few more days. Then, on Saturday, we'll have Doc Wilson check you one more time. If'n he says you're fit to start doin' things again, we'll see about the young'uns then."

"Yes! Oh, yes!" she replied.

❧

Marva came that afternoon. She arrived clutching a letter in her hand. Rushing past Smith with nothing more than a quick hello, she hurried into the bedroom and bounced onto the end of the bed.

Hattie sat in the rocking chair. Her morning's adventure had exhausted her. She'd slept for two hours before waking again.

"Look what I've got!" Marva exclaimed, waving the pages in her hand. "A letter from Berk! And guess what!"

"What?"

"He's comin' for the family picnic!"

Hattie's eyes widened. "Really? That's wonderful! When are they comin'?"

Marva's gaze dropped to the letter. "Let's see—here it is...he and Nan are coming down the Thursday afternoon before Labor Day. He's taking Friday off. An' they're gonna stay with Carrie and Gene."

"Carrie never said a word when she was here yesterday. That sneak! Reckon she was gonna surprise us?"

"Prob'ly. Anyway, here's what he says: *Me and Nan can't wait to come down. Little Gene is excited about the trip, but I think he's more excited about starting school when we get back—first grade.*

Hattie laughed. "He and Dulcie will have plenty to talk about then. She's excited about school, too."

Marva read on. *Poppy's the cutest thing you ever saw. I think her hair gets redder by the day! Just wait 'til you see her, Marva. You'll fall in love, or my name ain't Stoneworth! She's already got a mind of her own, too. Nan has to fix her hair just right, or she fusses. And she's got to have ribbons at the end of her braids every day, not just on Sundays!*

Hattie clapped her hands and laughed again. "He's gonna have his hands full with that little girl!"

Marva looked up from the closely written pages and grinned. "Don't he sound proud?"

Hattie nodded. "What else does he say?"

Besides being with all of you, I'm just looking forward to being out of the factory for a few days. Sometimes I have to force myself to go inside that monstrous building! I must confess I find myself longing for the days when I used to putter around the yard at home, feeling the sun on my back and the warm earth between my hands, and watching the growing things almost sprout before my eyes. Still, what I'm doing is honest work, and I'm thankful for a steady job in these uncertain times. I don't complain, with so many folks out of work and wondering how they'll feed their children. So far, that's a worry I don't have to think about.

Hattie interrupted. "Poor Berk! He was always moving bulbs and transplantin' things. How sad to dread what you do every day!"

"I know," Marva agreed. "But he's right. As long as he's able to take care of his family...This is a depression, after all. It's tough on all of us."

"What else does he say?"

Marva turned to the back of the last page. "That's just about it."

Hattie settled deeper into the rocking chair, a dreamy smile on her face. "Just think, we're all gonna be together."

Suddenly her eyes flew open wide. "You think Smith'll let me go, don't you? I mean, you don't think I'll have to stay home from the picnic, do you?"

Marva's face reflected her compassion. She leaned forward and squeezed Hattie's knee.

"We'll work on him, honey." She giggled. "You know Carrie can get him to agree to just about anything! Besides, you're doin' so much better than you were even a week ago. An' there's still two more weeks until the picnic. I 'magine he'll let you go."

"I don't know. He won't even let the young'uns come home until Doc Wilson says so," Hattie said.

Marva's brow furrowed. She answered slowly, "Well, I can understand that. Doctor Wilson told all of us that you can't take any risks of getting sick, with your body still so weak. Smith's just bein' careful, that's all."

She leaned back against the bed post. "I will tell you this, *if* Smith agrees to let you go, you aren't gonna do any of the work this year. Me, and Chloe, Willa, Carrie and Lalie already talked it over. We'll do all the food. You're just gonna be a spectator, you hear?"

"But..."

"No buts, Hattie. You're still weak as a kitten. An' you're white as a sheet."

At Hattie's protest, Marva gave her a firm look. "Now listen, that's the deal. You agree to just enjoy yourself, and let the rest of us do the fixin's, or we'll tell Smith..."

Hattie threw up her hands and laughed. "All right, all right. Don't you go tattlin' on me! I'll be good."

"'Course you will. We wouldn't expect anything less."

Marva paused. She looked at her lap, nervously smoothing the lines out of her dress. "I'll run home and bring the young'uns down after a while, but I really wanted to talk to you alone for a few minutes."

Hattie's heart sank. She was pretty sure she knew what Marva was going to say. She'd been dreading this confrontation since realizing that the Dunford children had gone home with Marva.

"Now, Hattie, don't get excited. Just listen."

Marva fidgeted in her chair, then said, "Conroy and I would like to keep the Dunford kids, if Deke don't want 'em."

She rushed on. "I know you want 'em, too. But, just hear me out. I promise, I...I won't take 'em from you. I just want you to hear what I have to say about it. That's all."

"All right. I'm listening."

Hattie clamped her mouth shut and crossed her arms over her chest.

"Won't be long 'til Dulcie and Jackie come home. An' you've already got your hands full with Dalton—him bein' so small an' all, an' you havin' to feed him every two hours."

Marva clasped her hands together in her lap. "Smith's about beat down tryin' to keep up with the house and you and Dalton. You're not gonna fare any better, Hattie. You're still tryin' to get your strength back..."

Her eyes searched Hattie's.

"Me an' Conroy were talkin'. We've had the kids for a while now, an' we've watched 'em—how they act with each other, an' how they react to any kind of scare, or threat. They need an awful lot of the right kind of attention to...to undo what they been taught. 'Specially Digger."

Hattie gripped the arms of the rocker.

"An' you don't think Smith and I can give 'em that?"

"'Course you could. You worked wonders with 'em in the short time you had 'em. But..."

"But what?"

Marva seemed to choose her words carefully. "Hattie, you already got three kids of your own..."

"So it's only fair *you* get the Dunfords?" Hattie snapped, rocking forward in the chair.

Her sister's eyes filled with tears. "Oh, Hattie. Don't get mad! Please! I'm not sayin' that. You know I'm not."

"Then exactly what *are* you sayin', Marva? That you an' Conroy would make 'em better parents than me and Smith?"

"No!"

Hattie watched silently while Marva tried to control her emotions.

"You've already got three children," she repeated. "They deserve every bit of love and attention you and Smith can give 'em. Conroy and I just wondered if Becky and Digger and the little girls don't deserve the same thing—love and attention that's...that's just *theirs*. That they wouldn't have to *share* with your kids—where they wouldn't feel like, I don't know, like...like add-ons, I guess."

Hattie didn't say a word.

"With us, they'd still be their own little family, but with different parents, that's all," Marva continued. "We just thought it might not be so hard on 'em."

Hattie knew there was truth in what Marva was saying. She fought her own tears, as helplessness and frustration ruled her thoughts.

"An' this don't have anything to do with the fact that you an' Conroy haven't had children of your own?" she asked quietly.

Marva threw up her hands. "Of course it does. I'd be *lyin'* if I said it doesn't. But honestly, Hattie, we're thinkin' about what's best for the young'uns, too."

Hattie grasped for any shred of an argument that would dilute Marva's logic. "An' exactly where would you put 'em, Marva? Your house is smaller than ours."

"We'd close up the porch. You know our screened porch? We'd make it into one big room for the girls, an' Digger could have the small room off the kitchen all to himself."

Marva ran her hand across the quilt that hung on the end of the bed and waited for Hattie to respond. The obvious fact that she and Conroy had done a *lot* of talking about the Dunford children's future lay between the two sisters like an open grave—

dark and ominous.

"Seems to me you got it all worked out. Got it all tied it up in a pretty bow." Hattie sniffed. "Why'd you even tell me, if you'd already decided you was gonna keep 'em?" She batted angrily at the tears that ran down her cheeks.

Marva dropped to her knees in front of Hattie and grabbed her sister's small hands between her larger ones. "We ain't takin' 'em, Least'un. Not if you don't agree. I *promise* you we won't do that."

Hattie pulled her hands away, and threw her head against the high back of the rocking chair. She closed her eyes.

"Go home, Marva. I'm tired," she said.

❧

Hattie curled onto her left side and hugged Smith's pillow. She tried to sleep. Instead, Marva's words replayed over and over in her mind. *Conroy and I just wondered if they don't deserve love and attention that's...that's just theirs. That they wouldn't have to share with your kids—where they wouldn't be, I don't know, add-ons, I guess.*

Hattie pictured Mary Claire's little face, smiling up at Marva, her pudgy hand clinging to Marva's skirt. She saw Dorie, Mary Claire and Digger, each little blond head bent reverently in prayer around Marva's and Conroy's supper table. Tears stung her eyelids.

Off in the distance she heard the four o'clock whistle blow at the Black Diamond Mine. Hattie flopped onto her back and threw one arm over her eyes.

Of course they'd do better with individual attention. Of course they'd flourish under Marva's sweet mothering. Of course Conroy would be wonderful with them all—so why is it so hard to admit it? Why does it hurt so bad? Why am I so bent on keepin' 'em myself?

She saw herself walking with the children up through the orchard, Dalton on her shoulder, Digger and Becky laughing and chasing after Jackie and Mary Claire. She pictured Dorie's head tipped at an angle toward Dulcie's cupped hands, listening to a whispered secret—a soft breeze entwining Dulcie's ebony curls with Dorie's golden ones, like the sunshine and shadow of a late summer day.

And somewhere in a deep dark corner of Hattie's mind she saw Deke Dunford lying in wait for them. Waiting for the opportunity to snatch his children back—and in some demented, obscene moment of rage, to do to them what he'd done to Mamie. Her heart pounded.

She saw Becky's terrified face, and Digger's small angry one. She saw Dorie cowering, her soft arms wrapped protectively around Mary Claire, as Deke....

Hattie's eyes flew open against the horror of the nightmarish scene that played through her mind. A cold sweat trickled down between her breasts. Finally, her heart racing, she fell back on the only thing she knew to do. She prayed.

Please, Lord, no matter what else happens, keep 'em safe. Keep 'em outta Deke's reach. Please don't let him get the children. I...I don't want to be selfish. I don't want to do anything outside Your will. An' I don't want to hurt Marva, either, Lord. Maybe You do mean for her to have them, but...I don't know if I can just let 'em go. I...I want 'em, too. Help me to do the right thing...even if it's not what I want. Even if it means they go to Marva. But mostly, Lord, somehow, please save 'em from Deke.

Hattie rolled over and sobbed into her pillow.

❧

Marva waited until supper was over, then loaded the children into her car for the drive down to Hattie's. They pulled down the hill and up the drive. Digger lifted Jackie down from the seat, and reached back to help Mary Claire. Becky and Dorie scampered across the yard.

Dulcie climbed out and plodded to the door.

Smith held the screen door wide for them and greeted them one by one. He tousled Digger's hair, and teased Becky. He tugged on Dorie's braid, and chucked Mary Claire under the chin. He grabbed Jackie and threw him into the air and caught him, then sent him on into the house.

When Dulcie approached, he squatted down and held his arms out. "How's Daddy's girl? I sure been missin' you, sugar."

Dulcie laid her head on his shoulder and wrapped her arms around his neck. Smith hugged her tight, laying his cheek against the smooth skin of her neck. As quickly as he'd pulled her to him, he held her out at arm's length and looked at her more closely. The little girl's face was flushed, her eyes glassy.

"Marva, Dulcie's awful hot," he said.

"She's been just fine all day..." Marva placed a hand on Dulcie's forehead, then tipped her chin up. "Honey, don't you feel good?"

She shook her head. "Not too good."

Marva checked Dulcie over for spots, or any obvious sign of serious illness, then shrugged. "She's not broke out, so I don't think it's measles, or scarlet fever. But I think you're right. She's runnin' a temperature."

Smith scooped up the feverish child and bundled her back into Marva's car.

"She can't come in Marva," he said firmly. "We just can't take the risk that Hattie or the baby might catch something."

Marva slid in on the driver's side. "No, of course not. It's prob'ly just a summer cold, but I understand. I'll run her home, and come back for the others later."

Dulcie began to cry. Smith squatted down by the open car door. "You can come see your mama as soon as you feel better. All right, honey?"

The sick little girl crawled across the seat. She laid her head in Marva's lap and refused to look at Smith. He could still hear her crying as the car went back up and over the hill.

21

Marva was right. Dulcie had a miserable summer cold. Her nose dripped, and turned red. Her little body ached, and her throat hurt.

For the next four days, Aunt Carrie came and sat with Dulcie, or else Uncle Conroy stayed with her while Jackie and the Dunfords went to visit her mother. She was sad, and she was lonely. They wouldn't let the other children play with her for fear that they might get sick, too. She missed her mama. She missed her house and her room. She missed Jackie. And as hard as she tried not to, she even missed Smith and baby Dalton.

Marva brought her letters from Hattie. Just little notes, really, but sweet messages of love and longing to see the little girl. Smith always added a few lines at the end. And signed each, *Loving you SO much, Daddy.*

On Wednesday, he sent a small paper twist of lemon drops with the note. On Thursday, he tucked in a pretty leaf and sent along a huge fragrant peony blossom from the bush in the front yard. On Friday, it was a small box with five rattling walnuts. On Saturday morning he saw a fluffy caterpillar on the smokehouse porch. He found a jar, and with a hammer and a nail punched holes in the metal lid. He stuffed the jar with milkweed, then gently added the caterpillar.

Every night Marva sat on the edge of the bed and read the notes to Dulcie.

...The lemon drops are to remind you that you are my sunshine—sweet and bright...

...By the time this flower wilts, you'll be feeling better and come home to your mama and me. You're the prettiest bloom in our garden...

...These walnuts are from last year, but I'm already planning a special day for us to gather walnuts this fall. Remember how much fun we had when we got these?...

...This funny wiggle-worm looked lonely. Bet he was missing you, just like I am...

Saturday afternoon, while the rest of the children played in the small back yard, Dulcie sat up on her bed and looked at the fading peony in the jar of water that sat on top of the dresser. Already a few of its petals had dropped off to lie sadly on the floor until Aunt Marva came to scoop them up and throw them away.

Dulcie was a very confused little girl. She had cried all the way back to Aunt Marva's house on Tuesday. She'd cried through supper. She'd cried until it was time for bed, and then she'd cried herself to sleep. Grandma Crowe was right. Smith *was* getting rid of her. He didn't want her any more. That's what she'd thought then. But now, four days later, she wasn't as certain. If he didn't love her, why would he send her letters and presents? Why would he bother if he didn't love her? The small, thoughtful gifts delighted her. Mama didn't send them. Smith did. Aunt Marva told her so. And she showed Dulcie the letters. Mama's careful, neat handwriting was different from Smith's larger, squarish scrawl. *He* had written her every day. Why? It didn't make any sense, unless...maybe Grandma Crowe was wrong. A tiny flicker of joy tried to ignite in Dulcie's confused little heart...but no. He couldn't love her. Grandma wouldn't lie to her. She must be right. Still...

Dulcie listlessly flipped the dog-eared pages of her Raggedy Ann and Andy book. The colorful pictures didn't hold her interest long, and soon it was laid aside. Dulcie flopped onto her stomach and kicked her bare feet up behind her. Cupping her chin in her hands, she gazed out the window and watched the other children play.

❧

Doc Wilson smiled. "Tired of this ol' bed, I hear."

"Tired to death!" Hattie responded.

"An' she's gettin' cranky about it," Smith teased.

Doc Wilson's eyebrows shot up. "You cranky, Hattie? I can't

imagine you bein' difficult."

Hattie blushed. "Maybe a little bit."

The doctor laughed. "That put some color in your cheeks. I'm glad to see it. It's a good sign that you're on the road to recovery. How's your energy?"

"I...I don't have a lot yet," Hattie admitted. "But I'm getting better."

"Uh-huh. And you haven't been exposed to anything?" He looked from Hattie to Smith and back again.

"Not that I know of."

Smith shook his head. "Dulcie's got a cold. As soon as I realized she was sick, I stopped letting her see her mama. She's stayin' with Marva."

The doctor nodded. "Wise choice. No fever, Hattie?"

"No. I feel fine. I get tired pretty easy, but I feel fine. Honest!"

Smith continued. "I been keepin' a close watch on the other young'uns, too—watchin' 'em for runny noses, or fever. They've been fine so far."

Doctor Wilson laid a hand on Smith's shoulder "Sounds like you've been a good watchdog, Smith."

He reached into his black bag and retrieved his stethoscope. "All right. Let's take a look at you, Hattie."

Smith excused himself and paced back and forth in the kitchen until the doctor called him back into the room.

"She looks good," The doctor said.

Hattie beamed. "Guess what! Doctor Wilson says the children can come home tomorrow!"

The doctor held up a cautionary hand. "Now wait just a minute. What I *actually* said was, *if* the baby looks as good as you do, and *if* Dulcie's past the worst of her cold, the children can come home tomorrow."

Hattie slid off the bed and happily padded into the kitchen after the doctor and Smith. She watched anxiously while Doctor Wilson examined Dalton.

The baby solemnly watched the doctor's face, then suddenly broke into a gummy grin.

"Well, look at you!" the doctor exclaimed. "You are gonna be a charmer."

He checked the baby over thoroughly, then handed him to Smith.

"How often is he nursing?"

"Every two hours!" Hattie and Smith replied together.

The doctor laughed at their response. "Well, his lungs sound great. I believe he's ready to come out of the box. It's warm enough now. I think he's maintaining his temperature on his own. He can go into the cradle."

Doctor Wilson, poked a finger at Dalton's double chin. "It's obvious he's eating well. Those were my biggest concerns. Underdeveloped lungs, his body temperature, and that he gain weight at a reasonable rate. Looks like he's doing all three."

The older man turned to Smith. "You've done a remarkable job here, Smith. Congratulations."

Smith looked prouder than proud. He shifted the baby to his left shoulder and wrapped his right arm around Hattie's waist.

"We done it together. Hattie kept him fed. I just did the haulin' back and forth between the box and the bedroom..."

Hattie gazed up at her husband's face. "An' you did the diapers, an' the washin', an' the chores..."

Doctor Wilson smiled. "You two are quite a team."

He began stuffing things back into his bag.

"Tell you what. Just to be on the safe side, I'll run to Beech Creek and take a peek at Miss Dulcie. Better to be safe than sorry."

He glanced up at Hattie. "I still have concerns about you getting sick."

At Hattie's protest, he fixed her with a firm look. "You still need to be careful. You are doing remarkably well, but it wouldn't take much to knock you off your feet again. Keep drinking plenty of water to stay hydrated—you need more than ever while you're still nursing. And lots of nourishing food."

He pulled a small pad out of his pocket and wrote down a few instructions. "I'm gonna write out a recipe for baby milk that you can bottle-feed Dalton if need be. You might want to let Smith take a few night feedings so you can get some uninterrupted sleep."

He hesitated, then went on, "You can go to church if you feel up to it, or take a ride in the country, but *no* heavy work, and no *extras*. Just the minimums. Your rugs will have to wait to be beaten, and the walls can wait 'til next year for a good scrub. You hear me?"

Hattie nodded reluctantly. "What about Labor Day? We have the Stoneworth family picnic comin' up."

"Let's see—when is that? A couple of weeks from now?"

Hattie nodded again.

Doc Wilson looked her up and down.

"You should be strong enough to go by then, if you *promise* not to overdo. You understand? You've got enough kinfolk to take care of the details. You just sit in the sun and enjoy yourself. Hear me?"

"Yes, sir. But surely I could bake a jam cake, make a few sandwiches..."

"Smith, you're gonna have to take a firm hand with her. I can already tell. Give her an inch and she'll take a mile," Doc teased.

Smith threw back his head and laughed. His loud guffaw startled the sleepy baby. He howled. Smith cringed, shamefaced, then pulled out a chair and pointed Hattie into it. He handed Dalton to her.

"Honey, why don't you sit right there and hold Dalton while I walk the doctor out."

They left her happily kissing Dalton's little toes.

The two men walked to the black sedan waiting outside. Doc tossed his bag onto the seat and would have followed it, but Smith laid a hand on his arm.

"'Bout your bill, Doc. I, uh...I don't have much cash money right now."

"You and just about everyone else in Muhlenberg County," the doctor laughed ruefully. He shrugged his shoulders.

"Don't worry about it, Smith. I got a special deal running right now. Babies under five pounds are free. And didn't Hattie tell you? Stoneworths get a group discount, just because there's so many of 'em. They keep me in chickens and pies, if nothin' else. Never hurts to have a Stoneworth praying for you, either."

"Thank you, Doc. Thanks for everything! As soon as I can, I'll come up with somethin'. Mebbe a jam cake. Suppose I could mix and bake one with Hattie lookin' on and instructin'? Anyway, Doc, we're mighty grateful!"

The doctor waved away Smith's gratitude.

"I know, I know."

❧

Hidden in the shadows of the woods beyond the smokehouse, a man squatted in the weeds, concealed behind a woodpile. The litter of cigarette butts around his feet showed he'd been waiting there a long time. Beside his left foot, from an opened half-filled fruit jar wafted the stench of cheap moonshine whiskey.

When the breeze blew just right, the sound of laughter floated up from the house. A movement from the back door caught his attention. From the watcher's vantage point, Smith and the doctor were clearly visible as they walked outside.

The man's fist tightened around the stock of the high-powered rifle he held in his hands. His fingers shook slightly. Carefully raising the gun to his shoulder, and steadying the rifle between two split logs at a gap in the upper course of the woodpile, he sighted down the barrel. Smith stood in the crosshairs.

22

Deke Dunford's finger tightened against the trigger. A squirrel barked and jumped from a branch of the oak tree behind him. Startled, the man hesitated. Smith ambled down the drive and stood beyond the doctor's car. The moment passed. Slowly Dunford lowered the barrel of the rifle. He swore viciously under his breath, then melted silently into the shadowy woods.

❧

Later that afternoon Sheriff Westerfield hoisted his girth from the driver's seat of his black Chevrolet sedan and crunched across the drive to Hattie's house.

"Hello?" he called.

His broad hand dwarfed the wooden spool that served as a handle on the screen door. Swinging the door open, he stepped heavily onto the porch.

Hattie climbed up the single step from the kitchen onto the raised screened porch, drying her hands on her apron.

"Why, Sheriff Westerfield, come on in!" Hattie's welcoming smile faded when she saw the grim look on the man's face.

"Oh, dear. This is an official call. I can tell just by looking, you're not here to visit," she said.

Hattie watched as he swung his head from side to side, scanning the back yard and surrounding area.

"No, ma'am. I'm sorry to say I ain't." the sheriff replied. "Smith around?"

Hattie's heart lurched in her chest. "He's up on the hill, but I 'spect him back any minute." She gulped hard "Is...is he in trouble?"

The big man turned his attention back from his apparent surveillance of the property to Hattie, and the deep lines of his face softened.

"Don't fret yourself, Miz Hattie. I ain't had no trouble from Smith since you took him on. You been doin' a fine job tamin' him."

Hattie's shoulders dropped in relief, then stiffened again. "It ain't about Eldon, is it? He's not..."

Hattie's oldest brother, Eldon, suffered with a horrid condition that many long-time miners had developed. Over time, particles of fine coal dust filled the tiny sacs of the lungs, cutting down oxygen intake and turning the lungs black. Once a tall robust man of huge proportions like the rest of the Stoneworth men, Eldon now looked like a stooped skeleton with skin. He still worked the mine every day, but the disease was taking its toll.

The sheriff placed a huge hand on Hattie's shoulder, and smiled gently.

"I ain't here to give you bad news about Smith, nor any o' your kinfolk. I just need to talk to Smith about something that happened last night."

Hattie said a silent prayer of thanks. "In that case, set yourself down and I'll pour you a cup of coffee."

The sheriff lowered his massive body onto one of the small wooden chairs at the table while Hattie gathered two cups and the coffeepot from the kitchen. After she'd poured them each a cup of hot coffee, she placed the old metal pot on a folded dishtowel on the scarred table and sat down on the opposite side from the visitor.

"Sure has been hot, ain't it?" the sheriff asked over the rim of his cup.

"Mighty hot. If my flowers get any droopier, they're gonna fall over. Smith hasn't had time to water 'em, with the new baby an' all."

The Sheriff let his eyes drop to Hattie's now-flat stomach. "I thought you looked diff'rent than you did last time I saw you."

Remembering her mad dash to the outhouse during his visit when Mamie was dying, Hattie blushed furiously. "Kind of you to notice," she answered dryly.

The sheriff laughed. "Now, don't you go getting shy on me,

Miz Hattie. I got a wife and young'uns. Reckon I seen a woman with morning sickness a time or two before you come along..."

He leaned forward and whispered confidentially. "I even delivered me a couple of young'uns in the line of duty. Let me tell you! Ma Richards weren't too happy with me, but I got the job done."

Hattie laughed. "I reckon you did."

The sound of someone whistling interrupted their conversation, and turned the attention of both of them to the figure making his way from the orchard toward the house.

"There's Smith now," Hattie said.

Sheriff Westerfield spoke quietly, "He's still limpin' awful bad. It's been almost two years since he was crushed at Coaltown Mine. He still in a lot of pain?"

Hattie nodded. "Every day," she answered simply. "Not that he'd ever say so, but I see it in the lines on his face. And every now and again when he thinks I'm not lookin'."

"Takes a real man to bear up and not complain," the sheriff replied.

By then, Smith was at the edge of the yard. Hattie rose and held open the door.

"Smith, we got company. Come on in," she called.

"Hidy, Sheriff!" Smith held his hand out.

"Smith." The Sheriff wrapped his huge paw around Smith's hand and shook it hard. "Good to see you. Got a few minutes for me?"

"Always got time for you," Smith grinned. "Seems to me it's a wise man that makes time for the law."

The sheriff threw his head back and laughed.

There had been a time when he and Smith were adversaries, but those days were long past now. They held each other with mutual respect these days. The Sheriff had even testified *for* Smith at his murder trial the year before.

The large man sobered and swung his heavily jowled face from Smith to Hattie and back again. "I need to talk to you, Smith." He cleared his throat. "Might be better if'n it was just you an' me.

Some of what I got to say..."

Smith frowned and shook his head. "Ain't no secrets in this house, sir. Anything you got to say, I'll be tellin' Hattie, so you might as well just spell it out."

Sheriff Westerfield seemed to consider each word as he spoke it. "Do you know who Little Jenny is?"

Smith's eyes cut toward Hattie, then he nodded slowly.

"She's dead. Murdered last night," said the sheriff.

Smith leaned forward in his chair. "What's that got to do with us?"

Hattie gasped, "Oh my! Who was she? What happened?"

The Sheriff appeared to become very interested in his tie. "Little Jenny Foster was a..." He coughed and then continued, 'a lady of the night.' She lived in Hopkinsville."

Hattie gasped again. Her eyes widened as she looked at Smith. "And...and you knew her?"

Smith reached toward Hattie and squeezed her hand. "Honey, I said I knew *who she was*. I didn't know *her*," he answered firmly.

He turned back to the sheriff. "I heard she was a sweet little thing, and I'm sorry she's dead, but, again, what's that got to do with us?"

The sheriff steepled his fingers under his chin. "The man described as bein' the last one with Little Jenny sounds an awful lot like Deke Dunford. The sheriff over in Hopkins County says he's got a witness that heard Little Jenny scream and then saw Deke run out of her place. The witness went in and found her."

The sheriff shifted in his chair and looked uncomfortable. "It appears she'd been brutally..." again, he cleared his throat, "uh...compromised. And then beat to death."

Hattie's hands flew to her face. She closed her eyes against the vision that danced in her imagination—another woman bloodily beaten to death by Deke Dunford, and this time...Horror and revulsion mixed with pity and sadness. "Oh, that poor woman." She moaned. "Oh, Smith!"

Hattie turned toward her husband. "I can't believe it. I just *can't*!"

Sheriff Westerfield pushed back his chair and stood up. "You better believe it, Miz Hattie. The witness is a credible one.

"I feel a bit guilty saddlin' you with responsibility for his young'uns, but from what I hear they seem to be doin' mighty well with you and the Fentons. They sure don't need to be at the county poor farm."

Smith rose too, and walked to stand behind Hattie's chair and rested his hands on her shoulders. He moved his jaw from side to side as he did when in deep thought.

"Sheriff, if Deke killed Little Jenny, then you got 'cause to arrest him now."

"That's right." The Sheriff sighed deeply. "We've issued a warrant for Dunford's arrest. After all, there ain't many Clark Gable look-alikes runnin' around this part of Kentucky. Especially ones that drive a 1934 Studebaker Coupe like was seen speedin' away from where Little Jenny was murdered."

"No, I reckon not." Smith shook his head.

"He's layin' low," the sheriff continued, "but we'll get him. Reckon y'all can keep his young'uns a while longer?"

"Of course," Hattie replied.

The large man looked at Smith. "I know how frustrated you were when I couldn't get him for Mamie's death. But this time..." He left the sentence hanging.

Smith held up one hand. "Wait a minute, Deke's not stupid. He knows these hills like the back of his hand. He ain't gonna be easy to catch."

"You're right about that, too, Smith." The sheriff nodded. "But eventually we'll get him."

Inside the house, the baby cried.

Hattie glanced toward the sound. "I need to check on Dalton."

The sheriff started toward the door. "That's all right, Miz Hattie. I need to be on my way. Just wanted to let y'all know about Deke."

Hattie thanked him and stepped into the house.

As soon as she disappeared, Sheriff Westerfield jerked his head toward the outside door.

Smith glanced toward the house and said, "I'll walk you out."

He followed the officer to his car.

The sheriff climbed into his car, then leaned on the window frame. "Listen, Delaney, Miz Hattie may be in some kind of danger. Deke's gotten more an' more irrational since Mamie died. I'm 'bout positive he's been breakin' into houses and even a store or two. You know he got throwed out of the Black Diamond mine that afternoon before he went home an' beat Mamie?"

Smith nodded. Gossip spread like wildfire in the small mining communities.

The sheriff continued, "I figure that's what set him off that night. They suspected he was stealin' equipment, an' sellin' it at Jockey Day in Greenville. When they asked him where he was gettin' his sellin' goods, he got purty ugly with Mr. Boggs. So Boggs fired him on the spot. Said he wasn't about to take abuse from the likes of Deke. These days, there's too many good men lookin' for work to keep a thief."

"Yessir," Smith answered. "Times are mighty hard for most of us right now."

The officer reached across the seat and picked up his hat. He pulled it down over his brow and said, "Anyway, with him on the loose and crazy enough to start stealin', I been keepin' my ear to the ground. First off, Deke's been hitting the liquor purty hard, but what I'm hearin' most often is how he's sayin' harsh words about Miz Hattie."

Smith stiffened. "He'd better be careful what he says."

The sheriff's eyes bored into Smith's. "An' you better be careful you don't try takin' the law into your own hands!" he warned.

At Smith's growled response, the older man sighed. "Listen here, you said before you didn't know Little Jenny. That true?"

Smith, confused by the sudden change of direction from the sheriff, replied stiffly, "I heard tell of Little Jenny when I was workin' in the mines—usually from the younger men. But I ain't never laid eyes on her myself."

"Just thought you should know," the sheriff said, pumping the gas and simultaneously pivoting his foot to press the starter, "she had black hair and deep, dark eyes, just like your Hattie."

22

The distinctive thunk of car doors slamming jolted Hattie from her journal writing. She raised her head and closed the book just as Dulcie raced through the open door and launched herself into Hattie's arms.

"Mama!"

The little girl's voice was muffled against her mother's shoulder.

"I missed you!"

"I missed you, too." Hattie hugged her daughter tightly. "How are you feelin'? Are you all right?"

Dulcie leaned her head back and gazed up at Hattie's face. "Yup. Doctor Wilson said so."

Hattie laughed. "Well, if Doc Wilson said so, it must be true."

A movement caught her eye. Looking up, she saw the five other children crowded into the doorway watching.

Jackie sat on his bottom and scooted down the one step into the kitchen.

"Hi, Mama. See my rock."

He reached deep into his pocket and fumbled a smooth flat stone out of it. He held it out to his mother in his dimpled hand.

Hattie ran her fingertips across the surface. "My goodness. Isn't that pretty. Where'd you get it, honey?"

"Digger finded it. He gived it to me."

Digger grinned. He shuffled his feet.

"Just an ol' rock," he mumbled.

Hattie shook her head. "Oh no, Digger. It's a lot more than that. It's a gift that you gave a little boy. Look how happy you made him. You've got a generous heart."

Dulcie twisted on Hattie's lap and reached up to pull her mother's face back toward her. "You all better now, Mama? Can we live here again?"

The obvious longing in Dulcie's hopeful expression tugged at Hattie's heart. She leaned down and pressed her nose against Dulcie's.

"Yes!" she whispered.

"Yeah!"

Hattie set Dulcie down and looked at the clustered children. "Where's Marva?"

Becky answered, "She dropped us off. Said to tell you she had errands to run, but she'll be down tomorrow."

"Oh." Hattie looked at the bags and bundles the children held.

"How 'bout we get your things back upstairs where they belong. Then we'll take a walk."

She watched each little face as the children trooped by. They were so sweet, so precious.

"Oops!" Hattie reached out and snagged Jackie around his middle, scooping him onto her lap. "Not you, little boy! You're not ready for those steep stairs yet."

"Am too," Jackie giggled.

"Are not!" Hattie teased, tickling his little round belly.

Jackie curled himself around her hand, laughing. "Stop! That tickles!"

Dalton woke up and started to cry. Becky clumped down three steps, then squatted and peered through the stair rail.

"Miz Hattie, Aunt Marva said we was supposed to help out. Want me to get the baby?"

Aunt Marva? "Sure, Honey. That...that would be fine."

Hattie absently handed Jackie a stub of pencil and tore out a blank sheet of her journal notebook for him to draw on.

Becky came the rest of the way down the stairs and picked up the fussing baby. She jounced him on her shoulder until he quieted, then leaned against the doorjamb.

"He's so sweet, Miz Hattie! Aunt Marva says..."

Hattie only half listened to what Becky said after that. *Aunt Marva! There it is again...So that's the way it is,* she thought sadly. *They've already chosen Marva and Conroy over me and Smith. Somehow, during the last few weeks they've stopped thinking of this as home...maybe they never did.*

"Miz Hattie?"

"Hmmm?"

Becky's face came sharply back into focus. She stood waiting expectantly for some response.

Hattie forced herself to smile at the little girl. "I'm sorry, Becky. I guess I wasn't listening. What did you say?"

Concern flickered across Becky's face. "Are you all right? I mean, Aunt Marva said we shouldn't tire you out."

The little girl bit her lip. "Are you tired already?"

Hattie laughed softly. She stood up and put Jackie on the chair she'd just vacated. She went to Becky and hugged the worried child. "No, honey. Just excited that you're all home again. Guess I was just daydreamin'."

Becky shifted the baby to her other shoulder. Her eyes got soft and dewy. "My mama used to woolgather, sometimes. That's what she called daydreamin'."

The little girl wandered to the side door and looked out. "She'd just stop whatever she was doin' and sorta gaze off in the distance. I...I always wondered where she went."

Hattie started at the mention of Mamie. Since the burial, the Dunford children had mentioned her only rarely. And just in passing, almost as though she'd been only a vague, peripheral part of their lives, rather than their mother. It had worried Hattie, but she hadn't known what to do about it, so she'd left them alone.

She walked over to stand behind Becky. "Where do you think your mama was dreamin' about?"

Becky glanced up at her, then back out the window, blinking hard. "I don't know. Maybe...a big house with a maid and a chauffeur, like you read about in books. Or...maybe she went to a foreign land...like...like New England."

If the little girl hadn't been so deadly serious, Hattie might have laughed.

Becky tightened her arms around Dalton and gently rocked him back and forth. "I...I think mostly she...she just went somewhere my daddy couldn't go. Where...where she was safe," she whispered against the baby's soft head.

Hattie caught her breath at Becky's unthinking admission of Deke's cruelty. She smoothed Becky's blond hair, then wrapped her arms around the little girl and the baby. "I think you're right. I think that's exactly where she went."

She rested her chin on top of Becky's head. "And you know what else I think? I think you are a mighty smart little girl to have figured that out."

She turned Becky, held her out from her, and studied her face. "I think wherever she went in her daydreams, she made sure she had you, Digger, Dorie, and Mary Claire, with her. Your mama would never have left you on purpose. You know that, don't you?"

Becky leaned into Hattie for a quick moment, then loosened her grip on the baby with one hand and wiped at her tears. She gave Hattie a watery smile. "That's what Aunt Marva said, too."

"Aunt Marva's a wise woman," Hattie admitted.

"Yes, ma'am. She sure is."

Overhead, a loud thump and raucous laughter sounded from the other children. Dorie squealed, and Dulcie yowled. Jackie raised his head from his artistic creation and craned his neck toward the sound.

"Digger?" Hattie called. "Are you pickin' on the girls?"

Dulcie scampered halfway down the stairs. "No, ma'am. We're pickin' on *him*!"

Dorie followed Dulcie onto the steps.

"He's our prisoner. He was tryin' to escape! See?"

Coming down the stairs behind the girls, under the watchful eye of his three-year-old guard, Digger allowed Mary Claire to lead him. Both his hands were stuffed together into one large sock.

"Handcuffs," Mary Claire announced sternly. "He's bad!"

Jackie hopped off his chair at the kitchen table and stomped over to the bottom of the narrow stairs. Making a fist with his right hand and pounding it down into the palm of his left hand, he glared up at Digger.

"Proverbs 10:1-3, The proverbs of Solomon. A wise son maketh a glad father: but a foolish son is the heaviness of his mother. Treasures of wickedness profit nothing: but righteousness delivereth from death. The LORD will not suffer the soul of the righteous to famish: but he casteth away the substance of the wicked."

Dead silence descended on the house as the little boy powerfully quoted Scripture. All eyes were on the toddler.

Hattie snorted, then laughed. The rest followed. Soon the house rang with the sound.

❧

Late that night, Smith and Hattie lay side by side talking through their day.

"I'm tellin' you, he quoted it word for word!" Hattie whispered.

Smith laughed so hard he shook the whole bed.

"Shhhh! You'll wake the children!" Hattie giggled.

"Cain't help it. That boy! I can just see him standin' there, righteously shakin' his finger at Digger."

Hattie smothered a laugh. "Oh, no! He wasn't shakin' his finger, Smith. He was poundin' the pulpit, just like Brother Belk at the revival last spring. I wish you could have seen that boy. He was a picture! An' you should have seen Digger's face! His eyes were huge, like judgment was really rainin' down on him."

"Digger's come such a long way since you brought those kids home back in June. Just playin' with the girls is a huge milestone for him. You've worked miracles on them young'uns!"

Hattie sobered. "I'm not so sure, Smith. Marva and Conroy have done an awful lot, too."

The admission was hard for her to make, but to the very roots of her soul, Hattie was honest. She told Smith about the conversation she'd had with Becky.

"Before they went up to Marva's, those children avoided any talk about their mama. Marva helped 'em open a...a door somehow."

Smith rolled onto his side facing Hattie and brushed a hand down her cheek.

"You feel like you failed 'em, 'cause it didn't happen here?"

Hattie thought a moment. "No, not exactly. It could have been just a matter of timin'. Before I had the baby, they weren't ready yet. Another few weeks went by and then they were."

She looked at Smith. "I'd rather it had been under our care, 'stead of Marva's."

"Why? Because Mamie sent the young'uns to you? You think you should'a been the one that that got 'em to open up?"

Hattie's eyes flew open. "That's not it. I mean, I do feel like they're my responsibility. Mamie did send 'em to me. But it's more than just feelin' obliged. I love those kids."

She punched at her pillow.

"Guess I'm jealous. I...I feel guilty about that," she whispered. "I've never been jealous of any of my brothers or sisters before. It's just wrong."

Smith gently tugged at a strand of Hattie's dark hair.

"The stakes ain't never been this high. There's four little lives involved in this mess. It's not like Marva got a new hat, an' you didn't."

"I know that! But I don't like feelin' so selfish."

She picked at the cuff of her nightgown. "I mean, shouldn't I want to do what's best for those 'little lives'—not just be thinkin' about how hurt I am?"

"You're mighty hard on yourself, Hattie."

He reached for her fidgeting hands and captured them between his own. "You're the most unselfish person I've ever met in my life. You want them kids, and so does Marva. I think what you're feelin' right now is pretty normal."

Smith yawned hugely. "'Sides, now that Deke's up for murder, a judge is gonna have to make the final decision about them young'uns. It ain't really up to you *or* Marva. You're borrowin' trouble you don't need, honey. Why don't we just try to enjoy whatever time we've got with 'em, while we can."

"You're prob'ly right." Hattie sighed.

She rolled away from Smith and let him gather her to his chest, one arm draped across her body.

Smith yawned again. "Try to sleep, honey. Dalton's gonna be hollerin' in a couple of hours."

Hattie stared into the dark. "Just wish they'd call *me* Aunt Hattie..."

23

Gideon, pushing back from the table, said, "Another fine meal, Miz Hattie."

"Thank you, Gideon, but Smith did it all. He still won't let me lift a finger," Hattie replied.

"You did all this, Mr. Delaney?" Darlin asked.

"Cain't take too much credit," Smith answered. "Hattie's sisters are still sendin' food down. I just sliced the tomatoes and cucumbers, and put everything on plates."

Hattie adjusted the baby on her lap and leaned forward. "Oh! Speakin' of plates, I'm supposed to ask y'all to our family picnic on Labor Day. You'll come, won't you?"

The slender mountain girl beamed as she responded, "That's mighty nice—more'n nice, Miz Hattie."

"Sounds like a family gatherin'," interrupted Gideon. "Wouldn't want to horn in on your kinfolk, ma'am."

"Oh, no! Not at all," responded Hattie. "You are family to us. We'd be honored to have you. You wouldn't be hornin' in at all."

"'Course not," agreed Smith, "We're gonna be at Ol' Airdrie."

"What's Ol' Airdrie?" asked Gideon.

"It's sorta like a ghost town on the Green River a mile or so below Paradise," said Smith. "But..."

"You mean there's really a town named Paradise?" Darlin interrupted.

Smith laughed softly at the look on Darlin's face. "Sure is. Legend has it that folks traveling up and down the Green River in olden times thought it was about the purtiest place they'd ever seen. They called it 'paradise' and the name stuck. A whole community sprung up there."

"If it was so wonderful, how come it to die out, then?" asked Gideon.

Smith leaned back in his chair and draped his arm across the empty one next to him. Hattie watched his face. He was obviously enjoying the opportunity to spin a tale.

"Paradise didn't die out. Airdrie did. You see, down the river a ways from Paradise, a wealthy Scotsman found iron ore and decided to build an ironworks like they had back in Scotland. So he bought up the countryside and brought workers over from the old country."

"But it didn't work out," added Hattie.

"Sure didn't," Smith continued. "It's a shame, too. A short ways back from the river, at the base of a bluff, they built a fancy furnace and brought in the finest equipment—the stone shell of that furnace is still there."

"Just the shell?" Gideon asked.

"Yep. And they built a tall, three-floor engine building outta cut native stone—it's still standin' too, sorta majestic like, but lonesome, with the roof and wooden floors and machinery all long gone."

"My gracious. All that money they put into it, and it's just fallin' down?" Darlin' asked.

"Sure 'nuff. Up the side of the hill about the level of the top of the furnace stack, the hill steps back a short ways, and makes a shoulder-like flat area that runs along the side of the bluff. From that ledge, they tunneled back into the hill for coal and iron. They built a long, sixty-step stairway running down the bluff to the base of the furnace and machine house."

Hattie refilled their coffee cups. "On top of the hill," she said, "they built a whole village with homes, hotels, a store—there was even a post office. It was some kind of showplace in its time,"

Gideon gave a low whistle. "Sounds like they was plannin' for it to be there a long time. So what went wrong?" he asked.

"Stubbornness." Smith leaned forward and took a sip of his coffee. He picked up the napkin from his lap, folded it and laid it on the table. "Well, better get to the chores."

Gideon's and Darlin's mouths dropped open.

Hattie poked Smith. "Stop teasin' these young'uns!"

She turned to the McBrides. "Serve him right if you got up

and went home. He's waitin' for you to beg him to tell the rest."

Smith stuck his bottom lip out playfully. "That woman ruins all my fun," he mock-complained to no one in particular.

He leaned forward on his elbows and went on with the story.

"Old man Alexander and his men were stuck in their ways. Tried to do everything just like they did in Scotland. But this weren't Scotland, and they needed to adapt. Alexander wouldn't do it. Neither would the men he brought in. Just fired up the furnace and tried a few times. He didn't have much success, so the old boy threw up his hands and said 'Forget it!' He took off to Lexington to raise thoroughbred horses."

"Well, ain't that a shame!" said Gideon. "So it all went to ruin?"

"Yep, but not for a quite a while. For many years Yankee General Don Carlos Buell had a fancy mansion right on the brow of that hill, overlooking the river. Once he died back early in this century, Airdrie went downhill fast. Years went by an' the site got to be known by the locals as 'Ol' Airdrie'."

Smith rocked his chair onto its two back legs.

"It sure left us an ideal place to have our picnic—oh, did I mention that there's a mighty fine spring there? Just wait'til you get a big draft of that delicious spring water!" he grinned.

Hattie choked on the mouthful of coffee she'd just taken, and cut her eyes toward her mischievous husband. She'd tasted the mineral-laden spring water. It smelled like rotten eggs and left a metallic tang in the mouth.

Smith pounded on Hattie's back. "Sounds like you need some of that spring water yourself, Hattie. They say it's good for whatever ails you."

He winked.

"It sounds so excitin'—the buildings, the stairs, and the mines going back into the dark. I'd love to go along," said Darlin wistfully. "What do you think, Gideon? Can we go?"

Gideon reached over and squeezed his young wife's hand. "I reckon."

He looked from Smith to Hattie and back again. "If'n you're

sure you don't mind us buttin' in."

❧

On the Saturday before Labor Day, Smith and Gideon went with Gene Beckwith and Forrest and Berkley Stoneworth to Airdrie to clear away fallen limbs and brush. They cleaned out the spring, built a loose stone fire pit, and made general preparations for the picnic.

Berk, Nan, and their children, Little Gene and Poppy, had arrived late Thursday from Louisville. It was obvious that Berk was happy to be out in the countryside. Smith and Gene found him wandering through the underbrush, gazing at the honeysuckle and renegade grapes that grew wild all over the hillside.

"What's the matter, Berk? Ain't never seen a tree before?" Forrest teased.

"Not lately I haven't. Up in Louisville—well, seems like they're cuttin' 'em all down to throw up more houses."

Smith beckoned the other two men. "Y'all come on. Gideon's found us the perfect tree for hangin' a swing."

Soon they all stood at the base of a large tree. It stood right on the bank of the Green River. High off the ground hung heavy horizontal branches swooping out from the trunk.

"Looks like a good one to me," said Gideon, eyeing the huge canopy.

"Son, have you lost your mind?" Forrest asked incredulously. "Those branches are thirty-five, forty feet up! Even if I was a youthful Cy Young an' pitchin' for the National League All Stars, I couldn't chuck a rope that high."

"Don't need to pitch nothin'. I'll carry the rope up there."

Berk laughed. "You gonna sprout wings and fly?"

Gideon grinned and pulled a ball of twine from a rucksack slung over his shoulder. He found the end of the string and threaded it through one of his belt loops.

Handing the ball to Berk, Gideon said, "As I climb, you just keep unwinding it for me."

He pointed to a broad branch that pushed out parallel to the river. "When I get out on that limb up there, tie the string to the end of the rope, and I'll pull 'er up and tie it nice and tight."

The older men watched skeptically as Gideon dropped his rucksack at the base of the tree. He locked his arms and legs around the trunk and shinnied up the tree.

"Look at that boy go!" said Forrest, pushing his hat back on his head.

"He's somethin' else," said Smith proudly.

Before long Gideon reached the area where he could climb from branch to branch.

"He sure reminds me of someone..." said Berkley. He leaned his head back and shaded his eyes to watch Gideon move higher and higher into the tree. Suddenly he snapped his fingers and laughed out loud. "Give him a beard and a top hat, and add a few years, he'd look just like Abe Lincoln!"

"Yep," Smith agreed. "An' he's every bit as honest."

Gene Beckwith joined the conversation. "Must be close to six feet, six inches tall, and cain't weigh more'n a hundred and sixty pounds."

"Don't matter. He's tough as ol' shoe leather," commented Forrest.

By this time Gideon was scooting out on the big horizontal limb.

"Tie the rope onto the string," he called down.

Berkley pulled out his knife, cut the string from the ball, and tied the end around the rope.

Gideon pulled the rope up, wrapped it around the limb four times, then reached down and tied the loose end tightly to the rope hanging down.

"Tied it with a bowline knot, nice and snug," he announced. He swung himself from the limb onto the rope and slid down hand over hand like a circus acrobat.

"Fine job, Gideon," said Smith, patting him on the shoulder.

He reached for Berkley's knife. "Now let's cut her off two or three feet from the ground, tie a big knot in the end, and we'll have ourselves a mighty good swing!"

❧

Right after the men left for Airdrie, Marva arrived at Hattie's house with boxes of groceries.

Hattie sat and watched while Marva prepared their part of the meal that they would all share the next day at Carrie and Gene's house. She knew that Carrie and the rest of her sisters and sisters-in-law were cooking, too.

The pair chatted happily back and forth about Berkley and Nan and their children, and who was going to bring what to the Sunday dinner at Carrie's. They laughed over Lalie's latest beau and clucked over President Roosevelt's latest struggle to revive the nation's economy.

Before long, Hattie grew restless. It bothered her that she wasn't allowed to help. She chafed at her restrictions.

"Seems like I could peel potatoes, or somethin' easy like that," she suggested hopefully.

"You're not peeling an orange. I'm under strict orders to keep you still, and so are you," Marva said in a no-nonsense tone.

"Smith and Forrest both cornered me at Radburn's store this mornin'," she continued, "If you even step foot out of that chair I'm supposed to pack up and go home. Now, which way do you want it?"

Marva arched an eyebrow at her younger sister.

Hattie sat quietly.

"Why don't you piece your quilt?" Marva suggested. "That's something you can do sitting down."

Hattie leaned on one elbow. "I don't have one cut out right now. I could finish binding the one we quilted last month, but it's too hot to have it layin' across me."

"Have any mendin'? You could..."

"Except for edgin' the quilt, I don't think there's a piece of handwork left undone on this side of Muhlenberg County. I've done it all. That's about the only thing Smith allows me to do." Hattie smiled ruefully.

Marva smiled in return. "Poor Hattie. Waited on hand and foot by the man she loves. Bless your heart, you poor thing!"

Hattie laughed. "That's me, all right. 'Bout as pitiful as they come."

Marva sifted flour into Hattie's heavy mixing bowl, then dumped in the rest of the ingredients for a jam cake.

"I know this won't turn out as well as if you'd made it, but you can walk me through it, and hopefully no one will turn up their nose. You have such a light touch with bakin' goods."

Hattie watched Marva closely. "And you have a light touch with children. Becky talked to me about her mother the other day. She said the two of you have been doin' some talkin' about her, too."

Marva didn't meet Hattie's eyes. "Becky's a sweet little thing. I think she's carried a heavy load for an awful long time."

With her back to Hattie, Marva opened the firebox on the stove. She poked at the coals and added wood to heat the oven. "Did you know Becky always took the children up to the old cabin whenever Deke beat Mamie? She would gather 'em up like chicks and hustle 'em outta harm's way. She told me she felt like she had to protect 'em, 'cause her mama couldn't."

Hattie hadn't known. Her heart squeezed with pain for the little girl who'd seen too much.

"About the children, Marva..."

Marva whirled to face Hattie. "Not today, Hattie," she begged. "I...I don't want to talk about it today."

❧

By the time Smith and Hattie and the children pulled up outside Carrie and Gene's house on Sunday afternoon, there were already cars and trucks lining the road.

Smith made a face. "All them Stoneworths got the best parkin' spots. Tol' you we should have been here earlier."

On the contrary, from the time they had returned home from church, Hattie had been champing at the bit to get to her sister's house. Smith, however, had puttered around the property, poking into the smokehouse and wandering around the yard. She'd even seen him out by the stacked wood at the edge of the woods. He'd knelt down behind the woodpile, then raised up, his face set in stone. He'd seemed distracted ever since.

Hattie reached over Jackie's head and brushed her fingers

across the back of Smith's neck.

"Is everything all right? Are you...what's going on, honey?" she asked worriedly.

Smith glanced at his wife. Her face was wreathed with concern. He swallowed hard.

"Everything's fine, Hattie. I'm just out o' sorts, I reckon. Sorry 'bout that."

"You sure?"

Smith grinned and leaned across the seat. He planted a kiss on Hattie's cheek. "Yep. Now let's go have a good time."

Jackie shoved them apart like Samson pushing down the pillars of the Philistine temple.

"Hey! You is squishin' me!" he complained.

The tension in the truck cab evaporated. Smith and Hattie laughed at the little boy's consternation.

❧

Eldon Stoneworth held court on the front porch swing. The skin of his ravaged face was pulled taut across his cheekbones. In spite of his obvious illness, he was still a fine-looking man—and still head of the clan.

Forrest and Berk sat on straight-backed chairs. Gene and Chloe's husband, Ray, leaned against the wall, well under the shade of the porch roof. Smith joined them just as they all roared at the punchline of Eldon's joke. Smith held the door open for Hattie, then sat down on the top step. He listened to the other men banter back and forth.

Chloe and Ray's teenagers huddled with Eldon and Rose Ellen's older children in the side yard. Ben Stoneworth, Eldon's 18-year-old son, stood just inside the white picket fence watching the little ones, including Jackie, Mary Claire, and Poppy. Forrest and Vida's two-year-old son, Clifford, was there, too. The rest of the youngsters chased and ran, then flopped in the shade of the oak trees to cool off.

None of the goings-on touched Smith. All he could think of was what he had seen behind the woodpile. Deke Dunford had obviously spent a considerable amount of time sitting there, watching the house. The evidence was irrefutable.

Smith was angry. He'd known that Deke was skulking around once in a while, but now he was apparently lying in wait. But waiting for what? That was the question. Was he waiting until Hattie was alone so that he could do to her what he'd done to Mamie—what he'd done to Little Jenny?

Stark terror and fury, unlike any he'd known before, roiled and burned, nearly choking Smith with its ferocity.

What am I gonna do? How do I deal with a madman? Smith asked himself. *Dear Lord, please help me protect Hattie and the young'uns. Please don't let Deke get 'em. Somehow, Lord, if he comes after 'em, help me to find him first....*

Out of the corner of his eye, he saw Marva and Conroy arrive.

Conroy apologized for their lateness. "We had a baptism. Couldn't miss that!"

Digger flew around the corner of the house and skidded to a halt.

"Hey, Uncle Conroy!"

"Hey, yourself."

"Wanna play catch with me?"

Conroy reached out and grabbed the little boy in a huge hug. "You bet I do. I been lookin' forward to it all week! How you been, buddy?"

"Fine," Digger beamed. "Did you bring your catcher's mitt?"

"Sure did."

Their voices faded as they walked around to the back of the house.

Smith returned to his reflections about Deke. His stomach turned at the thought of Deke watching Hattie move through the house. When had Deke been behind that woodpile? Had it happened more than once? How long had it taken to smoke the cigarettes that littered the ground? Smith had found the telltale footprints in the dirt. He'd smelled the fruit jar Deke had left behind.

Smith clenched his jaw. Had Deke watched the house at night? Had Hattie been silhouetted against the lamplight wearing her pretty white nightgown? Had Deke run his eyes over her body? Had he seen her then?

He shuddered.

"Goose walk across your grave, Smith?" Forrest asked.

"Huh?"

Smith turned toward Forrest. His brother-in-law's face was quizzical.

"Who you plannin' on killin', Smith?" he asked quietly.

Smith shook his head ruefully. "Was I that obvious?"

Gene and Eldon nodded.

"Looked like you was about to leap off the steps," said Berkley. "What's goin' on?"

Smith didn't know what to do. He'd always been able to handle whatever trouble came down the pike all by himself. In fact, most of the time the scrapes he'd gotten into had been of his own creation. But this time it was different. He wasn't the one in danger. He hated to worry Hattie's brothers, but this was big. Really big.

He glanced toward the front door to make sure none of the women were in sight, then checked to see where the children were.

Stepping back up onto the porch, he started talking in a low voice.

"I ain't plannin' on killin' nobody, but I got reason to believe Deke Dunford may be after Hattie..."

24

The Stoneworth clan began arriving at the end of the road at Paradise at ten o'clock Labor Day morning. Because it was more than a mile walk back to the picnic site, two rowboats bobbed in the Green River, waiting to carry the women, the babies, and the food down the river to Airdrie. The teenage boys had been shanghaied into rowing their mothers and aunts. Dire warnings were fired at the boys, with threats of terrible consequences if they splashed the woman or soaked the food—and woe to him who dared to race. All this took place amid much laughter.

Hattie and Dalton were handed into young Ben's boat. Darlin and Levi were already seated at the far end with Rose Ellen.

"Don't worry, Aunt Hattie, I'll take good care of you," Ben announced, wiggling his eyebrows up and down while shifting his weight gently from side to side. The boat rocked slightly.

Darlin squealed and clutched the side with the hand that didn't have a chokehold on Levi. Hattie sat down quickly, her brown eyes wide.

"Quit that, Ben Stoneworth, or I'll tell your mama." she threatened. Her dimples flashed, completely removing any fear that Ben was in danger of his mother's wrath.

Ben chuckled. He glanced toward his mother, then leaned over to whisper, "Uh, Aunt Hattie. I'm six foot four. An' I weigh over two hunnerd pounds. What you reckon my mama could do to me at this point?"

From her seat next to Darlin, Rose Ellen heard him, and laughed. She narrowed her eyes, and pantomimed swinging an oar at his head. "I heard that, young man! Don't you try my patience, or I'll show you what I can do."

Ben reached for the hamper that Eldon held out to him. A

look passed between them. Ben nodded almost imperceptibly, and set the covered basket in the space between the seats, then helped Forrest's wife, Vida, over the edge of the boat. She was ungainly with her advanced pregnancy, and lowered herself carefully onto the seat next to Hattie.

"Forrest is gonna piggyback Clifford over the hill. Honestly, I'm glad. That boy's about to wear me out," she complained good-naturedly.

"I understand." Hattie grinned. "Wait 'til the new baby comes. You'll find out what tired really is!"

Vida groaned. "Don't tell me. I don't want to know. My ankles are swollen, and my fingers are so puffy I had to take off my weddin' ring—or risk losing a finger. I look like Mr. Hammer's prize heifer. I just can't take any more bad news."

Rose Ellen leaned toward the other two women. "Could have twins. That would keep you hoppin'," she teased.

"Bite your tongue, Rose Ellen," Vida exclaimed. "They'd have to send me to the asylum!"

The women watched the river slowly go by while Ben rowed the boat downstream. None of them noticed him scanning the shore, the rocks and hills, and the dark spaces between the close-set trees. None of them knew that tucked into the hamper at his feet, between his mother's coconut cake and a jar of her bread-and-butter pickles, he carried a loaded Colt 45.

❧

On the other side of the river, melting from tree to tree, Gideon and Pride silently followed the boat's slow progress. In his right hand he carried his rifle. Like Ben Stoneworth, he, too, scanned the hills and the trees along the river's edge.

Early that morning, Smith had come to the small McBride cabin. He'd called Gideon outside and clued him in. They'd stood next to Smith's truck while Smith told him about the visit from Sheriff Westerfield and about the woman called Little Jenny. He'd told Gideon about finding Deke's watching place behind the woodpile.

They had both agreed that Hattie was a sitting duck on the

open water, but she wasn't up to walking the mile back to Airdrie from Paradise. Gideon volunteered to walk the bank on the far side. Now he used stealth to keep himself hidden, not only from the women on the boats but also from other eyes that might be peering from the dense woods.

❧

Walking the trail to Airdrie with the other men, and the children, Smith ran Hattie's river progress through his mind. *Now she's past the big sycamore...should be beyond the inlet now...now they're...*

Like the other men, he carried a rifle. His senses were on high alert; every snap of a stick, or creak of the wind in the trees, tightened his grip on the gun.

By rights, with his bad leg, he could have justified riding in the boats with the women, but his pride, and the fact that it would have worried Hattie, had made the trek a necessity. He gritted his teeth. *Should be past the sandbar...*

Dulcie and Dorie skipped ahead, with Jackie and Mary Claire pumping their fat little legs up and down, trying to keep up. Mary Claire stumbled on a root and went down hard. Smith hurried toward the crying child, but Conroy was already there, laying his rifle on the ground to scoop her up. Smith watched the little girl wrap her arms around Conroy's neck.

Conroy brushed the dirt away from her skinned knee and gently blew on the scrape. He kissed her tears away and sent the toddler into a giggle fit.

"She all right?" Smith asked.

"Sure she is. She's a trouper, ain't you, honey?" Conroy answered.

Mary Claire smiled up at Conroy and nodded.

"Want to ride on my shoulders?" Conroy asked her.

"Yes!"

Conroy picked up the little girl, lifted her high above his head and lowered her onto his shoulders. Mary Claire squealed and clutched at his head, partly covering his eyes.

Conroy pretended to stumble. She squealed again.

"All right, settle down up there." Conroy laughed. He squatted to pick up his rifle and set off again with the delighted child riding on her high perch.

Ahead, Forrest spoke quietly to Ray, then handed Clifford to Chloe's husband, and dropped back from the center of the pack to walk with Smith.

"Any sign of Deke?" he asked softly.

Smith shook his head. "Nope."

"You know, Smith, our women are in the boats, too. If Deke takes a shot..."

"He'll never get the chance. Gideon'll get him first."

Forrest's face was grim. "Sure hope you're right about that."

Smith lifted his bad leg over a fallen limb. "I'd never have put Hattie on the boat if'n I'd thought otherwise," he said.

"You sure got a lot of faith in that boy."

"Yep."

"Hope it ain't misplaced."

Smith pinned Forrest with a hard look. "It ain't!"

❧

The clan gathered amid a cluster of huge oak trees that spread their canopies together. Even in the heat of September, the temperature under the shade was comfortable, with the breeze blowing off the river.

Hattie and the women shook out their bright quilts and spread them on the ground. They tucked their knees modestly under the skirts of their summer dresses and enjoyed the break in their normal routines.

The men and children trickled into the grove.

"Aunt Marva! Aunt Marva! Look at my knee," Mary Claire cried. She pushed her bottom lip out pitifully. "See? See?"

She pointed to the roughened skin.

Marva clucked and petted the little girl. "Oh, look! How'd you do that, honey?"

"I fell down," the little girl said sadly.

Conroy winked at his wife. "About twenty minutes ago she fell down."

"It still hurts," Mary Claire cried.

Marva gathered the little girl in her arms. "Of course it does. Poor thing."

She returned her husband's wink, then said over Mary Claire's head, "Too bad you won't be able to run in the sack race."

Mary Claire lifted her head from Marva's shoulder. "Huh?"

"Well, if you're hurt *that* bad..."

Mary Claire's face was a study of conflict. It was obvious she really enjoyed being the center of attention, but on the other hand, there was the sack race to consider.

She bent double to peer at her knee, then back up at Marva, smiling brilliantly.

"It's all better now," she pronounced.

Marva laughed. "My goodness! Well, I'm sure glad."

Marva set the child on her feet.

"You run on now. And stay away from the river!" she called after Mary Claire, as she scampered off to play with the other children.

By this time all the men except Gideon had made their way into the clearing.

Hattie leaned back on her arms and closed her eyes. "Feel that breeze? It's so peaceful!"

Carrie came to kneel beside her, her eyes scanning the clearing.

"What, with all these men walkin' around with their rifles? Looks like an armed camp," she declared.

"Shootin' contest," Ray, Gene and Forrest answered at the same time.

The women looked from the men to each other and burst out laughing.

"You ain't excited about it are you?" Carrie teased.

"Yeah, Ray, y'all could put the guns down," Chloe added.

"Watchin' for copperheads," Ray muttered. "Gotta keep an eye out for snakes down here by the river..."

"Copperheads!" Nan exclaimed. She tucked her feet tightly under her skirt. "We don't have copperheads in Louisville."

Marva flashed her deep dimples at Conroy. "Does feel a little like we're under armed guard, honey."

Hattie jumped in. "Or bein' held hostage," she said.

Eldon cleared his throat. "Uh, I suggested we carry the rifles. Hate to leave 'em layin' around as long as there's so many young'un's..."

"Or you could just unload 'em." Rose Ellen fired back.

The banter went back and forth among the adults.

Jackie stood in the center of the group, turning in circles as each adult spoke. Finally he walked over to Eldon. He tugged his uncle's pants leg until Eldon finally leaned toward him.

"Psalm 34:6: *This poor man cried, and the LORD heard him, and saved him out of all his troubles.*"

Jackie shook his head solemnly and walked away, leaving the adults with their mouths hanging open.

Vida was the first to speak. "How does he *do* that?" she asked Hattie.

Hattie grinned and shrugged. "I have no idea. It's not just Scriptures he remembers, either. The other day while I was changin' Dalton's diaper, I called off a grocery list to Smith. Last thing I told him was to get a couple of pencils for Dulcie. When he got back from Radburn's, Jackie asked him if he'd remembered the 'pound of coffee, one bag of white beans, five-pound bag of cornmeal'—he just went right down the list. I thought Smith was gonna bust his sides laughin'. There were thirteen items I asked for, an' he didn't miss nary one. It's a wonder to us, too."

"It sure *is* a wonder!" Vida exclaimed. "Clifford's only three weeks younger'n Jackie, an' me'n Forrest are still tryin' to get to *him* to tell us what the cow says."

"Moooooooooooo," said Clifford.

❧

All the children lined up on the starting line with burlap bags pulled up to their waists for the sack race. Forrest yelled "Ready, set, go," and they were off—all except the three little ones. Poppy, Jackie and Clifford stood in their sacks and hopped up and down on the starting line, going absolutely nowhere. Jackie lost his balance and toppled over onto Poppy, who fell on Clifford. Clifford put his hand down on one of Poppy's braids just as she tried to sit up. She yowled. Soon a toddler free-for-all was under way. Jackie bit Clifford, Clifford pinched Poppy, and Poppy took a swing at Clifford and clobbered Jackie in the eye. Carrie and Gene's eight-year-old son, Junior, won the race.

It took the three mothers a good ten minutes to untangle the two-year-olds from their gunnysacks and one another, and to soothe their hurt feelings. Carrie's sugar cookies did the trick.

Ben Stoneworth came and took the battle-scarred threesome to see a particularly wonderful tree frog he'd found, and the women relaxed again on their quilts to watch the three-legged race.

Berk's wife, Nan, apologized for the black eye Jackie was going to have the next morning.

"Don't be silly, Nan," Hattie exclaimed. "They're just babies. Those things happen."

"Never thought I'd see the day when Poppy would be brawlin' with the boys," Nan said.

Carrie hooted. "Just you wait! One time my Lindy walloped the little boy down the road. He'd been teasin' her for months. Just silly things, like name-callin' and pokin' her. But he pushed her down once too often. Time came, Gene got tired of it and took her out back. He showed her how to deal with that little bully. Lindy's fifteen now, and you know, that boy comes knockin' on the door real regular."

Nan still looked horrified. "It's just...she such a *girl*! I mean, she's so...so prissy!"

The other women laughed.

"Could be worse," Lalie said. "Remember what a tomboy I was? I'll never forget pullin' on that pair of Berk's pants 'cause I thought it'd be easier to ride that old bicycle Daddy brought home from who-knows-where. My skirts kept getting in the way."

Hattie's eyes went wide. "I remember that look on Mama's face when you came down the stairs!"

Hattie collapsed onto the quilt, laughing. "She looked like she'd seen a haint!"

Lalie smiled ruefully. "Yep, and what she did next will 'haint' me for the rest of my days!"

Willa and Chloe looked at each other blankly.

"Why don't we know this story? Willa asked.

Hattie gulped, holding her sides. "You must have been at school or something."

Lalie interrupted. "No, y'all were off with the Bennett girls, I think."

"So what did your mama, do?" Darlin asked.

Lalie laughed. "Let's just say I never tried to wear britches again! I learned to ride that bike in my skirts."

In the early afternoon, the woman began opening the hampers and laying out the platters of ham and fried chicken, jars of pickles, and plates of deviled eggs. They took out tins crammed to the top with homemade cookies, and uncovered cakes and pies.

Soon all were assembled around the food. They held hands and Eldon offered thanks. "Lord, we sure do thank You for this time together. We celebrate this family and the parents that raised us to believe in You. We thank You for the joy of bein' out here in Your beautiful creation. We ask Your protection and Your guidance. Thank You for this food. In Your Son's name, Amen."

A chorus of amens followed. Then they got down to the serious business of eating. No one seemed to notice that when Forrest finished eating he picked up his rifle and walked over to where Ray stood. Only then did Ray fill his own plate.

Gideon and Smith took their food and sat under a tree just a short way from the women.

"Don't know, Smith," Gideon commented quietly. "I sure didn't see hide nor hair of Dunford when I was on the other side of the river. Mebbe he didn't know y'all was comin' out here."

Smith swallowed the bite he was chewing. "He knows about it, all right. The Stoneworth family picnic has been a tradition for at least thirty years."

"Yeah, but seein' as he ain't a Stoneworth..."

Smith shook his head. "Trust me, son. He's out there somewhere. I can feel him."

❧

"Little Gene, your Mama says you're startin' school tomorrow. Looking forward to it?" Hattie asked.

"Yes, ma'am." The bright-eyed boy nodded vigorously. "'Cept, Aunt Hattie, I ain't Little Gene no more. I'm Eugene now."

Hattie's eyebrows flew up. "Is that right?"

"Yes, ma'am. Pudgy Brown said I'm fatter'n he is, so I cain't be *'little'* nothin'. I'm gonna be Eugene instead," the boy said proudly.

"Well, that's fittin'," Hattie replied. "Eugene is your name."

"Uh-huh. I'm named after Uncle Gene. That's his name, too."

Hattie nodded. "That's right."

Dulcie interrupted. "Can we go swimmin' now, Mama?"

"Not yet. You need to wait a while after you eat. Otherwise you'll get cramps."

"Why?"

Hattie shrugged. "I don't know. But that's what they say."

"Who says that, Aunt Hattie?" Eugene asked.

"Why...everybody, I guess."

"Shoot," said Dulcie. "I wanted to go swimmin' now."

Hattie patted the quilt beside her. "Why don't you sit next to me and watch your daddy win the shootin' contest instead."

"Hey, that sounds like a challenge, Hattie," Gene called. "You reckon Smith's gonna win this year?"

"Well, he did last year." Hattie answered proudly.

The men lined up at the edge of the grove with their rifles and the good-natured ribbing started.

"Eldon, you should just sit down. You're eyes ain't what they used to be."

"My eyes is just fine, thank you. It's my back that's goin'."

"Berk, you been in that factory so long, let me show you how to hold that gun."

"Forrest, you bring BB's for that pea shooter?"

The women laughed at the men's teasing. Even in the midst of the verbal horseplay each man handled his rifle with care.

The contest started with lumps of coal being thrown high into the air. Each man had three lumps and three shots. Eldon hit two of his. Forrest hit one, then got to laughing and missed the next two throws. Gene hit the first and the last throws, but missed the middle one. Ray stepped up to the firing line and lined up on his shot. He fired and missed, then hit on both of the last shots. Smith, Gideon and Ben Stoneworth all scored on each throw. The rest of the men sat down and catcalled at the three final shooters. Three more throws and Ben missed his last shot. Then it was between Smith and Gideon. Ben threw for them.

They each took six shots and scored on each.

It seemed to be a stalemate until Forrest called, "Two at a time, Ben."

Ben grinned and picked up two small pieces of coal. He hurled one, then the other.

Smith got the first, recocked the rifle, swung it toward the second target and fired. He missed.

Ben looked at Gideon. "Ready?"

Gideon nodded.

Ben reared back and threw the first lump. The second followed quickly behind it.

Gideon peered through the notch sight on his rifle and fired. He yanked the lever, re-sighted and fired again. The second target exploded right behind the first.

The men whooped and hollered. Smith clapped the grinning boy on the shoulder.

"Good for you, son!"

Forrest stomped over. "Lucky shot," he teased. "Think you can do it again?"

Gideon raised his rifle back to his shoulder. "Ready when you are."

Forrest threw this time. He repeated the double throws four times. Eight shots fired. Eight targets exploded.

Forrest whistled. "That's the finest shootin' I ever saw! How do you do that?"

Gideon shrugged. "Started young, I reckon."

"We all started young," Eldon responded. "An' I've had 'bout thirty years practice ahead of you. Sure cain't shoot like that."

Gideon looked a little uncomfortable with all the attention, but proud, too.

"I ain't never studied on it, but I reckon there's three things you gotta have to shoot steady-like. Good eyes, a calm hand, and a way to make 'em work together," he said.

Darlin stood next to Smith. "He's sure got the eyes. His uncle, Little Anse, had a Victrola. Gideon could read the letters on the record while it was spinnin' 'round! Even the little bitty ones on the bottom of the label."

Dulcie tugged at Hattie's sleeve. "Can we go swimmin' *now*, Mama?"

Hattie called to Smith, "You ready to take these young'uns swimmin'?"

"You bet!"

Everyone moved down to the water's edge. The men took turns swinging out over the river and dropping off the rope they'd hung from the oak tree on Saturday. The boys followed right behind them.

Smith stayed in the shallows with the smaller children. His bad leg worked much better in the buoyant water. He splashed and teased the youngsters, then allowed the delighted children to dunk him under the cool water. He came up sputtering. They piled on him again.

"Hey, Gideon," he called to the young man on the bank, "come on in!"

Gideon shook his head vigorously and shuddered. "I ain't real partial to water. I'll stand here an' watch."

"Suit yourself," Smith laughed.

Berk climbed up the bank and grabbed the rope swing. "Watch this!" He called.

He pulled the swing back as far as possible, jumped on it and held on until it reached its apex high over the water. He let go and executed a perfect jack knife, slicing the water cleanly.

The crowd erupted in applause.

"Do it again, Daddy!" Eugene shouted.

Berk swam to the shallows, then walked back up to the swing.

This time, when he let the rope go, he performed a swan dive.

Again the family applauded.

Smith kept one eye on the children frolicking in the water around him and the other on Berk. For the first time all day, he allowed himself to relax a little.

The water brilliantly reflected the hot sun. The breeze blew softly. In that brief moment, all seemed right with the world.

Hattie's scream shredded the calm. Time froze. The shot rang out before her cry died away.

25

Gideon, poking the snake with the barrel of his .22, said "Ain't a copperhead. It's a cottonmouth."

The crowd gathered around the snake. It had been shot cleanly through the head. Hattie stood to one side, tightly clutching a shrieking Dalton.

"It was crawlin' right toward the baby," she cried. "I don't know what made me look over an' see it comin'. I was watchin' Berk dive. But I glanced back and there it was!"

Hattie's face was ashen.

Smith gently pried her fingers from the baby and took him from her. He pressed her down to the quilt at her feet. "Sit down, honey. You look like you're gonna pass out."

Smith quickly examined the baby. "He ain't bit, is he?"

"No! I...I scared him when I snatched him up like I did," said Hattie.

Gideon stepped forward. "Reckon my rifle shot scared him, too."

Hattie pushed herself up to her feet and hugged Gideon tightly. "Thank you! You saved him. You saved his life with your rifle shot."

Gideon awkwardly patted Hattie's shoulder. "That's all right, Miz Hattie. Just glad I heard you scream and saw the snake in time."

Hattie's hands flew to her mouth. "Oh, Smith. We could have lost him—we could have lost Dalton..."

"But we didn't, Hattie. He's fine. See?" He held the baby where Hattie could see his now-calm face.

Carrie put her arms around Hattie. "Smith's right. He's just perfect, thanks to the Lord, and Gideon. C'mon, honey, please sit down 'fore you fall down."

Hattie let her sister ease her back down onto the quilt. "I just keep thinkin' about how he was so little an' we worked so hard to keep him goin'...an' then the snake could have..."

"I know, I know," crooned Carrie softly. "But it didn't get him."

Hattie took a deep steadying breath.

"You're right. It didn't. She smiled shakily. "I'm just..."

"You're just bein' a mama. That's all," Carrie answered.

Smith handed the baby to Nan. "Hold him for me a minute, will you?"

"Sure will."

"Gideon, thank you," Smith said. He reached out to shake the young man's hand. "You saved the day."

Gideon kicked at the grass. "You would'a done the same for my boy."

Smith threw back his head and blew out a long breath, the fear finally draining from his body.

"I sure would've tried."

Digger poked the dead snake with a stick, then sliding the branch under the carcass he picked it up. A devilish look came to his eyes. He turned toward the little girls.

"I'll take that, Digger."

Ben Stoneworth's hand descended on Digger's. He took the stick with the drooping snake back into the woods and flung it deep into the trees.

"Awwww!" Digger exclaimed.

"I know, son." Conroy patted Digger's shoulder. "Would've been kinda fun to see you chase the girls with that dead snake, but it wouldn't have been very nice."

Digger grinned sheepishly. "Guess not."

"Race you to the river instead," Conroy offered.

Digger whooped and tore off toward the water, Conroy hot on his heels.

Several others began moving back toward the river. Others stayed at the quilts and snacked on the leftovers. Berk made a few more spectacular dives, then returned to where the women sat. He shook the water from his hair like a wet dog.

"Hey! Quit, you big lug!" Willa cried, swatting at her brother's leg.

Berk laughed and flopped down on the quilt beside Hattie.

"Hey, Least'un, I'm gonna follow y'all home, if it's all right with you."

"Sure. That's fine."

"I'm gonna take some cuttings from the pear tree."

He snitched the last deviled egg from the plate, and popped the whole thing in his mouth. He closed his eyes and made "mmmmm" noises while he chewed. Hattie rolled her eyes.

Berk stretched out on the quilt. "My yard ain't bigger'n a postage stamp, but I'd sure like to see if I can get a couple of those trees to grow. What do you think?"

"I think if anyone can make 'em grow, it's you."

"All right then, that settles it."

❧

The afternoon wore on. They lit a fire and toasted marshmallows for the children. They sang together, as was their tradition—first old standards and mountain songs, then hymns. Their voices blended, as only the voices of blood family can, into beautiful harmonies, and somehow the terror of the snake incident faded into just another story to tell at next year's picnic.

Before the sun went down—when it would be too dark to safely wander through the woods—the time came to head home. As he had that morning, Gideon slipped away first. Ben quietly ferried him across the river to watch the women make the boat trip back upstream.

The rest of the men gathered their rifles and their exhausted children, and began herding them toward the trail back to Paradise.

Smith lingered. He took the bucket they'd brought and walked to the spring to fill it for dousing the fire.

There, beside the water, deeply imprinted in the muck, was a familiar shoeprint, its sole cracked across the instep.

The hair on the back of Smith's neck stood on end. He knelt

and filled the bucket, then casually made his way back to the fire pit. He poured the water over the lingering embers, then turned and walked to the trail. It felt as though every nerve in his body was on fire. The morning walk down to Airdrie had unnerved him, just thinking that Deke was out there, somewhere. Now he *knew* Deke was there. Lurking. Just as he had done at home. Waiting....

Smith's heart hammered in his throat. He caught up with Eldon and told him about the footprint. Smith took up the rear guard for the loose column of men and children. Eldon's long-legged stride quickly took him forward up the left flank. He passed the message on to Gene and Ray. Gene strode to the front of the group and held his rifle at the ready. Forrest caught sight of what the other men were doing. He nudged Berk. They quickly moved from the center of the pack to the right side. In this way, with two men on each side, one at the front and another at the rear, the fathers and uncles and brothers, with unspoken, almost military precision, escorted their precious children through the deepening gloom of dusk and on to safety.

26

The morning after the picnic was a mad scramble of children getting ready for the first day of school. Hattie made a good breakfast for them all, but the youngsters were almost too excited to eat.

She and Smith were enjoying one last cup of coffee on the screen porch while the children retrieved their school supplies, when a small fracas erupted in the kitchen.

"You can't go, Jackie!" Dulcie cried.

"Can too."

The wire handle of Dulcie's lunch bucket was clutched tightly in Jackie's hands. She grabbed the other side of the handle and tugged.

"Give me it! It's mine."

"No. *Mine!*"

"You can't go, Jackie. You're too little!"

"Am NOT!"

Hattie looked at Smith. Smith looked at Hattie.

"You goin' in there? Or is it my turn?" Hattie asked.

"I'll do it." Smith clumped into the kitchen. He plucked Jackie and the lunch bucket off the floor.

"Hey, you. You're too short a horse to go to school, Jackie-boy."

"But I want to go," said Jackie. "I'm a big boy."

He smiled his best cherub-smile, and opened his huge brown eyes convincingly.

Smith chuckled. "Yes, you are. But you're only two years old. You have to be six to go to school."

Jackie didn't look convinced that age was a factor.

His daddy gently untangled Jackie's fingers from around the

lunch bucket handle, and handed it to Dulcie.

"You'll get to go to school soon. But not today, son."

"But I *want* to go," Jackie repeated. He sniffed pitifully.

Dulcie took her lunch bucket and haughtily marched over to the rest of the waiting children.

"He's such a baby," she announced to Dorie.

Smith glanced away from Jackie's sad face to Dulcie's triumphant one.

"He's not a baby, Dulcie. Jackie's a mighty smart little boy. He's been hearin' the rest of you talkin' 'bout school and seein' all your new things. Must seem unfair that y'all get to do somethin' wonderful and new while he has to stay home."

Dulcie lifted her chin high. "Well, Mary Claire don't get to go, an' she's not carryin' on about it."

"Mary Claire's not Jackie. An' Jackie's not Mary Claire."

Smith looked back at Jackie's crestfallen face. "He's really upset, Dulcie. Don't you think you should be sweet to him, instead of makin' fun?"

Dulcie dropped her eyes to the floor. "Sorry, Jackie," she mumbled.

From the moment of his birth Dulcie had adored her little brother. She'd been his protector and his teacher. Smith watched her expressive face. He saw her emotional battle. Finally she came to stand in front of Jackie.

"Tell you what. When I get home, I'll tell you all about it, 'kay?

Jackie sniffed again. "'Kay."

"Wanna carry my lunch bucket 'til we get there?" she offered.

"Yes!"

Smith set Jackie on the floor beside his sister. She solemnly handed the covered tin pail to the little boy.

The small crisis averted, Smith went to the kitchen door.

"You 'bout ready, honey?"

"Uh-huh. Just about. While I get the baby, will you run to the smokehouse and get those canned peaches for Carrie? Might as well drop 'em off while we're in town."

Hattie swallowed the last of her coffee and went to get Dalton while Smith herded all the children outside to the truck. He perched Jackie on the seat, still clutching Dulcie's lunch bucket, then walked to the back of the truck.

"Today's special 'cause it's the first day. Y'all know that tomorrow you'll be walkin', right?" Smith asked.

The children all nodded eagerly.

Digger waited politely until the older girls were all seated, then picked up Mary Claire and stood her in the truck bed.

"Hang on a minute, honey," he said in a near-echo of Smith's respectful tones. "You can sit with me."

He clambered over the tailgate and sat down on the wheel well. He gathered the little girl onto his lap. "Hang on tight. Don't want to lose you."

Smith's heart soared with pride. He quickly walked to the smokehouse, blinking unexpected tears. *That boy's come a long way!*

He turned the wooden latch on the door and stepped into the building. The only light inside came through the open door and a window on the frontside. The walls were lined with shelves, each loaded down with jars of home-canned fruits and vegetables. Smith found the peaches, grabbed two jars, and started for the door.

A small noise outside alerted him. Smith jerked his head toward the sound. He saw nothing through the window. Quickly he crossed the threshold and leaped off the porch to peer around the corner at the back side of the building, then walked its length. There was nothing there. Turning back to retrace his steps, he laughed at himself. *Got me jumpin' at shadows,* he thought.

That's when he saw it. There, in the dirt at his feet, lay a still-smoldering cigarette butt.

❧

The door of Sheriff Westerfield's office slammed back against the wall.

Smith marched to the man seated behind the desk.

"You got to do somethin'. Deke's lost his mind. He's..."

"Whoa! Slow down, Smith. What's goin' on?" the startled

sheriff demanded.

Smith pounded on the desk with his fist.

"You got to find Deke. He's...he's *stalkin'* Hattie," he shouted.

The lawman leaned forward and waved Smith into the wooden chair. "Calm yourself. Now, what do you mean he's stalkin' her?"

Smith eased down onto the chair. He told the sheriff about finding the hiding place behind the woodpile. He related the incident at the spring at Old Airdrie, and described the cigarette butt he'd seen that morning.

"He's like a...a wildcat after a rabbit. He's watchin' her all the time, followin' us wherever we go." he raged. "You got to *do* somethin'!"

Sheriff Westerfield steepled his fingers and pursed his lips.

"I know you're upset, but you have to realize, there ain't no law agin' watchin' someone."

Smith sputtered, "But...but he's trespassin'..."

"Well, I s'pose you could make a case for trespassin', but I don't recall your land bein' posted."

"No...no, it's not, but..."

"Have a mighty hard time makin' that stick, then."

Smith jumped back to his feet. "Well, what are doin' to find him? He's up for killin' that woman in Hopkinsville...why ain't you caught him yet?"

"Sit down!" the sheriff thundered. He jabbed one meaty finger at the chair.

Smith sat.

"I know you're upset," the sheriff repeated. "I ain't thrilled about it, either, but Deke Dunford ain't the onliest case me an' my men have to work on." The large man waved away Smith's protest. "'Sides Deke, I got the usual stupidity that goes on every day around here, and this rash of break-ins all over the county. Last night it was the store at Paradise."

"But he was *there* yesterday!" Smith interrupted. "I *saw* his footprint at the *spring*. I *told* you that."

"I heard what you said, an' I'm filin' that piece of information, but I don't have no proof that it was Deke."

The sheriff threw up his hands. "'Til I do..."

"How in the world is he gettin' away with it?" Smith rose again, and began pacing the small office. "You'd think somebody would've spotted his coupe. Ain't too many Studebaker coupes tearin' up the roads of Muhlenberg County..."

"We got the coupe. It's sittin' in Grady's garage in Central City. Couple of hunters found it back of Jacksontown a week or so ago."

"What?"

"Yep. Found it big as anything. Just sittin' down by Pond Creek, back in the woods. Engine was stone cold."

Smith nervously pushed his hands through his hair.

"Well, what are you doin' about it?"

"I cain't tell you that. It's an open investigation. You're gonna have to trust that I know how to do my job."

Smith gazed out the window at the American flag and the flag of the Commonwealth of Kentucky flapping on the poles outside.

"Other than the Lord Hisself, I don't know what to trust any more, " he said flatly.

He wheeled on the sheriff. "I'm tellin' you right now, if you don't find him soon, I'm gonna round up the Stoneworth men, an' we'll find him ourselves. We know these hills as well as Deke does. *We'll* find him. And when we do..."

"Do that, Smith, an' I'll lock you up myself. You, an' every other male member of Hattie's family. You know that, don't you?" The sheriff sighed. He rubbed his hands over his jowls. His red-rimmed eyes stared back at Smith.

Smith's rage faded into helpless frustration. "What am I *supposed* to do, then? Just sit an' wait for him to come get her?"

"I...I just don't know."

The man leaned back in his chair and swiveled it slowly from side to side. He was silent for a long moment while he seemed to consider what his next words should be.

"You got cause to be angry," he finally said. "And you got reason to be scared. I don't think less of you for feelin' that way, but you cain't take the law into your own hands."

He leaned forward onto his elbows.

"Tell you what you *shouldn't* do," the sheriff continued slowly. "Until Deke's locked up tight, you shouldn't leave your wife unguarded for even a minute."

For the first time since entering the office, Smith really looked at the sheriff. He saw a man defeated. He saw the lines around the older man's eyes and the creased corners of his mouth.

"Why? What is it? What ain't you tellin' me?"

Sheriff Westerfield rose and lumbered around from behind the desk. He placed one hand on Smith's shoulder.

"There's been another murder. I got the call last night. Ain't even been home to bed yet."

Smith's eyes searched the Sheriff's worried face. "Who?"

"Another lady of the night."

Smith felt the blood drain from his face.

"What'd she look like?"

"Small—and dark, just like the last one."

27

Smith called into the kitchen, "Hattie, I'm gonna walk up to Clarence Hunt's."

He sat in the living room, lacing up his new shoes.

"Clarence said he had another one of those old seven-bullet tubes for the Spencer rifle somewhere. Mentioned it to me last Sunday."

Smith stood up and took a couple of tentative steps. He rocked up on his toes to break in the leather of the shoes, then took a few more steps.

"I figure, if Clarence found it," he continued, "Jordan Pickens will pay top dollar for it. That would be a nice addition to the rifle Gideon traded to Jordan for his truck."

The clatter of dishes and the giggles of several female voices, mostly little girls, pealed through the house.

Hattie stuck her head into the doorway. Flour liberally covered her hands, apron, and left cheek.

"You gonna be long?"

"Couple hours prob'ly."

"Why don't you take Digger along. I'm baking sugar cookies with the girls. I think he's feelin' sorta left out."

"Sounds like a deal. Save us a few of those cookies."

Hattie smiled. "'Course we will."

Smith took a few more steps in his new shoes.

"Well, what do you think?" he asked.

He walked around the room. The heel of the right shoe was two inches taller than the left. It compensated for the shortened length of Smith's bad leg. It had healed badly after the mine cave-in and accounted for most of his limp.

Hattie watched Smith's gait. He moved with ease.

"Why...look at you! You're not hardly limpin' at all!"

"Nope!" Smith grinned. "Bill Shemwell built up the heel just right. B'lieve that'll make all the difference in the world."

"Let me see you!" Hattie exclaimed.

Smith did an awkward half jig.

Hattie clapped. "It's wonderful, honey. I'd throw my arms around your neck, but I don't want to get flour all over you."

"I don't care!" Smith grabbed his wife around the waist and swung her around the floor.

Hattie kissed him soundly, then shooed him out the door.

Smith stopped to talk to the pair of long legs that were sticking out from under his truck.

"Hey, Gideon, as long as you're gonna be here this afternoon, I'm runnin' over to Hunt's. Will you stick around 'til I get back?"

Gideon wormed his way out from beneath the truck frame and stood up.

"Sure will," he said wiping his hands on a rag. "You know I won't leave Miz Hattie alone. 'Sides, it's gonna take me a while to figure out what's goin' on with your engine."

Smith clapped him on the back and went to find Digger.

The boy was flopped on his stomach across the board swing that hung from the oak tree in the front yard. He pushed the ground with his toes and moved slowly back and forth.

"Digger, how 'bout you an' me take a hike up to Jacksontown? Wanna go?"

"You bet! Can we take Pride?"

The dog lay gently panting at the base of the tree.

"Go ask Mr. McBride." Smith laughed.

Soon Smith and Digger, with Pride trotting along beside, followed the postal route through Mondray valley to the north, then west, to where it climbed the ridge and went on to Jacksontown. Clarence's house sat on the very brow of the hill that overlooked the tiny village. Most of the way the boy and the dog ran ahead to take side trips, checking out things of interest.

A short distance before they got to the town, Smith called to Digger. "Son, just ahead, take that path to the right. We'll go up to

Mr. Hunt's from the back side."

"Okay," the boy yelled back.

Smith watched them dash off the road and down the path. By the time he started following along the path, he heard Digger shout. The two came running back toward him.

"Hurry, Mr. Delaney! Wait 'til you see what we found!"

About fifty yards down the trail there was a newly made cross path where a car had driven off the road and into the woods. It was apparent that the new trail had been used several times.

"When we got right here," said Digger, "Pride stopped. He started to whine, then turned down this way."

He pointed to the right. "I followed him, and look what we found!"

Digger shielded his eyes with his left hand and pointed up into a large old maple. In a crotch twenty-five feet or so above the ground, someone had built a platform. Lying on the ground beside the tree was a five-foot-long two-by-four timber.

"Would you just look at that!" said Smith. "You did find something! That's quite a tree house."

"Can I climb it?" asked Digger eagerly. "There's a ladder on the back side."

"Well, let's take a look."

They made their way to the back of the tree. Short crosspieces had been nailed to the tree anywhere there were no limbs to provide footholds or handholds.

Smith examined the makeshift ladder carefully.

"Maybe I'd better try it, son. Some of those holds are pretty far apart. If you fell and got hurt, your mama would..."

He caught himself. "Hattie would be mighty upset at me—and I would too."

"Aw! I could do it," Digger said, kicking the dirt.

"You prob'ly could, but I think I'd better try it first. Let me check it out. If we can figure who built it, we'll ask permission for us to use it. Maybe we could even nail on another hold or two so we can both climb it."

Smith reached up, grabbed a crosspiece and pulled himself

up. He carefully made his way to the platform. After a couple of moments he came back down.

"Yep, somebody's built a real solid tree house up there—just a platform, really. But maybe we could add walls and a roof to it."

"Think so?" asked the delighted boy.

"I 'magine. First we gotta find out who owns it, though," Smith said as they continued along the path.

He glanced around to get his bearings. "Don't think we're to Clarence Hunt's property yet...Nope." He pointed. "See that ol' fence row? That's where his land starts."

An ancient split-rail fence extended from either side of the trail into the woods. "He might know who put that tree house up. We'll ask him—right after we discuss the bullet tube he told me about."

❧

"Looks like we got us three mysteries," said Clarence.

He and Smith sat drinking coffee on the front porch of his home. They watched Digger and Pride investigating a groundhog's den at the far end of the yard.

"First, me and Nell have looked everywhere. We cain't figure what coulda happened to that old bullet tube. Second, I don't have any idea who built the platform in the tree, and third, I ain't got a clue why Jeb Sawyer was seen pulling out from Jackson Chapel late Saturday night."

After Smith had filled his friend in about the tree house, Clarence had told him how his neighbor's teenaged boys, and their dates, had seen Jeb Sawyer on Saturday night sitting in his truck in the drive at Jackson Chapel. They'd pulled in to see if he was having car trouble, and he'd torn out as though they had spooked him.

"Clarence, I got more to tell you about that tree house," said Smith quietly. "I didn't want to mention it while Digger was here, but at the base of the tree I found boot prints. They were Deke's. Some of the prints had the crack across the sole that we know is his."

"Well then, you ain't likely to be wrong about that," said

Clarence.

Smith took a sip of his coffee. "There's more, my friend," he continued. "I didn't let on to Digger, but that platform is loaded with stuff—I got a purty good idea it's stolen goods."

"You mean it?" said Clarence, "And him a deacon in the church!"

Smith snorted. "Not any more, he's not. 'Sides, he was a deacon in name only. Sure wasn't by action. Looks to me like he's been carrying load after load up that tree. Mine stuff, groceries, household goods, and more. It's not even well hid. That man's mind is sure messed up!"

Clarence scratched his chin. "You reckon...you reckon Jeb Sawyer's in on it?"

"Cain't say," replied Smith, "Wouldn't surprise me, though. There's an old sayin' that goes, 'The enemy of my enemy is my friend.' As bad as Jeb hates me, he prob'ly figures if Deke don't like me either, they can be bosom buddies."

"Could be," said Clarence thoughtfully. "How 'bout we walk down to the church and see if we can find any proof they're in this together."

The long time friends made their way down the long curving drive that led down the hill to Jacksontown Road. The Jackson Chapel building was a long block to the right of the junction with the Hunts' drive. They checked out the building, which was never locked, and came up with nothing.

Standing on the steps, Smith said, "There's gotta be something. Let's look around out here. Jeb Sawyer was here for a reason. An' it sure wasn't to attend prayer meetin'. He's never darkened the door of this church. An' I don't b'lieve he drove all the over here from Coaltown to watch the stars."

He scanned the eaves and the front of the building. "Is there any way to get under the floor? The front is built up off the ground."

Clarence frowned. "Yeah, there is. There's a small cut-out door on the lower side, near the front."

As they approached the door, Clarence said, "Lookee there, Smith, we're on to somethin'! There's the tracks! Some of 'em have the split sole."

Smith leaned down and pushed open the small door. "Man, oh man! This is it!"

In the dry crawl space was Deke's hideout. There was a tan straw-tick mattress, a kerosene lantern, a plate and utensils, and a number of boxes with food and clothes.

"If that don't beat all!" said Clarence. "But how come we never seen him coming or going?"

Smith squatted down and peered into the gloom. "The way I figure it, most of the time he must hide out here during the day. He most likely don't come out 'til dark, when he can prowl for places to break into. Prob'ly parks his car down in the woods by the tree house, and slips in and out of here on foot."

The air coming out of the crawl space was fetid. Smith pointed to the filth of the hideout. "How does he stand it in there? He's got to be crazy to live like this."

Clarence backed up a couple of steps. "You're right about that! I don't want a thief, 'specially one who's off his rocker, living next to us! What do we do now?"

"First thing we're gonna do is call in the sheriff." said Smith firmly. He closed the door. "He can stake out the place and nail 'im."

"Hey, are you down there, Mr. Delaney?" Digger called. "Wait 'til you see what we got!"

As they climbed the hill, they could see an excited boy holding a groundhog by its hind legs, and a battered but happy hound by his side.

"We got 'im!" said Digger, dancing around. "We dug 'im out! Him and Pride went at it. You shoulda seen 'em. He almost got away, an' he got a couple of good licks in on ol' Pride. I...I clobbered 'im with a stick. We got 'im!"

Smith and Clarence nearly collapsed laughing at the boy, the dog, and the groundhog.

"Son," said Clarence, "when I sent you down there, I didn't expect you to catch anything."

❧

Nell Hunt was roped into bringing out a plate of her oatmeal cookies to celebrate the successful groundhog hunt. Digger munched happily until Smith noticed that time had gotten away from them. He sent the boy hurrying ahead to let Gideon and Hattie know that Smith was on his way home. Clarence volunteered to go to Radburn's to call the sheriff and report what they'd found.

Smith was just passing the old rail fence when he heard a commotion ahead. He heard an angry male voice, and the smack of skin on skin. Pride barked savagely. Then he yelped and went silent. Smith heard Digger cry out.

"No, Dad, no! You hurt him!" he sobbed.

Smith broke into an awkward run. He burst around the turn into the new cross path. There, under the big maple was Deke Dunford. On the ground was the crumpled form of the dog. Deke was shaking Digger by one arm, and slapping him repeatedly. He drew back his fist to hit the little boy when Smith yelled.

"Stop it, Deke! Don't you hit 'im again!"

Deke froze when he heard Smith's voice. He viciously shoved Digger to the ground, then whirled at the man who was rushing at him.

"Just been waitin' to get my hands on you, Smith Delaney," he spat. "Now's the time!"

He squared himself to meet his foe.

"No, Daddy, please, Daddy!"

"Shut your mouth, Digger!"

Deke swung a wild right at Smith. Smith ducked under it, and slammed Deke in the midriff with a solid right, followed by a powerful left uppercut that sent Dunford reeling backward. He crashed into the maple tree and slid to the ground. He shook his head and grabbed for the two-by-four lying beside him.

Smith lunged toward him, but his good foot caught on a root and he stumbled. He scrambled to his feet, looking up just in time to see Deke swing the board. He tried to duck, but the two-by-four slammed into his left shoulder and then his head. He went to his knees, then lurched forward into the leaves on the ground. Stunned, he heard Deke's voice screaming for him to get up.

Smith's body seemed to move in slow motion. He raised his head enough to see Digger bury his face into the side of the unconscious dog, sobbing.

"Get up, Delaney!" screamed Dunford. "Get up and face me. I'm gonna kill you. Get up and face me like a man!"

Smith pushed himself up to his knees, then dragged one foot up under him and tried to stand.

"That's it, Delaney. Get on your feet and take what's coming to you. Take it like a man!" Deke taunted.

Through blurred vision, Smith saw Deke crouched in fighting stance right in front of him. He was holding the club, ready to strike, and shouting obscenities. Beneath the rushing in his ears, Smith heard another voice—one speaking in broken English.

Focus, Smith. Focus, spin, leap, kick; focus, spin, leap, kick; focus, spin, leap, kick!

I can't do it, Hiro. Been too long.

Hattie's sweet voice drifted through his consciousness. *I can do all things through Christ which strengtheneth me...*

He heard Jackie lisping his way through the Twenty-third Psalm, *Yea, though I walk through the valley of the shadow of death, I shall fear no evil...*

And under it all, the unbroken refrain came again and again: *Focus, spin, leap, kick; focus, spin leap, kick; focus, spin, leap, kick!*

Smith staggered to his feet.

Instantly, Deke charged and swung the club at his head. Smith summoned every last bit of strength he had. Somehow, he avoided the brutal swing of the club, and whirled. He leaped at Deke, and kicked. The built-up heel of Smith's new shoe caught Deke flush on the side of his head. Deke dropped like a stone—and lay still.

Digger raised his tear-streaked face.

"Did you kill him?" he whispered.

Smith staggered to the fallen man and knelt beside him. He felt for the pulse at his neck.

"No, his heart's beating and he's breathin'. We'll get him a doctor. Let's go. You get my cane. I'll carry the dog—is he alive?"

"I...I think so. Maybe I can carry 'im."

"No, son, I'll do it. You tell me what happened."

They started down the path and into the road.

"Me and Pride hurried down the trail just like you tol' me, and when we got to the maple tree, there was my daddy climbin' down from the tree house. He had a sack of stuff. I was so glad to see him I ran to 'im. I...I tried to hug 'im like Jackie does you..." Digger choked.

"It made 'im mad. He...he started cussin' me and callin' me names. Pride began growling. When Dad slapped me, that's when Pride attacked 'im. Bit him on his leg. Then Pride jumped up and bit his side. But Daddy grabbed 'im and choked him 'til he was just a rag, then he threw him on the ground an' stomped 'im. He kicked 'im in the head."

Digger began sobbing again. "Oh, Mr. Delaney, is Pride gonna die?"

Smith was just trying to understand the words that were flying past his addled brain. Everything sounded like a Victrola running down: slow and murky.

"Don't know, son," he slurred. "His right front leg looks mighty bad—must be where Deke stomped 'im. But a minute ago, I think he whimpered a little. That's a good sign."

"Oh, he's just gotta live!" Digger cried.

"He was just pertectin' me. Shouldn't'a had to pertect me from my own daddy. I was tellin' Daddy I loved him. But when he kicked poor ol' Pride, I tried to stop 'im. That's when he started beatin' me. An' then you got there."

"It's over now, son." Smith wiped the cold sweat from his brow.

"I ain't makin it very fast carryin' this dog..." he muttered.

A wave of dizziness swept over him. "Tell you what—why don't I stop and rest a minute."

He sank down on the low bank beside the road with the dog in his lap, and took in a deep breath in through his nose.

"Digger, you better...you better run tell Gideon to come an get me and Pride with his truck. Better send Becky to..." Smith fought the blackness that was creeping into his brain. "To...to Radburn's. Tell Doc Wilson to come in a hurry. Think I got myself a mighty big knot on my head...Maybe Doc can fix Pride, too. Then he can come over here and check out your dad."

"I'll do it, Mr. Delaney, real quick. But, sir, he ain't my dad no more. He killed my Mama, an' just about killed you and Pride."

Digger shook his head firmly.

Smith saw a tear running down the boy's cheek.

The last thing Smith heard was Digger's voice.

"He ain't my dad no more. Gonna find me a new dad."

He glanced at Smith's still face.

Then he ran.

28

Doctor Wilson later told Hattie that when he came past Henry Johnson's house, he saw a frantic little figure in the middle of the road near the top of the hill. Digger danced a nervous jig, his right arm windmilling a signal for him to hurry.

When he reached the lad, Digger jumped on the running board of the slowing car. He grabbed the window frame by the driver, and hung on. He begged the physician not to spare the horsepower.

"Mr. D. ain't doin' no good a'tall. We fetched 'im home in Mr. McBride's truck, but Mr. Delaney ain't talkin' right. His eyes are lookin' all queer. Miz Hattie says his head's hurt real bad. Please hurry, sir!"

Digger stopped to take a breath, then rushed on. "An' poor ol' Pride! He's just the pitifullest thing, all broke up an' cryin'! Keeps tryin' to gnaw at his shoulder— Mr. Gideon had to put a muzzle on' 'im! Said it like to broke his heart to muzzle that dog. He's goin' after my daddy with his rifle. He said that soon as he gets back he's gonna have to put Pride away! That means he'll have to kill 'im!"

The near-hysterical little boy grabbed the doctor by his sleeve.

"Please, Doc, don't let him do it. Cain't you fix 'im? It's all my fault. He was tryin' to pertect me! You just gotta fix 'im. Just gotta. An'...an' Mr. Delaney, too. You gotta fix him. I'll give you all my money. I ain't got much—but I'll even give you my birthday money next month, if I get any."

Doc Wilson had looked for an instant from the hill's rutted road to the earnest, tear-streaked face of the pleading lad. He patted one of the hands clinging to the car's window.

"We'll fix them, son. God being our helper, we'll fix them, both."

When Doc's car slowed as it approached the end of the drive near the back porch, Digger jumped off and ran ahead to open the screen door. Before he got there, Hattie, concern deepening her already dark eyes, swung open the door.

"Thank you for hurryin', Doctor! The sheriff should be on his way, too."

"Where's my patient Hattie?"

He walked past her and across the long porch.

"Living room."

When the doctor started through the kitchen door, he glanced at the cluster of children on the side porch. Squatting around a muzzled, whimpering dog, they were speaking soft words of encouragement to the poor hound. Standing above them, leaning against the roof support and watching with concern was Digger.

"This here's Pride, Doctor Wilson," the boy said. "Please hurry, he's hurtin' real bad."

Doctor Wilson walked to the door. "You just keep an eye on him for a few more minutes. I'll be with you in a little bit."

❧

"Doc, I'm so relieved that you think Smith's gonna be okay," Hattie said a half an hour later. She gave a grateful smile.

Together, Hattie and the doctor had moved Smith to the bedroom. He was propped up on the bed, his head and shoulder well bandaged.

"You know," Hattie continued, "the minute you drive over that hill, he's going to think he needs to jump up and take on the week's chores. You need to tell him he's gotta take it easy for a while. I'll never get it through his thick, busted-up skull."

"Hattie's right, Smith. This one's serious. The contusion on your shoulder is a deep injury. Without X-rays I'm not certain you don't have a fracture. I want that arm in a sling for at least ten days."

"Aw, Doc…" Smith responded.

The doctor narrowed his eyes. "I'm not through yet...as I told you, you have a fracture of the left temporal bone—the part of the skull above your left ear. You're lucky to be alive."

Smith wasn't in much shape to argue. "How long am I outta

commission, Doc?" he mumbled.

"Long enough to heal—I'll be able to give you a better answer when I stop by tomorrow. Meanwhile, remember that you're the patient. No sudden movements. Stay in bed or just sit around for the next few days. Then you should be able to ease around a little. But no lifting anything that weighs more than a couple of pounds."

"Aw, Doc..." Smith repeated.

"Listen here, son, your biggest responsibility is to your family. You get yourself well. Good and well. You bullied Hattie into behavin' after she had Dalton. Now I'm givin' her permission to bully you back. Hear me?"

Smith smiled weakly. "I hear you."

Doc Wilson placed his instruments back into his black bag.

"Now, I reckon I need to see my next patient—the four-legged one on the porch."

❧

Doctor Wilson joined the children squatting around the dog. Hattie stood just outside the door watching.

Digger dropped to his knees beside the dog.

"Let me help you, sir. He knows me real good."

"He's very good with the dog," Hattie assured the doctor "and Digger is quite strong."

"That'll be fine. I'm always glad for an assistant. Think you can hold his back legs for me, son?"

Digger nodded.

"It's gonna hurt him a little when I started prodding on his shoulder."

"No use, Doc," said a strong bass voice. Gideon McBride walked up behind them, his rifle clutched tightly in his hand.

Hattie rushed to him. "Did you find Deke? What happened? Did you get 'im?"

"Weren't no sign of 'im, Miz Hattie. He musta come to, an' run."

Gideon knelt by the dog.

"Pride's pretty busted up, sir. Better let me take 'im out in the woods and put 'im away."

"Oh, no!" Digger cried. He put his hands over his ears, shaking his head and looking up at Gideon in horror.

"Please, Mr. McBride, won't you let the doctor just *see* if he can fix 'im? He *promised* he'd try," he begged.

Doctor Wilson's right fingers probed the left shoulder and chest of the writhing dog.

"Mr. McBride, you're right about him being pretty busted up."

The doctor pointed to the broken leg. "This leg is shattered just below the shoulder—and he's got a couple of broken ribs. Dunford stomped him, from what Smith told me. We can't save the leg, and I'm no dog doctor, but I think I can save your hound."

The doctor looked up at Gideon. "I'll have to take off the leg, but he should make it just fine."

"I don't know, sir," Gideon wavered. He blinked his eyes rapidly.

I *am* awful partial to that dog...I'd hate to..."

"Please, *please*, give 'im a chance," begged Digger. "I'll help hold 'im for the operation if you want me to, an' I won't cry, or...or nothin'. I promise. I'll do whatever you want me to! Don't you see, Mr. McBride, if'n Pride dies, it'll be all my fault."

"What do you say, Mr. McBride?" the doctor asked. "He's your dog."

Hattie placed a hand on Gideon's arm. "Please let the doctor try, Gideon. For the boy's sake, if nothin' else. Pride will still be a fine companion for the children and a good guard dog."

Gideon took off his cap. He gently scratched Pride under the chin.

"In two-three months," Doc Wilson said, "you'll be amazed at how well he gets around. Why, at the first Westminster dog show in New York City, nearly half a century ago, they featured a *two*-legged dog! 'Wagner's Nellie' didn't have *either* one of her front legs, but she got around just fine on her back legs, She practically stood upright—and was smart as a whip!"

Gideon looked doubtful, but said, "All right. Let's try it. Pride deserves a chance."

❧

Hattie sent the younger children to play in the front yard with instructions not to come back until called. Gideon brought a small table from the back porch and covered it with newspaper. Hattie found an old sheet. At the doctor's instructions, they tore it into strips. The doctor went to his car to retrieve the items he would need, then, the trio of Doc Wilson, Gideon, and Digger washed up.

Hattie prayed.

Doctor Wilson brought out a cone and bottle of ether from his black bag.

Gideon stood beside his favorite—his Pride—and talked softly to him for a little while. When he was ready, he nodded to the doctor.

Doctor Wilson held the cone over the dog's nose and slowly dripped the ether into it.

"Digger, this is a mighty big job. You think you can handle it? You'll have to watch carefully and make sure he doesn't get too much."

Digger nodded solemnly. He took the cone and bottle from the doctor. He concentrated hard to do it exactly as the doctor had.

"That's the way, son. Not too fast, not too slow," the doctor encouraged.

Soon Pride was still, and the surgery began. The helpers did what they could as the doctor called on them. They mostly watched intently as he carefully removed the damaged limb, sutured the incisions and sewed flesh and hide back into place.

Hattie noted with pride that Digger did not blanch—though she did—at even the goriest parts of the surgery. When the work was finished, and the dog bandaged, she brought fresh water for the after-surgery clean-up.

As they dried their hands, Gideon, who had not spoken a word during the entire procedure, said, "Doctor Wilson, that was something else. Never seen anything like it. If Pride makes it, I'll be eternally grateful—in fact, I already am. You done a fine thing."

"You're welcome—I think he's going to be all right."

"Doctor Wilson," said Digger, extending to the doctor a just-dried hand, "I'm mighty grateful, too. You promised, and you did it. You kept your word."

Hattie, looking on, noticed the tears that welled up in the eyes of the tremulously smiling child.

The doctor shook the boy's hand and said, "You're welcome, Digger. You were quite an assistant. Thanks for your help."

Digger started to turn away, but spun back to face the doctor squarely.

"You don't reckon...I mean, do you s'pose, sir, there's any way I could be a dog doctor when I grow up?"

The doctor reached out and tousled the boy's hair.

"I have a feeling you can be anything you set your mind on. You're a bright boy. Anything is possible."

He smiled and patted Digger on the back.

"And, son," he continued, "if you do decide you want to be a veterinarian, you come see me. I'll do everything in my power to make sure you get a chance."

Hattie hugged Digger tight. Over his head, she beamed her thanks to the doctor.

❧

Within a few short weeks a happy three-legged dog was tripping and traipsing along after Gideon wherever he went. But Pride spent longer and longer periods of time at the old Stoneworth place. The entire household grew fond of the brave little hero-dog. Especially Digger and Smith.

Gideon talked as though he had left the dog there to keep him from hurting himself in trying to keep up with the other dogs at his house. But he confided to Darlin that as long as madman Deke Dunford was on the prowl, he *wanted* the dog at the Delaney house. No dog would better know Dunford's smell. None would sense his presence quicker. None would make it known more aggressively. Soon the Delaney home was Pride's home—at least for the time being.

29

For Smith time seemed to creep by. His bandaged shoulder ached, and the sling got in his way. Although his blurred vision had finally cleared, he wasn't in a very good mood the following Saturday morning when Eunice Crowe, unexpectedly, came to call.

Outside, an October rain poured from the eaves. Eunice arrived beneath a huge battered black umbrella. She carefully lifted her long old-fashioned skirts, and picked her way to the door.

Hattie met her. "Good mornin', Mother Crowe. This is a surprise."

Eunice's face grimaced into something that resembled a smile.

"Surely I don't need an invitation to come to call? I heard your man was hurt. Come to see if I could be of any help."

She shook her umbrella vigorously, spraying the porch, and Hattie, with cold rainwater.

Hattie graciously welcomed the old woman into the kitchen and poured her a cup of hot coffee.

When Hattie turned to retrieve the sugar bowl, Eunice ran one black-gloved finger along the top of the wooden chair rail that ran along the wall, peering intently at her fingertip.

"See anything interesting, Eunice?"

Eunice Crowe jumped like she'd been shot and whipped around. Casually leaning on the doorframe behind her stood Smith.

A rusty, barking laugh emerged from her pursed lips. "Hello, Smith."

Eunice brushed her hands together as though to shake off filth. "You'll have to forgive an ol' woman," she said. "Ol' habits die hard, I reckon. I've always been particular 'bout cleanliness. Don't guess it's right to judge other folks by my standards."

Hattie's eyes widened. She looked away from her former mother-in-law and quickly scanned her spotless kitchen, looking for anything out of place.

Eunice reached across the table and patted Hattie's hand.

"I s'pose, with a new baby, an' all them...them Dunford young'uns, it's hard to keep up." Eunice didn't seem to realize how insulting she was.

Smith walked past the woman and opened the Hoosier hutch. He took down a cup and poured himself some coffee, then leaned against the side door.

Eunice continued, "Speakin' of them young'uns, where are they?"

Hattie explained, "Marva and Conroy have the Dunford children today. Digger's workin' on a school project an' Conroy's helpin' him."

"Ain't it fine to have an educated man to help?" Eunice commented.

Hattie saw Smith grind his teeth.

Digger's project was to build a birdhouse. Smith could have helped Digger make an elaborate multistoried house with turrets and Victorian gingerbread—or even an authentic log cabin. But with his arm in a sling he wasn't able to saw the wood. Poor Conroy was going to try to slap some boards together into a box. He was hopelessly inept at anything that had to do with a hammer and nails, but had eagerly volunteered to help. Digger had accepted the offer, knowing that he probably wasn't going to get his best marks on the project. He'd be lucky, in fact, if the thing held together until he got it to school.

"An' where's my grandchildren today?" Eunice asked politely.

Hattie leaned toward her. "I'm so sorry, Mother Crowe. Dulcie's been fightin' the sniffles again. She's sound asleep upstairs. Jackie's playing in the front room."

Hattie started to rise. "I'll get him for you."

Eunice gestured for her to stay. "No, don't do that. I'll see him 'fore I go, but I really come to talk to *you*."

Eunice rummaged in her large black purse and withdrew a

thick sheaf of what were obviously legal papers.

"Now, Hattie, I know this Deke Dunford bizness is unpleasant for you, but we need to face facts."

"Deke's a problem, all right," Hattie answered slowly.

"Well, if he gets you, you need to know the young'uns will be taken care of."

"What?"

"Eunice..." Smith warned.

The old woman looked from Smith to Hattie. Hattie's obvious confusion seemed to delight her.

"He's out for you. You know that, don't you?" she said triumphantly. "Comin' for you. That's what I heard."

"WHAT?" Hattie exclaimed again. She turned to look at her husband. "Is that true? Is...Deke...?

"We don't know that for sure, honey," Smith rushed to assure her. He came to stand behind Hattie, and glared at the vindictive old woman.

"You ain't got no call to upset Hattie."

Eunice's face was a study of innocence. "Why, I would *never* worry Hattie on purpose. Ferd an' me heard all about it from that nice-lookin' young deputy over at Greenville. It's common knowledge. Reckon I just assumed Hattie knew, is all."

"Knew *what*, exactly?" Hattie asked.

"Well, that Deke's killed two women…'course they was the worst kind of sinners..." she added, as though their killings hadn't really mattered much.

"...An' the rumor is he might've killed Mamie, too." She didn't appear to believe that part of the story.

Eunice fiddled with the fluff of worn lace at her throat. She pinned Hattie with a look.

"Anyway, that nice young deputy said that Deke's been comin' around down here. Lookin' at you. Everybody says you'll be next. That's why I'm here."

She patted the papers she'd brought.

"I had these drawn up over in Central City. Now, if you'll sign right..." she leafed through the documents, then stabbed at a line on the bottom of a page. "…here, then I'll be able to take the young'uns home with me, if anythin' happens to you. I mean, if Deke should..."

"Wait just a minute, Eunice," Smith bellowed.

Hattie patted his arm. "No, Smith. Mother Crowe is exactly right. The children need to be taken care of," she said with much more calmness than she felt.

She turned and faced Eunice square on. "I appreciate all the time an' effort you put into this, Mother Crowe. It musta cost you a pretty penny to have the lawyer draw up these papers. I know, because when Smith and I wrote our wills, it cost us plenty. Thank goodness we already took care of the children."

"But...but, Hattie," the old woman sputtered. "You never tol' me."

"No, ma'am. I didn't. I just went about my business and took care of it. I would never leave somethin' so important to chance."

"So...I'm goin' to get the young'uns?" Eunice asked. "Is that what you're sayin?"

Hattie stood up. "No. That is most assuredly not what I'm sayin'. If anything happens to me, Smith will raise the children. He loves them, an' they love him."

"He cain't!" Eunice squealed. "You cain't let him do that. He ain't blood kin!"

"I can, and I will," Smith responded firmly. "They're my babies, now."

Eunice narrowed her eyes. "You didn't even give 'em your name, Smith Delaney. You didn't *never* want them young'uns!"

"Listen here, you ol'..."

Once again, Hattie laid her hand on Smith's arm. "Mother Crowe, Smith didn't adopt my children, because *I* wouldn't let him...He offered to adopt them—begged me, in fact, but *I* said..."

"See there!" Eunice crowed. She jabbed a finger in Smith's direction. "Even your *wife* has better sense than to let *you*..."

"...Because, *I* wanted to respect Jack's memory!" Hattie interrupted.

Eunice's mouth dropped open.

"Mother Crowe, Jack was a fine husband, and a wonderful father. *I* wanted the children to know that. It doesn't mean Smith isn't just as wonderful. Or that he's not fit to be their father. It was a matter of respect for Jack's name and his memory. But, if you think that Smith *should* adopt the children, we can do that."

Hattie had trumped Eunice's ace. The old woman turned an ugly shade of scarlet.

"No! I don't want 'em wearin' *his* name," she spat.

"Oh. All right, then. We'll leave things as they are."

Hattie sat back down and picked up her coffee cup. Over its rim she eyed Eunice cautiously.

Smith reached under the table and squeezed Hattie's hand. She squeezed back. All was quiet for a moment.

Smith dropped Hattie's hand, and casually picked up a plate from the center of the table. He offered it to Eunice.

"Cookie?"

❧

Out of sight, Dulcie stood barefoot at the top of the stairs. She'd heard what Hattie and Smith had said about adopting her and Jackie. Smith *did* want her. He'd wanted her all along. A slow smile spread across her little face.

❧

Smith and Hattie saw Eunice to the door a short time later. Hattie turned on Smith the moment the old truck drove over the crest of the hill.

"Why didn't you tell me about Deke?"

"Aw, Hattie..."

"No! *Why* didn't you tell me?" she demanded to know.

"Just didn't want you worryin' about it, I reckon." He faltered.

Hattie was angry. Angrier than she'd been in a long time.

"You've known about this for how long? An' I have to hear about it from *Eunice*? How could you do that to me?"

"Honey..." Smith tried to take her in his arms. She pushed him away. He let his arms drop to his sides.

"Look, Hattie," Smith said quietly. "I was tryin' to protect you. I was wrong. I should've tol' you. I see that now, but I didn't want you worryin' yourself about it. I've been keepin' a sharp eye out, an'..."

Hattie stared blindly past the screened wall to the rain outside. The last few weeks ran through her mind like a moving picture at the Bijou. Everything made sense now. All the times when Gideon had hung around while Smith had gone to run errands. The times Smith had dragged her along with him when she could have stayed at home.

"An' every time you went to town, you left me with Gideon, or took me to Forrest and Vida's, or Carrie and Gene's. You made sure I was under lock and key the whole time."

"It weren't like that..."

She wheeled back to Smith. "It was *exactly* like that! Oh, I can't believe how stupid I've been..."

She narrowed her eyes. "An' the picnic...Is that why y'all were marchin' around Ole Airdrie with your guns all day long? Has it been goin' on that long?"

"Yes."

Hattie marched over to face him. "Do you mean to tell me that everyone in my family, and even Gideon, and Darlin, knew what was goin' on, everyone except *me*?"

"No, no, Hattie. Just the menfolk."

Hattie laughed bitterly. "Oh, well then. As long as it was just the men..."

Smith pleaded, "Honey, you have to understand..."

Hattie's mouth set into hard lines. "I do understand, Smith. B'lieve me, I do. You didn't trust me."

"Hattie, that's not it at all! Be fair..."

"*You* be fair, Smith—*you* didn't trust me enough to treat me like an adult. *You* didn't trust me with my own safety."

Fighting angry tears, she turned on her heel and left him standing there.

Smith's shoulder throbbed. He kicked savagely at a shoe lying on the porch floor. Finally he walked out of the house and threw himself down on the side porch swing. He leaned forward and rested his elbows on his knees, and buried his face in his hands.

Hattie found him still sitting in that position several minutes later. She sat down next to him.

"I...I'm ready to listen," she said.

Smith raised his head. She was so little sitting there next to him, all prim and proper. Her eyes were red and puffy.

"Aw, Hattie."

Smith gathered her into his arms. They rocked back and forth slowly for a few minutes. Then Smith started talking. He told her everything—from the first footprint he'd found under the bedroom window to his recent visit with Sheriff Westerfield. He told her what Little Jenny looked like. He told her about the other woman Deke was suspected of killing.

When he'd finished, Hattie was still for a moment.

"Oh, my," she said finally. "No wonder you didn't tell me."

Smith lifted her chin. "I was wrong, Hattie. No matter how much I thought I was protectin' you, I was wrong."

Hattie agreed. "Yes, you were, but now I understand."

She suddenly shivered.

"You cold?" Smith asked, wrapping his good arm around her more tightly.

Hattie shook her head.

"No. I'm scared."

30

Late that night after the children went to bed, Smith and Hattie sat talking in the living room. Hattie sat with the quilt she was binding draped over her legs. Smith wrestled one-handed with the newspaper. Their quiet conversation was interrupted when Becky and Digger slipped into the room.

"Miz Hattie, can we talk to you?" Becky asked.

"'Course you can."

Hattie laid the quilt aside and patted the couch next to her.

"Come sit with me."

Becky crossed the room and sat on the very edge of the couch. She stared at the floor.

"Becky, what is it?" Hattie asked. "Are you in trouble, honey?"

"No, ma'am." Becky wouldn't meet Hattie's eyes.

Digger stepped forward.

"See...um. We was wonderin'...I mean....We waited 'til the kids was asleep, 'cause...."

Becky turned to Hattie and blurted out, "You been so good to us. We just love y'all to death, but...well..."

Digger interrupted, "They don't have no young'uns—not even one..."

"An'...well, we thought maybe it would be better..." faltered Becky.

"...Y'all got three kids," Digger added.

Smith folded the paper and dropped it onto the floor beside his chair. He stood up and walked over to Digger. Placing one hand on the boy's shoulder, he turned the child to face him.

"Slow down, son."

Becky started to speak. Smith hushed her, too. He looked from one child to the other and waited.

"All right, now that everybody's calmed down, let's try again—one at a time."

Smith looked at the little girl. "You go first, Becky."

Becky lowered her eyes again. "We was talkin'—me and Digger and the little ones—Mary Claire's *real* partial to Aunt Marva. She's *so* happy at their house, an' they seem to like us, too."

Hattie closed her eyes. The moment she'd been dreading had arrived. She felt her heart squeeze hard.

"Not that you ain't good with her, too," the girl rushed on. "It's just...you got Jackie and Dalton. An' they take an awful lot of your time. But, Aunt Marva's got all the time in the world to baby Mary Claire. She's still so little. She needs that. Don't you see?"

Hattie reached over and squeezed the girl's hand. "'Course you're right. Mary Claire needs lots of attention—Dorie does, too."

Digger said, "See, Miz Hattie, Uncle Conroy don't hardly know how to build stuff. I could help 'im with that. An' he don't know nothin' at all 'bout dogs. Me and him could get us a dog an' I could teach 'im al! about 'em. Mr. Delaney already knows how to do carpenter work, an' he knows dogs 'most as good as Mr. McBride." Digger's eyes begged their understanding.

Becky leaned against Hattie. "An' Aunt Marva, she's just the best thing. She's *so* sweet. I...I think she gets lonesome for us when we're not there. You know, when we're down here? She's always so sad when we leave her and come home. I...I think *she* needs us more'n *you* do."

Hattie blinked hard to hold back the tears that threatened to spill down her cheeks.

Digger wriggled out of Smith's grasp. "Uncle Conroy says we cain't go less'n you say so, Miz Hattie. He says he won't take no part in hurtin' y'all, so, me an' Becky was wonderin' if maybe you could...well...well, could you decide you like the idea of us goin' to them? Then it wouldn't hurt you none, right?"

Hattie wished it were that easy to mend a broken heart. "Is

that what you want? All of you? Do you want to go to Marva and Conroy?"

"Oh, yes, ma'am!" the children answered together.

"I was hopin' you'd be happy here," Hattie said sadly.

"We *are* happy, Miz Hattie. Happier than we've *ever* been, I reckon," said Becky. "But you'd still get to see us. I know we wouldn't get to be Dulcie's and Jackie's and Dalton's brother and sisters, but cousins is almost as good, ain't it?"

Hattie took a deep breath and slowly blew it out. "Yes, it is. You're right about that."

"So...what do you think?" Digger asked. "Can we go? Can we be Aunt Marva and Uncle Conroy's kids?"

Hattie looked at Smith. He nodded over the children's heads.

"If that's what you want," Hattie said finally, her voice thick with emotion.

Digger rushed to Hattie and perched on the arm of the couch next to her.

"Please don't be sad, Miz Hattie. We'll still come see you. Me an' Mr. Delaney got plans for that tree house we found. Don't we, Mr. Delaney?"

"That's right, son. We sure do," Smith responded.

"An' Miz Hattie, we love you, too," Becky was quick to assure her.

Hattie forced herself to smile through her tears. "I know that. An' I love you."

Hattie swiped at her eyes. "I'm just...I'm just thinkin' how happy Marva's gonna be! Won't she be tickled?"

Digger reached over and took his sister's hand. "There's just one more thing. Me an' Becky been hearin' stuff at school 'bout our dad. Ain't no chance he could come get us, is there? I mean after all this time, he don't want us, right?"

Smith walked over and sat on the other end of the couch. "I...I don't think it has anything to do with wantin' you, or not."

He leaned over and placed a hand on Digger's shoulder.

"You two are old enough to understand that your dad's in bad trouble. He's...he's probably goin' to prison, when they catch him," he said quietly.

"Yes, sir, but what if he don't?" Digger asked.

"I don't think there's any way he'll get out of it."

Becky looked up at Smith, and then at Hattie.

"Did he really kill those women? That's what Ann Wadell said. She's in sixth grade. She said he killed 'em dead as a doornail, an' never looked back, just like our mama."

Hattie answered carefully, "We don't know for *certain* whether he killed them or not. We do know that the sheriff *thinks* your dad is the one who..."

Digger interrupted, "...Killed 'em dead as a doornail."

He kicked at the rug in front of the couch. "You reckon the sheriff's right? He should know, shouldn't he?"

Hattie shrugged. "I s'pose so. Either way, when they catch your father, there'll be a trial. If they find him guilty, he'll lose his rights to the two of you, an' the little girls."

"Then Aunt Marva and Uncle Conroy could have us for sure, right? He couldn't *never* come back an' get us, right?" Becky asked.

"That's right."

Hattie didn't think her heart could be broken in more pieces than it already was. She was wrong. It shattered into shards when she saw the relief written on the faces of Deke Dunford's children.

❧

Hattie knelt beside her bed. *Lord, I'm askin'. Would you do what Digger said? Would you change my heart, so that it doesn't hurt me to give the kids up? I don't want to be bitter, and...* She buried her face in the covers. *...and have hard feelin's for Marva and Conroy. I reckon you had your hand in this all along, or the young'uns would be contented here. But, they ain't, an' I...I can't get over it, Lord. It hurts me so. If you would just help me make up my mind to be happy about it, maybe it won't hurt me so bad. Just like Digger said.*

Hattie felt the bed sag as Smith kneeled down beside her. His arm draped around her and pulled her to his chest. His voice took over where hers left off. They prayed together.

31

Marva and Conroy firmed up plans to enclose the screened porch on their house and turn it into a bedroom for the Dunford girls. Smith spent his spare time working on the renovation, but he always made sure someone was with Hattie. He heeded the sheriff's warning that she never be left alone.

Most of the time, Gideon came to stay with Hattie at the small house under the hill. He did odd jobs as a trade for food. Smith and Hattie didn't have much money, but there was always a surplus of fresh or canned vegetables and fruit. Sometimes he brought dogs along and put them through their paces.

Once in the late afternoon about a week after Eunice's visit, Smith caught sight of Deke across the road standing on the rise in the Sumners' field. Deke was silhouetted against the setting sun. Even shading his eyes, Smith couldn't make out the man's features, but he knew it was Dunford. It couldn't have been anyone else. By the time Smith got his gun, the man had vanished.

The first frost came the last week of October. The following Saturday, Smith took the children to gather walnuts from the large trees in Mr. Hammer's front pasture. They pulled their wagons behind them up the hill and began picking up the nuts, piling them with satisfying "clunks" into the metal wagons.

"Yuck!" said Dulcie, shaking her hand vigorously. "This one was mashed. I got yellow stuff on my fingers!"

"Yep," said Smith, "and that juice will stain your fingers, an' anything else it touches. If the hull is broken or mashed, pick 'em up real careful. Just toss 'em in the wagon."

"And don't let 'em touch your clothes," Digger warned. "It'll turn 'em black."

"I'm gonna have to run up to Conroy's and work on the new

bedroom," Smith told the children. "You fill these two wagons, take 'em back to the house and put the walnuts in the wooden bin on the smokehouse porch. I reckon if you do that twice, it'll be enough for today. Soon as I get a chance, I'll show you how to hull 'em without gettin' stain all over the place."

Gideon was tied up with a dog sale that morning, so Harwell Radburn had agreed to stay with Hattie until Gideon wrapped up his business in Twin Tunnels. The storekeeper arrived just as Smith came down the hill from the Hammers' pasture to the house.

"Sure do 'preciate you takin' the time to do this, Harwell," Smith said, shaking the man's hand.

"Shoot, Smith, me an' Annie's crazy 'bout Hattie. Always have been. You know that. Whatever we can do to help..."

Smith smiled warmly. "It eases my mind, knowin' you'll be here 'til Gideon comes."

He called into the house.

"Honey, I'm leavin'."

Hattie came to the door.

Smith leaned down and kissed her on the cheek. "I'm runnin' to Beech Creek. Be back shortly after noon. You behave yourself now. I sure do love my girl."

Hattie batted her eyelashes. "I will. Love you, too."

She welcomed her longtime friend.

"Come on in, Harwell." She showed him to the table in the kitchen.

"I'm sorry to take you away from the store. An' I don't know what you're gonna do 'til Gideon gets here. Me an' Dalton aren't very entertainin'," she warned.

"That's all right, Hattie," Harwell grinned. "I like comin' to your house. It's always so restful down here."

Hattie burst out laughing. "With me an' Smith, seven kids *and* a three-legged dog? This is restful? You must have some kind of wild life with Annie at the store."

Harwell grinned. "You know my Annie. I love her with all my heart, but she could talk the hind leg off a mule. 'Tween her, an' the telephone ringin', and customers comin' in all day long—

seems right peaceful down here with you. You mind if I sit out there on the porch and just listen to the birds?"

Hattie smiled. "Not at all. That's one of my favorite things to do, too."

She poured a cup of coffee and took it to him.

"You just enjoy your quiet time. I've got some things to take care of upstairs, if you don't mind," she said.

"That's just fine, Hattie."

"That right out there is all I need for company." He waved at the trees lined up in the orchard behind the house. They were ablaze with fall colors.

Hattie went upstairs and took out the clothes the children would wear for church the next day. She carefully wiped the dust from their good shoes, and brushed Digger's small suit jacket. She stopped to fluff the pillows, and smooth the hastily-made beds.

"Mr. Radburn!"

Hattie heard a boy's voice frantically calling. She ran to the window at the end of the room and looked out.

"Mr. Radburn!"

One of the Humphrey boys was on his bicycle, flying down the hill from town, yelling at the top of his lungs.

Hattie raced down the stairs and rushed to the door. The boy jumped off the bike and ran toward the porch. Harwell met him.

"What is it? What's the matter, son?"

The boy's sweaty face was crimson from riding his bike so hard. "There's a...a fire at the store," he gasped.

Hattie's hands flew to her mouth. "What?"

"Annie?" Harwell choked. "Is my Annie...?"

The boy gulped. "Don't know, Mr. Radburn. I...I didn't see her."

Hattie put her arm around Harwell. "I'm sure she made it out in time. Annie's smart, she would have gotten out."

The boy tugged on Radburn's sleeve. "My dad said that when he was in the store this mornin', you tol' him you was gonna be comin' down here. He's got the volunteers comin' and is roundin' up a bucket brigade. But he sent me to fetch you back."

Hattie gave her friend a gentle nudge toward his car. "Go. Go on! Don't you worry about *me* at a time like this. I'll be fine. 'Sides, Gideon'll be here any minute. I'll be prayin' for you an' Annie."

Harwell hesitated for only the briefest moment, then dashed to the Dodge.

Hattie watched as he spun gravel backing into the road and flew up the hill. The Humphrey boy, hurrying after him, strained to pump the bicycle up the steep slope. Hattie walked back inside the door.

Please Lord, be with Annie. Don't let her be hurt. An' be with Harwell, too. Give him your strength to deal with whatever's happened. And protect their store. They are such a blessin' to us all... she prayed.

Hattie glanced back toward town, then walked across the porch and stepped down into the kitchen.

"Hello, Hattie."

Calmly sipping coffee from one of her mother's best china cups, with his revolver pointed straight at her head, Deke Dunford sat at Hattie's kitchen table.

❧

"Hey, Beck, if you'll stay with the little ones, me'n Dulcie'll take these loaded wagons home an' empty 'em," Digger told his sister. "No point in all of us goin', just to turn around and come right back."

"All right. We'll just pile up the walnuts while we're waitin' for you. Might even have enough for the next load by the time you get here."

"Pride," Digger said, scratching the dog's chin. "You stay with Becky and the little ones. Sit, boy."

Pride's ears sagged. He looked pleadingly at the boy, but obediently sat down beside Jackie and Mary Claire.

Dulcie tugged at her wagon. It was hard to get started, but once it was moving she was able to pull the heavy load without too much trouble. She followed as Digger led the way down the trail through the woods.

Going down the slope, the wagons rolled by themselves.

"Don't let it get away from you, Dulcie," Digger warned. "If you think it's gonna run you down, let go an' jump outta the way."

"I will."

"We can always pick up the nuts again, if we have to. Don't want you gettin' runned over, though."

"I'm doin' all right."

Dulcie bit her lip and planted her feet firmly against the push of the wagon. Slowly, they crept down the hill.

The land finally flattened out, and they had to pull the wagons again. They walked together talking quietly.

"Wait a minute, honey," Digger said just as they got to the edge of the woods. "You're gonna trip over your shoelace."

He knelt in front of her and quickly laced up the small shoe. They were just taking up their wagon tongues when they heard it.

Hattie's scream shattered the silence.

Dulcie's heart hammered. She took off running toward the house. Digger came pounding right behind her. Through the woods she could see her mother. Deke Dunford had her by the arm. He was dragging her out of the house. Hattie fought to get free. Dulcie opened her mouth to scream. Before she could cry out, Digger caught her from behind, clapped his hand over her mouth and wrestled her down behind the woodpile.

"Shhhhhh! Don't let him see us," he whispered.

Dulcie's eyes were huge above his hand, but she nodded her agreement.

Hattie screamed again.

Digger and Dulcie peeked over the stacked wood. They could see Hattie fighting Deke with all her strength. At one point, she made herself collapse to the ground, almost taking Deke with her. He planted his feet and viciously jerked her upright.

Silent tears streamed down Dulcie's cheeks. She clutched at Digger's arm. "We gotta do somethin'," she whispered frantically. "He's *hurtin'* her!"

Digger put his arms around the trembling little girl. His face was set like stone.

"Shhhhh, honey. We gotta be real quiet. If he gets us, too, won't nobody know what happened. As soon as he's gone, we'll...we'll get help."

Hattie swung a small fist at Deke's head. He backhanded her. She fell to the ground. Deke yanked her back to her feet.

Dulcie covered her eyes. She didn't see Deke pull back his fist and slam it into her mother's face. When Dulcie opened her eyes again, she saw Deke striding quickly down the lane. Her mother was slung over his shoulder, head down—not moving any more.

32

Hattie's thoughts fought toward the surface from a deep swirling burgundy darkness. Throbbing pain on the left side of her face pulsated in rhythm with the roar in her ears. And motion, rolling, swaying, jarred her body.

Ever so slowly, Hattie realized that part of the roaring she could hear was mechanical. Above the pain, she recognized the sound of an engine—she was in a moving car! Disjointed bits of thought began to jell into cohesive understanding.

She tried to blink her eyes, but excruciating pain burned through the left side of her face where it was mashed against ...what? What was it? She didn't know. It was hard to breathe. She turned her head slightly and opened her right eye. The light hurt. Her eye watered uncontrollably. Through white-hot pain, she forced herself to focus on her surroundings.

She was lying on her left side in the back of a strange car. Curled in a near-fetal position, with her hands tied behind her back and feet bound together, she lay facing the front of the car. Above the top of the front seat she could see the back of a man's head.

Hattie blinked to clear her vision. *Deke...? Why...? Where's he takin' me?*

Her memory rushed back with force. She remembered Deke sitting in her kitchen. He'd thrown her mother's cup, and when she had turned to run, he'd knocked over a chair in his haste to keep her from racing out the door. It was Deke who had slapped her face, over and over. And then...Hattie remembered seeing the fist flying toward her. It was Deke's fist. Just as now, it was Deke's head she could see above the driver's seat.

Through pain she shifted to look out the passenger side of the car.

A brick building flashed past. *I...I know what that is! That's the top of the Drakesboro Bank Building! He's going straight through the intersection toward Paradise.*

The car lurched over the railroad tracks beyond the traffic light and sped into the country. Hattie squeezed her eyes shut against the pain that ripped at her with every bump and jerk of the car. The choking sensation eased a little. Only then did she realize there was a filthy rag tied across her mouth.

He gagged me? Hattie pushed at the rag with her tongue, trying to move it away. It didn't budge. She made herself breathe slowly through her nose.

If I can get his attention, maybe he'll take the gag off and let me talk.

She pulled her knees up and kicked lightly against the seat. Deke glanced in her direction over the car seat.

"So sleeping beauty decided to wake up," Deke said in a friendly voice. "About time. Guess you don't want to miss all the fall colors. " He cackled.

Hattie made a muffled cry.

"Aw, what's the matter? Miss High-and-Mighty Stoneworth don't approve of my chariot? Ain't *that* too bad."

Hattie could hear the underlying anger in his voice.

"One thing you ain't never learned is proper respect! If I pull that rag off your mouth you'll likely start telling me off like you was the Queen of England and I was your stable hand. Well, I ain't gonna do it. I'm on to you and..."

Deke hit the brake and swerved, screaming, "You idiot!"

Hattie crashed into the back of the front seat, then crumpled forward into the small space between the seats. The car spun in the gravel of the road, hit the shoulder, and careened back onto the road.

"Idiot farmer driving his cow let her bolt right in front of me. Like to have wrecked us!" Deke muttered.

He looked back at her. "Well, look at you—got you on the floorboard, huh? Good enough for you. Least you won't be seen as we go through Coaltown. Should'a thought of that m'self." He gave a snort that sounded something like laughter.

"Don't you get any ideas, Hattie-Hattie," he said in a sing-song. "Don't you try to raise up neither. You ain't gonna get away. You're gonna get what's coming to you. So's Delaney. That's for sure."

Hattie swallowed hard. Fear and the gag in her mouth caused nausea to rise up in her throat .*Calm down, Hattie, s*he told herself. *Mustn't agitate him. Think. Think! What would Smith do if it were him? Smith! Smith will get help.* Her head bounced against the floorboard. *Oh, no! He won't even be home till dark. How will he know where to look? And what about the children—what about Dalton? He'll be starved!*

"You listening, woman? You better be listening! I'm talkin' to you. It's your fault. You did it, you meddling, prattling do-gooder. You killed her. You and that feeble-brained, bossy old crone. You and old lady Richards killed her! You killed my precious Mamie!"

A stifled "Noooo!" sprang, unbidden, from Hattie's muffled mouth.

"Don't you contradict me, woman!" Deke screamed. "You shut up!" The car swerved as he raised up in the front seat and swung his right fist behind the seat in an arc that just missed her.

"You shut up!" he repeated. "You kidnapped my Mamie. Took her up there to your place and killed her. There wasn't nothin' wrong with her 'til you got your hands on her. Got a little outta line and I just dished 'er a little dose of 'straighten up and fly right.' "

The car passed the junction to the Coaltown mine. A large coal truck rumbled by. Hattie wondered if the driver, high in his perch, could see down into the coupe. Could he—would he see her lying there?

"I wasn't gonna have her start gettin' all highfalutin and actin' like *you*. Thinking she had a right to talk back to me. Thinkin'she was better'n me."

She could tell by his voice that he had turned and looked back toward her. "Couldn't have her settin' that kind of example to our kids. Not in a thousand years! So I just tried to jar a little sense into her. Just put her in her place. That's all. That's all!" he screamed. "That's all I did. You hear me?" He swung at Hattie again.

"That's all I did." His voice softened. "Then you killed her. Killed her to get our young'uns. Set me up to take the blame so you could take them. That's what you done—that's *exactly* what you done!"

Hattie cringed at his madness.

His voice raised to a higher pitch. "You took my kids! Took them for that sister of yours and her preacher-boy husband. You ain't gonna get away with it."

Hattie heard him sob, then sniff. Then he was quiet for a while. *He's out of his mind—clean out of his mind,* she thought. *Dear God, please deliver us from evil...*

"No! You ain't gonna get away with it! None of you are. None..." Suddenly he screamed, "Becky, I'm gonna get you! My own girl and you turned your back on your daddy! Ohhhh, you gonna pay! And you gonna pay good!" He pounded the steering wheel with the heels of both hands.

"She turned on me! My Becky snuck off and got you and Ma Richards. I'd warned her about that old...Ohhhhh! She's gonna get it. I'm gonna take my razor strop to that little gal. I'm gonna thrash her till blood runs into her shoes."

Hattie tried to shift her position to a less painful one, but the ranting of the driver compounded the agony. She felt the car turn left and leave the main road. They were now on a rutted dirt road.

"And Digger—how could he sic that dog on me? Delaney put him up to it, that's how. Then he stopped me from whipping my own boy. Who does your man think he is? God? Think he's gonna call the shots? That Smith Delaney! Don't even fight fair. Kicked me in the head. Well, won't be long till he gets what he's got comin'." He cackled. "Yeah, he's going to get it."

He accelerated the car, and it fishtailed as they climbed a hill.

"And Little Jenny. She smart-mouthed me. Said I didn't didn't own her. Didn't have the right to treat her rough just 'cause I look like Clark Gable. Stuck her face out at me. I slapped her. Ain't no woman gonna talk down at me like that." He snarled. "I hate 'em!"

Hattie shuddered.

"Slapped her face and punched her in the gut. She looked so much like you, I couldn't stand it. See what you brought on? See? Your fault. It's all *your* fault!"

The car lurched out of one more rut and came to a stop.

"We're not there," said Deke over the seat. "But a tree's down across the road. That means we park the car here."

He pushed the car door open wide, leaned the seat forward and looked down at her.

"Well, look at you! Sorta sardined in there, huh?"

Hattie's eyes were like saucers above the gag. She forced herself to be absolutely still.

He reached in, grabbed her shoulders and dragged her out, face up, and stood her on her feet.

Pain jolted through her back, shoulders, neck, and the left side of her head. And with the tight rope tied around her wrists she could hardly tell her hands were there. Being jammed between the seats had diminished the already limited circulation in her arms. Now new pain pulsed down her arms toward her hands.

He leaned her against the car and untied her feet, then shoved her ahead of him. "Get going. We got a way to go."

She staggered and almost fell, but he grabbed her right arm, yanked her upright and steered her ahead. They walked through overgrown fields toward the top of the hill. Stumbling along with limited vision through her black eye, and gasping for air, Hattie recognized where they were. *Just ahead is where the community of Airdrie stood. We're above where we had the Labor Day picnic.* She looked around. *Where is he taking me?*

"I guess I could take that gag off for a while." He stopped and looked down at her. "You promise you won't scream if I do?"

She nodded.

"You better not! We're more'n a mile downstream from Paradise and wind's blowing this way. If you scream, before a hunter or fisherman or farmer can get here, I'll slap you speechless and stomp you to death on the spot—you understand that?"

Again she nodded—and shuddered.

He jerked her around, untied the knot in the cloth, and pulled it from her face.

"Th...thanks," she whispered. Trembling, she filled her lungs with air.

"You're welcome. 'Sides, I want you in good shape for when your husband comes to visit us."

"Deke, please let me go—there's the baby... he'll be hungry..."

His eyes coldly swept her. Instantly she was sorry she had spoken. Anger rose in his face and swirled into rage in his eyes and voice.

"Your baby! *Your* baby*!* What about my babies, my four young'uns? You murdered their mama. You kept 'em from me, their daddy—and you talk about *your baby*!"

He grabbed her by both shoulders and pulled her to within inches of his face. She saw fury dancing in his eyes. "Woman," he hissed between his teeth, "I'll kill you right now!" His clawed hands dug into her upper arms. He shook her viciously. Suddenly he paused. "No, I'll wait. I'll wait and let Delaney see me do it. Then I'll kill *him*!"

A wave of revulsion swept over Hattie, but Deke spun her around and shoved her ahead of him down a path leading from the brow of the ridge. Part way down the hill it swung left onto the broad ledge that ran parallel along the face of the bluff above the old furnace works. Soon they arrived at the mouth of the mine that ran straight back deep into the hillside.

"Welcome to your home, Mrs. Delaney. Your home for the rest of your life." He laughed. "Walk right in."

Hattie hesitated, but he shoved her from behind. She stumbled into the semi-darkness, arms still tied behind her.

She turned to face him. "Deke, don't do this! Please don't take things into your own hands. You can get help." Pleas poured from parched lips. "Things can work out, Deke. The Lord can ..."

"Shut up!" He slapped her with a backhand. "Shut up! You get back there in the mine to that straw-tick mattress. Then I'm going to tell you a thing or two." He shoved her again.

Hattie staggered toward a light brown object on the floor near the right side of the mine. Deke followed. When she got to the mattress, she knelt, then awkwardly twisted down on it into a sitting position.

"Deke..."

"I told you to shut up!" He yanked the cloth from his hip pocket and tied it across her mouth again. He sneered at her. "You just don't accept the facts. You're a woman with no respect for men. You was told to shut up, but you just wouldn't do it. Now you're gonna listen to what's about happen, like it or not."

While retying her feet, he continued. "Your husband is going to come to see you die. I thought about building a fire in the old furnace and tossing you in from up on the landing. That's what they say happened to rebellious workers in the old days. Ain't gonna do it, though. The smoke might draw a crowd." He threw his had back and laughed. Then he was quiet for a moment.

"But back in the mine there's a deep shaft. The bottom is full of water that they say comes all the way from the Green River through a water-filled tunnel. They say that slaves were promised freedom if they survived a jump into the shaft and could swim under water to the river. Don't think any made it. You wouldn't either."

The picture he created horrified Hattie. Even more terrifying was the wild look in his eyes. He rubbed his hands together and licked his lips.

"You wouldn't make it, because I'd keep your hands and feet tied. You'd be standing there at the edge of the pit and I'd let Smith get a good look at you. Then a gentle push. But I'd have your gag off. He'd hear your screams as you fell down the shaft till you plunged under the dark water."

Hattie shut her eyes, shook her head, and tried not to see the images conjured by her captor. *Dear Lord, I know this is not a bad dream, but help it to end. Somehow deliver us from this madman. Help him to see...*

"But I have another plan. A better plan. First, I got to get Delaney to come to our party. Then he can enjoy the big surprise.

I want him to enjoy it as much as I enjoyed having you murder my wife and take my children."

Hattie shook her head and uttered a muffled a "No, Deke!"

He slapped her twice. She fell onto the straw mattress, writhing in pain.

"You lie still. I'm going to walk to Paradise and leave word for Delaney to meet us here. In case you should decide to try to squirm out of here, I'm tying this extra rope to your wrists and running it to that wheel from a mine car." He pointed to an iron wheel half-buried under debris. "Even if you could hobble along, you couldn't pull that!" He laughed.

"I'll be back soon. Then it won't be long till our company comes. How glad you'll be to see him!" He chuckled.

She watched him walk toward the light and turn right as he left the mouth of the mine. Hope leapt in her heart. *Surely I can untie these ropes, or wiggle out of them. Lord, please let me find a way. Let me warn Smith. And there's the children....*

Lying on her side, her hands bound behind her back, feet tied, and a rope running to the iron wheel, it seemed helpless. But she pulled her feet up behind her back to her hands. It took forever, but with numbed fingers she finally got the knot binding her feet untied. Her blood softened the ropes at her raw wrists. She twisted her wrists and pulled in spite of the searing pain. *If I can just...can't get to the knot at my wrists.* She stopped moving for a moment and took a few deep breaths to calm herself down. Her eyes landed on the wheel.

Hattie stumbled to the wheel and backed up to it. She squatted. *If I can untie the knot at the wheel, I can pick up the rope and carry it. Maybe I can get down the old stone steps and to the river. Maybe a fisherman will see me, or…*As she tugged frantically at the rope where it was tied to the wheel, the knot finally began to loosen. *Almost! I can feel it. It's almost loose!*

She started when she heard a noise at the mouth of the mine. Her eyes darted to the bright entrance. Her heart leaped in her throat as she saw the silhouette.

Deke was back.

34

Gideon McBride drove through Drakesboro on his way to Hattie's house. He whistled as he drove. The sale of dogs at Twin Tunnels had gone well, and he was a happy man.

A crowd milling into the street in front of Radburn's store blocked his way. He pulled to the side of the road and glanced at the wooden structure that housed the home of Annie and Harwell Radburn and their store. Smoke wafted from the rear of the building.

Gideon jumped from the cab of the pickup truck and pushed his way through the crowd.

Ahead, Clarence Hunt stood, his cap pushed back. Gideon walked over and greeted him.

"What's happenin' here, Mr. Hunt?"

Clarence answered grimly. "Ain't a fire sale—just a fire."

Gideon, head and shoulders above the crowd, surveyed the damage.

"Don't look too bad."

"It ain't. But it sure could've been. Somebody set fire to the storeroom in the back." Clarence pulled his cap off his head, and slapped it against his leg. "Dumb kids playin' with matches, prob'ly!"

"Is Miz Annie all right?"

"Think so. She's 'bout scared to death, but other than that...she'll likely be fine. She's the one that found the storeroom burnin' to begin with. She was tryin' to put it out when the neighbors realized what was goin' on an' come a-runnin'."

"An' poor Miz Annie was here all by herself." Gideon stated flatly.

Clarence looked up at the tall young man standing next to

him. “Didn’t take long for Harwell to get here. One of the Humphrey boys found him.”

Clarence jerked his head toward the store. “He’s back there now tryin’ to calm Annie down.”

A prickling sensation crept up the back of Gideon’s neck. Every hair stood on end. Maybe it was the underlying currents of distrust he’d lived with all his life, or perhaps it was just the timing of the fire that alerted him. Either way, a grim suspicion wrenched his stomach. Gideon grabbed Clarence’s arm and spun the older man around to face him. “Mr. Radburn’s here? He’s here at the store?”

Clarence shook off the Gideon’s hand and shot him a stern look. “’Course he is. Where else would he be?”

“He was supposed to be with Hattie Delaney.”

Clarence’s face went from blank confusion to stark horror.

“Call the sheriff,” Gideon shouted over his shoulder.

He was already running to his truck.

❧

Gideon ran from one end of the Stoneworth property to the other. He’d already searched the house. The only sign that anything was amiss was an upended wooden chair and a shattered china cup littering the kitchen floor—that and the lack of occupants.

He’d found the wagons loaded with walnuts in the edge of the woods. There were small footprints leading up and down the trail. There were more prints behind the woodpile. Some were small. Some weren’t.

Gideon carried his rifle. He’d grabbed it before getting out of his truck, then reached under the seat of the pickup to pull the ancient revolver from its hiding place. He’d tucked the loaded pistol into his waistband—just in case.

Armed and scared, he stood in the drive and waited for the sheriff.

The noon whistle blew at the Black Diamond Mine. Under its wail, faintly, then more urgently, came the siren of the sheriff’s car.

Sheriff Westerfield skidded to a halt at the top of the drive.

“Where is she?” he called out his car window. Dread sounded

in his voice.

"Gone." Gideon answered, "Her—an' all the young'uns."

❧

Old habits die hard. As soon as Dulcie and Digger, with Dalton wrapped tightly in his spindly arms, had raced back up the hill to the pasture and told Becky what had happened at the house, Becky kicked into survivor mode.

"All right, let's get these kids to the cabin, quick!" she'd said, taking the baby from Digger. "We need to get hid, 'fore he comes lookin' for us."

Now they were sitting on the dirt floor of the old cabin set in the woods at the foot of Pa Rhoads Hill. Becky rocked Dalton, trying to get him back to sleep. Pride lay next to her with his nose on his one front paw, his eyes open, moving from child to child.

Dulcie kept getting up and peering out the window.

"Why do we have to stay *here*? *Why* can't we go to Radburn's an' get *help*?" she asked for the third time.

"I done tol' you why!" Digger snapped. "If our dad comes lookin', he'll likely come right down that road. You want him to get us, too?"

"N...no," Dulcie shuddered. She started to cry. "I just want to help my mama," she wailed.

Becky answered softly, "Hush, Dulcie. The only thing we can do right now, is hide out. We gotta wait awhile. Then, when Daddy falls asleep, we'll go back to your place."

Dulcie knuckled her eyes. "But how will you know when he's asleep?"

Becky shrugged, her face old again—like when she'd first come to live at Dulcie's house. "It'll be a while. It's early yet."

She nodded toward Dorie and Mary Claire. "See how quiet they are? That's how you gotta be, too."

Jackie sat with the little girls. His eyes were huge. He opened his mouth to speak, then closed it again and leaned against Mary Claire.

Dulcie didn't want to be quiet. She wanted to scream and scream and scream until someone, *anyone*, came to help.

"Y'all can sit here, if you want. I'm goin' to Radburn's." She started for the door. Digger's hand shot out and gripped her wrist.

"You ain't goin' nowhere. No one is." He growled.

"Digger," Becky said, "would you get some wood, so I can light a fire. I'm gonna boil the eggs you snuck from the house so we can have supper after awhile."

Digger's eyes never left Dulcie's face. "I'm goin'. I'll be back. Don't you move. Hear me?"

At Dulcie's slow nod, he went to the doorway and peeked out, then slipped around the corner.

Dulcie rubbed her wrist. "Why's he have to be so mean?"

Becky sighed. "He's scared. When Digger gets scared, he don't cry or whimper. He just...I guess he just gets mad. Try not to fret 'im."

Dulcie pushed out her lip. "I'm scared an' I'm not bein' mean!"

"No, you ain't. But you *are* bein' kinda demandin'."

Becky sighed again. "Look here, we *done* this before. Trust me. This is the best way. We stay hid 'til it's safe to come out."

Digger came back in with the wood and piled it in the bottom of the old fireplace. There was an old fashioned cast-iron hook hanging from a chain on a bracket. It held a heavy pot.

"You need me to fetch the water, too?" he muttered.

"Yes, please."

He unhooked the pot from the chain and carried it outside to the spring.

Dulcie watched him from the window. He carefully wiped out the pot with leaves, then lowered an old gourd dipper into the spring and rinsed out the pot. He dipped water into the pot until it was full. Leaning against its weight, he carried it back into the cabin.

"It's gonna rain." He said flatly.

"Rain makes me tired," Becky said, leaning back against the wall, the baby to her shoulder.

Dulcie's eyes and mouth went into perfect O's. "Maybe it'll make your daddy tired. Maybe he'll go to bed early!"

Becky closed her eyes.

"Maybe," she said.

❧

Smith pursed his lips tightly around the nails he'd stuck between them, and hammered the upright stud into place. Kneeling, he slipped first one nail, then another, out of his mouth, quickly toenailing the two-by-four to the floor joist.

Stepping back, he surveyed the progress he'd made on the renovation to Marva and Conroy's porch. It was shaping up nicely. At the front, where it faced the street, he'd framed two large windows to let the sunlight pour in. He planned to build a shelf-like bench beneath the windows that would run the full width of the porch. When he was finished, there would be hinged seat-tops to hide extra quilts and out-of-season clothes.

One more two-by-four to cut to size and nail into place, then he'd be ready to start walling it all in. A neat stack of lumber sat behind him on the porch floor—planks for the walls.

Marva had already purchased the wallpaper she'd put up to finish the room—tiny yellow roses on a cream background. It lay in rolls on the dining room table. Next to it, there were yards of crisp matching yellow fabric for curtains and the pillows that would top the bench.

At the back of the house, the phone pealed twice, then stopped in mid-ring.

Smith measured and marked the last stud. He set it across his sawhorses and picked up the saw.

"Smith?"

He swung his head toward the sound.

Marva stood in the doorway, her face white.

"He got her, Smith—Deke got Hattie."

❧

"Stop blamin' yourself, Smith." Sheriff Westerfield told the anguished man. "You done everything you could. You never give him an opportunity to get to Hattie and the young'uns. He had to create one. That's why he started the fire—to get Harwell outta here. Leastwise that's the way I figure it."

"Don't matter what I did. I didn't do enough," Smith said

woodenly.

He stomped across the drive and back again.

"I hate this waitin' around. I need to be *doin'* somethin'!"

"We'll start trackin' 'em as soon as McBride gets back with his dog," said the sheriff.

"I can't believe it. I just *can't* believe it! How did he get 'em all?" Smith yanked his cap off his head and threw it on the ground. "Why didn't one of 'em *run*?"

The sheriff shrugged his shoulders. "Don't make no sense to me, neither."

Smith tipped his head back and watched the clouds building in the west. "If it starts rainin' the dog won't be able to track."

He slammed his fist against the hood of his truck.

"How'd he get 'em *all*?" he asked again.

The sheriff pushed his hat back on his head and scratched at the gray hair underneath. "Them Dunford kids, they're...well—it's been pounded in to them to do what their dad says—they do it without thinkin'. I reckon that's how he got 'em to go with 'im. Your kids prob'ly didn't have a choice. More'n likely he held a gun on all of 'em."

Gideon's truck appeared at the top of the hill. Smith paced as it maneuvered the incline and pulled up the drive next to the sheriff's car. Princess sat like a statue on the seat next to Gideon.

Smith snatched up his rifle and headed for the young man and the dog.

"Any word?" Gideon asked. Smith shook his head.

"Listen, Smith, you gotta understand somethin'," said Gideon, nodding toward the dog. "Princess ain't the tracker Pride is. She'll do her best, but..."

"As long as she starts us in the right direction, that's what matters for now," said Smith.

The sheriff nodded his agreement. Gideon shrugged and motioned the hound out onto the drive. There she sat politely and waited for her next command.

"Got the dress?" the lawman asked.

"Right here," Smith answered. He opened the porch door and

picked up a dress of Hattie's he'd laid on the bench just inside.

Gideon took the dress and knelt in front of the dog. He held out the flowered material and pressed it close to the dog's face. "Can you find her, girl? Can you find Miz Hattie?" The dog whined softly.

Gideon tossed the dress back to Smith and held the dog's leash in his right hand.

"Seek, Princess."

Princess snuffed the ground around the door, then turned toward the smokehouse. She circled around the top of the drive, then whuffed at the grass on the edge. Suddenly she raised her head and gave a quick yelp. She pulled Gideon down the drive, toward the lane. Smith and the sheriff followed close behind. They made a beeline down the lane and turned right where the road went toward Jacksontown. Princess pulled hard against the lead, then stopped. She circled and whined, then circled again. Finally, she lay down and looked up at Gideon.

"That's it, she lost the trail," Gideon said. "I sure am sorry."

The sheriff walked along the edge of the road and pointed. "Look! This is where he parked. There's tire tracks. That's why she lost the scent. He carried 'em off in a car."

Smith squatted by the tire track. "Hattie would *not* have gotten in a car with Deke. Not unless..."

He didn't finish the sentence.

The three men turned back toward the Stoneworth place.

Sheriff Westerfield's shoulders slumped. Well, he said, "I'll call the station house from Radburn's and alert everyone to be on the lookout for Deke, Hattie, an' the young'uns—and any suspicious car."

They were almost back to the house when Harwell Radburn's Dodge sped down the hill and turned up the drive.

He rolled the window down on the big car and leaned out to call, "Hey! Call just came in from Paradise. Y'all need to get out there quick!"

Smith and Gideon broke into a run, the heavy-set sheriff puffing up the drive behind them.

“What they say, Harwell? Give me every word,” Smith demanded.

Harwell jumped out of the car. “Store owner said he seen Deke Dunford tearin’ down the trail towards Airdrie. And that’s not all…”

35

The road from Drakesboro ended in Paradise where the ferry crossed the Green River. The town's main street—the only one of any length—paralleled the river for a short distance. At the down-river end of the street it ended where a tree had fallen across it. A path continued beyond the log.

The storeowner was on the porch in front of the Paradise General Store waiting for them when the sheriff's car screeched to a halt. Without a word, he shoved a crumpled note into Smith's hand as the anxious man hurried up the steps.

"You didn't see my wife?" asked Smith, peering intently into the older man's eyes.

"No, sir. I'm real sorry. All I saw was Dunford running down the trail after the rock with the letter tied around it crashed onto the porch. Like to scared me to death! Thought someone was shooting up the place."

"When was that?" the sheriff asked.

"Must be a little more than an hour ago," the storeowner answered. "You know, that Dunford was in here a couple days ago. Had the strangest look in his eye. Tol' my missus I didn't care if'n I never laid eyes on 'im him again."

Sheriff Westerfield leaned toward the old man eagerly. "You remember what he bought? Might be important."

Smith, unfolding the letter, listened intently.

The old man stared up at the porch roof, obviously thinking. "Yes, sir. He bought some grub, some shotgun shells and a couple boxes of fancy rifle shells. I remember 'cause I was real glad to get rid of 'em. I'd ordered them bullets special for some man from Owensboro that come in here a couple years back. He said he was comin' out here to hunt. Never picked 'em up. Dunford seemed real pleased to get 'em, though."

"That's fine. You got a good memory," the sheriff said.

"There's somethin' else—don't know that it matters, but the Dobbs boys was in here yesterday evenin'. Said they seen a strange car parked on the hill close to where old Airdrie town used to be. Seen it a couple of times."

Smith had heard enough. He sat down on an empty nail keg with the letter. Sheriff Westerfield, Gideon, Deputy Rainwater, and the storekeeper stood waiting.

Smith pushed his cap back on his head and started to read the message silently. Quickly sensing it's nature, he returned to the beginning and read it aloud.

Smith Delaney, if you want your woman to see another day, heed what I'm saying. We are in the old mine on the bluff above the Airdrie furnace. I am armed, and I don't mean a little. You come meet me. I got a score to settle with you. Come by yourself. And don't be toting a gun in here, either. I'll be watching, and if you do, I'm gonna kill your wife right in front of your eyes. One of you is gonna die anyway. Reckon it's your choice which it'll be. Maybe you both will. I ain't decided yet.

I'm a dead man already. Ain't that funny? You getting a letter from a dead man? It's just a matter of when and how I die. Maybe I'll kill you, then me. Maybe I'll just turn myself in after you're dead, an' let the law execute me. Either way, it don't matter to me.

Don't try sneaking up on me. Come from Paradise right down the river and up the side of the hill to the mine. Stop at the hickory tree by the mine entrance. Call my name. Don't try to rush me. One blast to your pretty wife's head at close range from my shotgun and she's dead. She won't be near so pretty then, will she? You follow my directions, and I might let her live. But you're a dead man, Delaney, just like me. Hurry. Let's get this over."

Smith turned the letter over. "It's just signed, 'Dunford' "

Smith's hands were shaking as he handed the note to the sheriff. "It's pretty plain, ain't it, Sheriff?"

"Yep." The officer stared at the paper. "He plans to kill you on the spot, then turn a gun on hisself. He don't want to live any more and he plans to take you with him. Or Hattie, if you don't play his game."

"That's about the size of it," agreed Smith.

The sheriff's deputy had pulled up while Smith, still sitting on the nail keg, was reading the letter. He'd heard most of it.

"Maybe he's bluffing," said Deputy Rainwater.

"Nope, he ain't," said the sheriff, shaking his head. "He ain't, but there's a razor-thin chance I can talk some sense into 'im. Let's give it a try."

"He said for me to come by myself."

Smith removed his flat, narrow-brimmed cap and ran his fingers through his hair. He looked toward the woods downriver from the village of Paradise, then stood.

"Y'all stay here—I'm goin' in alone, just like he said. Don't want to take a chance rilin' 'im."

"Smith, wait," Gideon interrupted. "That man's outta his mind. You cain't go in there alone."

The sheriff held up his hand.

"McBride's right, Smith," he said. "You ain't goin' alone. He's already riled out of his mind. He's blaming others, mostly you and Hattie, for everything that's happened. His wife's death. His getting' fired from his job. The kids being taken from him. To him, *you're* the reason, Smith. You and Hattie. I gotta try to talk some sense to him. He's outta his head!"

"I'm a little outta my *own* head at the moment." Smith said grimly. "Let me tell *you* somethin', Sheriff. If he harms one hair on Hattie's head, I'm gonna kill 'im myself. If I have to do it with my bare hands."

He wheeled on the lawman. "An' why didn't he say nothin' 'bout the young'uns? Is he plannin' on killin me in front of my kids? *And* his *own*? He's insane!"

"All the more cause to try reasonin' with him," said the sheriff.

"Rainwater, you stay here," said Westerfield. He pointed to the large car. "Turn this car crossways in the road. Don't let nobody past this point."

The sheriff opened the trunk of the car, got out a rifle, and tossed it to the deputy. He took out another rifle for himself. Smith saw him glance at Gideon. The youth stared down river with his old Winchester 22-rifle cradled across his body. It had not left his hand from the time he climbed into the back seat of the sheriff's car. His dog was sitting at his left heel.

"Annie Radburn knows somethin's going on out here," Westerfield continued, patting the holster and gun on his ample right hip, as if to make sure the weapon was there. "And she knows it involves Hattie. That means there's prob'ly a passel of Stoneworth menfolk cloggin' the road headin' this way. And they won't be bringin' slingshots. We can't have 'em swarmin' through the woods to Airdrie."

"That's a fact, " said Smith, pacing.

He stopped and looked the younger lawman up and down. "An' one pup of a deputy ain't gonna stop 'em. Let's get this over with, Sheriff."

Smith started toward the trail. "I don't want Deke any more spooked than he already is. No tellin' what he'll do if he thinks a posse is closin' in on 'im."

Smith stopped. He stood stone still for a moment, then walked back to the sheriff's car. He took his revolver out of his waistband and laid the gun on the car seat.

"I'll play the game his way. I'm goin' in unarmed."

"You ain't goin' alone. I'm goin' with you," said Gideon. "Princess'll take us right to 'im."

He reached down and patted the dog.

"Son, I appreciate the offer," Smith said softly, "but I'm gonna take the fall. That's the only way he'll let Hattie live. Gideon, I don't want you to see me die."

"Mebbe he won't have to," said Westerfield. "I'll talk to Deke. Mebbe he'll listen to reason."

He turned to his deputy. "Rainwater, use the store phone and call my office and tell 'em to get Dr. Wilson out here pronto. For sure, *somebody's* gonna get hurt. We'll wait 'til you get back."

Smith Delaney stared unseeingly across the river toward the cultivated fields and rolling hills beyond.

"Our kids gotta have their mama," said the small, wiry man. "Y'all can help 'em make it without *me*, but they gotta have their mama."

He shook his head. "What Deke did to Little Jenny an' that other poor woman proves he don't care any more. I can't stand to think of Deke and my sweet Hattie..."

He rapidly blinked his slate-blue eyes.

"I'll take the fall," he repeated. "Then one of y'all can take Deke out. It'll all be over."

"He says he'll turn the gun on hisself," said Gideon, "but you can't tell what he'll do once he starts shootin'. He might shoot you, then Miz Hattie, too, just for spite. He might try to get away. The dog will help us…"

"Hold on a minute, Gideon," said Westerfield. "You're right that we might have to chase him and—hold it! I'm gonna deputize you two. Then, no matter what happens in there, it'll be all legal an' official."

"No, sir!" said Smith. "You deputize Gideon. I'm not goin' in armed. Anything I do will be in self-defense," said Smith, clenching and unclenching his fists.

"Just get on with it. Hattie's in the mine with that man. There ain't no tellin'..."

He glanced down the river to where the ruins of the abandoned mining community lay hidden in the forest that covered the hillside and bluff. He shook his head. "We gotta go. Now."

"McBride, I don't have no Bible here to swear on," declared the sheriff, "so raise your right hand and say after me..."

Gideon raised his hand and solemnly intoned after the sheriff. "I, Gideon McBride...do swear...that I will do right,...as well to the poor…as to the rich,...in all things...pertaining to my office as deputy sheriff;...that I will do no wrong… to any one…for any gift, reward, or promise, ...nor for favor or hatred, ...and in all things…I will faithfully…and impartially…execute the duties…of my office … according to the best …of my skill and judgement.

"I do further swear...that I have never...participated in a duel..."

"Sir," interrupted Gideon, "does a feud or a coal mine showdown count?"

"Nope," grunted the big man. "Let's continue."

"I do further swear,...that I will endeavor,...to the best of my ability,...to detect and prosecute …all gamblers…and others violating…the laws of the Commonwealth of Kentucky,...so help me God."

"Amen," said Smith.

As Gideon completed the oath, he lowered his right hand.

The sheriff said, "You are deputized under the laws of the Commonwealth of Kentucky. Wish I had a badge for you, but it don't matter. You're official and legal. And we got witnesses."

They walked back toward the store, and paused in the street.

A small crowd had gathered around. A number of others stood watching from the porches of the small homes, and in front of the few businesses in the village.

"What's goin' on, Sheriff?" questioned a rawboned, deeply tanned older man.

"Trouble down at Old Airdrie, Gilmore. I'm orderin' all of you to stay this side of the log down yonder at the end of the road. We hope to be back shortly."

He nodded toward Gideon. "If I need you, I'll send this young man for you. Otherwise, stay back."

"Hey! Ain't that McBride, the dog man? I saw 'im at Jockey Day. Suppose he'd do a shootin' demonstration for us when y'all get back?"

"Doubt it, Haden" retorted Westerfield. "Got more important matters on our minds."

"Doc Wilson will be comin' right away, Sheriff," yelled Rainwater as he hurried across the porch of the store.

"Good job, son. You ready, Smith?"

"Been ready."

The sheriff turned back to his deputy. "Rainwater, nobody past the end of the road. Got that?"

"Got it, Sheriff. These are good folks. There'll be no trouble—but I'm ready." He glanced down at his badge, made a show of palming the handle of his revolver, then moved his rifle into position with his right hand on the trigger guard and the stock pinned against his side with his arm.

Westerfield glanced at Smith, who was kneeling and retying the shoe on his bad right leg. The sheriff turned to Gideon. "Dog ready?"

"Just a minute. Smith, can I borrow that letter? I'll give it right back."

Smith tugged Deke's letter from his shirt pocket. He handed it to Gideon, who unfolded it and held it down in front of the dog.

Mr. Haden called out, "I seen the wonder you did with Jeb Sawyer's beast at Jockey Day, son, and what you done with them huntin' dogs, but if you try to tell me that there dog's readin' that letter, I'm liable to b'lieve you really do 'witch them dogs."

Several laughed, but Gideon didn't respond. He turned red.

The dog sniffed the paper and looked up at Smith.

"No, Princess," said his master. He held the paper out to the dog again. She sniffed and wagged her tail, pranced about, and whimpered at her master.

"Seek," said Gideon. He walked the dog across the lot in front of the store and toward the ferry. The dog trotted along just in front of him, smelling the ground and slowly wagging her tail. After going a short distance, Princess stopped, sniffed both to the right and the left, then turned left and trotted down the street alongside the river. Suddenly she bayed loudly.

"Quiet, Princess!" Gideon said firmly. "Quiet. And slow. Easy, girl." Glancing at Smith and Westerfield, he nodded to the left and said, "Let's go."

The trio stepped over a log that marked the end of the road and followed the path leading along the river. The dog, her nose to the ground, led the way.

"It's a good thing most of the leaves are off the trees," the lad said softly. He waited for the older men. "If we keep our eyes peeled, there ain't much chance of Deke getting the drop on us."

"Don't figure he'll try," said Smith. "He's prob'ly a short distance back in that mine. In the front of the entrance there's just a narrow sloping ledge before the bluff drops off."

"Yeah," said Westerfield. He stopped and gingerly removed a blackberry briar that had wrapped itself around his left leg. "An' that bluff must be six stories high."

"So we can't get at him from the front," said Smith, "or from the hill above the mine. We'll only be able to come at 'im from either side. He'll have the drop on us for sure. And he's got Hattie for insurance."

Smith squinted through the trees. He moved his jaw from side to side, seeing the picture in his mind.

The men continued their single-file march across a bog area. At several points they saw Deke's boot prints. Once across the lowland, the trail climbed along the rise above the river, then half a mile from Paradise the trail swung down closer to the stream. Straight ahead, and sloping up the hill to the left, was second-growth timber. It was dense with underbrush, briars and honeysuckle. Princess slowed, then, sniffing the ground, left the path and followed a slight trail into the thicker woods. The men followed her up the hill.

Smith paused, bent forward, put his hand on his left knee and leaned to the side to stretch his bad leg and hip. Even with his new built-up shoe, it was difficult to negotiate the rough terrain. He had not thought to bring his walking cane. But on the ground he saw a stick he could use. He stooped to get it. Just as his hand touched the stick, a loud "rat-a-tat-tat-tat" rang down the hillside. He threw himself to the ground—and instantly felt foolish. Smith knew that sound. He looked past the equally prostrate sheriff and Gideon McBride, at a huge pileated woodpecker. Its head a blur, it hammered the trunk of a dead oak. Then, through an opening in the tree branches beyond the bird, he saw a movement high on the hillside. A man peered at them from the landing below the top of the bluff.

Deke Dunford slipped silently into the shadows and disappeared around the hill.

36

Dulcie had had enough. *I'm leavin'. If I can't go to Radburn's, I'll go to Aunt Marva's house,* she told herself. Uncertain of how to get to Beech Creek, she bit her lip, thinking.

"What's the matter with you?" Digger asked. "Why you frownin' that way?"

"Just wishin'..." Dulcie answered.

"Well, don't be wishin' you was goin' to Radburn's, 'cause you ain't."

Thunder cracked in the distance. Dulcie jumped. Digger sneered at her.

"I don't like storms," Dulcie admitted.

"They don't bother me at all," he bragged.

"Bet they do." Dulcie answered.

"You'd lose."

Dulcie thought hard. "Bet you wouldn't walk all the way to Aunt Marva's house in a storm."

"Would too."

Dulcie rolled her eyes and laughed. "It would take you hours and hours to get there. You don't even know the way!" she taunted.

"No, it wouldn't. And I *do* know the way. I even know a shortcut. I could make in an hour—hour and a half at the most."

"Sure you could, Digger."

Dulcie rolled her eyes again. "There *is* no shortcut to Beech Creek."

Please, please, please tell me how to do it. I just gotta find my daddy to go help my mama.

"Just 'cause I ain't tellin' you don't mean I don't know the way," Digger said.

"I don't believe you. Not for one minute. You couldn't find

your way to Beech Creek in a...a whole week."

"I don't care whether you believe me or not. *You* couldn't do it. You'd have to go through Ditney Hill. You know who lives there!" Digger made an ugly face.

Yes! Dulcie kept her face as still as possible.

"See! I knew you were just spouting off," retorted Dulcie, jutting her face at the boy.

"I happen to know the road past Ditney Hill turns toward Ebenezer after Mr. Sutton's place. Daddy took me with him one time to see if Mr. Sutton would come plow a field for us. He told me where the road goes. And I'm not either afraid of the people who live at Ditney Hill, even if their skin *is* a different color."

She glared at Digger, hands on her hips.

"Anyway," she continued, "that road don't go to Beech Creek. So there. You're a liar!"

"Listen, Miss Smarty-pants!" said Digger, clenching his fists. "Just so happens that across the road from Sutton's there's a path a-runnin' right on through the woods and across the fields to Beech Creek. It ain't far at all!"

Dulcie stuck her tongue out at Digger, but smiled inwardly. She had the information she needed.

A short time later, the sky opened up and rain began to fall.

Pride raised his head. He scratched at the floor with his one front paw and whined softly.

"It's all right, boy—you can go out if you want to." Digger said.

The dog hobbled over the threshold and out into the storm.

Digger paced the floor and peered out the window, looking for Pride.

Dulcie glanced around the room. The rest of the children were dozing on the old quilts Becky had taken from an ancient, broken-down bedstead that sat in a corner of the one-room cabin.

Dulcie stood up and walked toward the back door, stopping by the fire to rub her hands together briskly as though to warm them. She glanced back toward Digger. He was watching her, a suspicious look on his face. Dulcie sat down next to the hearth and leaned against the rough wall.

Maybe if he thinks I'm sleepin'... She forced herself to close her eyes. She waited what seemed like a long time, then peeped at Digger through slitted eyes. He was standing at the window, looking out.

Somewhere off in the distance, Pride barked. Dulcie saw Digger glance at the other children. He looked uncertain. Quickly she closed her eyes before he looked at her. She forced herself to breathe slowly. Pride barked again.

Dulcie heard, rather than saw, Digger leave. She slowly counted to ten, then jumped up and raced out the backdoor and down the path to the lane.

She hurried along the road toward Drakesboro, but turned up the lane that passed Mrs. Daisy Sumner's house, and on up to Mr. Pal Sumner's house, where the road ended. But Dulcie climbed the steep path beyond. She was out of breath and her side was hurting when she topped the hill and came to a road. It followed a ridge running from Jacksontown through the country and along the west side of Drakesboro. *Got to follow this to get to Ditney Hill,* she told herself.

She felt naughty for running away. And guilty, and a little scared. The rain stopped, but lightning flashed ahead of her. The thunder boomed right behind it. Her heart pounded. Dulcie choked back a sob.

Gotta find Daddy. I just gotta. He'll know what to do. He'll find that mean ol' Mr. Dunford! He'll take care of Mama.

The frightened little girl stopped and rested for a moment, leaning down on her knees to catch her breath. She pressed at the stitch in her side. Still gasping, she looked back across Mondray valley. Far on the opposite side of the valley she could see the Stoneworth place—her home—nestled among ancient elms and oaks. There was no sign of life there. *We're all gone. It looks lonesome.* The thought made her sad.

Her eyes swept way to the left, to the base of Pa Rhoads Hill. She couldn't see the cabin where the children were, but there was a thin wisp of smoke rising above the trees. She hadn't thought about anyone seeing the smoke at the old cabin. *Please don't let Mr. Dunford see it. Dear Lord, please keep 'em safe*, the little girl prayed. *Oh, I gotta hurry! I just gotta get to Aunt Marva's 'fore he finds 'em.*

She began running down the dirt road. When she heard a car chugging up the road toward her, she dashed into the bushes and, trembling, hunkered down out of sight until it passed. It wasn't Deke.

The sky's darkness deepened. Rain began to fall again. *Can't be night coming. I heard the noon whistle at Black Diamond Mine right after we got to the cabin. Must be a bad storm.* Dulcie shivered, more from fear than from cold.

Soon the road became Drakesboro's westernmost street and there were houses on each side. She made herself slow to a casual walk. *Act natural. Maybe no one will pay attention to me.*

At last she came to the Greenville highway. *Just follow it to the top of the hill and turn left.*

She looked down to see which hand had a small wart on the inside of the wrist. Smith had told her that the wart was on her *left* hand, and that even if the wart *left*, that hand would still be her *left* hand. And he had rubbed it gently with his forefinger and hugged her. She could still feel the rub. And the hug. She would always know which was her left hand.

Dulcie stuck out her chin defiantly. *Grandma Crowe is wrong—he does love me. He didn't have to show me which is my left from my right.*

I just have to go up the highway and turn left at that street. It'll take me to Ditney Hill. Digger says the path goes to Beech Creek. And I'll find Daddy and he'll find Mama. Dear God, help us find my mama!

She started up the right shoulder of the highway.

The steady rain turned into a torrent. Dulcie, soaked and shivering, kept going. She hugged herself and struggled forward, leaning into the wind. Abruptly she stopped. Fear and hypothermia had begun to take their toll.

Wait! Daddy says you should walk facing the traffic, so a car can't hit you from behind. I'm on the wrong side. She used both hands to create a hood over her eyes, and peered up and down the road. She dashed into the road just as a sheet of rain swept across.

A coal truck roared over the hill, hit the brakes, and skidded into the other lane, just missing the terrified child. She tripped and tumbled across the shoulder, skidding to a halt in the surging water of the shallow roadside ditch. Her head smashed against a rock.

Dazed, Dulcie dragged herself from the ditch. Sopping wet, bruised, and crying, she got to her feet and stumbled up the side of the road until she found the street leading to Ditney Hill. Her teeth chattered.

Gotta keep going. Digger says it's not far from Ditney Hill to Beech Creek. Soon she was hurrying, as best she could, through the small community.

I'm not *scared. Mama says these are fine folks. I know the Suttons an' the Fraziers. Ain't no reason to be scared. Mama says their skin may be brown or black, but inside they're just like us. God made 'em in His image. That's right. That's what Mama says.*

A nearby flash of lightning and the immediate thunderclap jarred her out of her thoughts. She was at the end of the road. There in front of her, right across from the Suttons', was the path. Right where Digger had said it would be. The little girl ran pell-mell down the narrow trail. She lost all sense of time and distance and finally slowed to a walk through the fields and patches of woods. She began to stumble.

Gotta find Daddy, the exhausted child told herself over and over again. Her knees buckled and she fell face down. Then pushed herself up. She forced herself to run on, though she wasn't sure why she was running any more. All she knew for sure was that it was bad. That's why she had to run. Something bad was out there and it was coming.

The downpour increased. Right beside her, lightning struck a tree next to the path. Dulcie shrieked and ran hard, glancing behind her every few steps, certain something was there, and pounding along the path after her. Turning toward Beech Creek again, she saw the obstacle in her way, but didn't have time to stop. She plowed into it and collapsed in the muck, a winded, shaking heap.

When Dulcie opened her eyes, a huge black face was pressed close to her own. She screamed and screamed and screamed.

37

Whoooeee!" said Gideon, rising to a sitting position on the ground. "That woodpecker sure put a fright into me! I allowed as how Deke had turned loose on us with a tommygun!" He patted the hound next to him. "Reckon Princess is the onliest one of us that weren't fooled by that ole bird."

"Wait," said Smith. "I just saw Dunford up ahead. I'll take the lead."

Smith stepped past the other two men.

"You sure, Smith?" asked Sheriff Westerfield, hefting his ample body upright.

Smith felt his skin crawl. "I couldn't hardly mistake him," he said. "It's me he's after, so I'll go in front."

He pointed toward the bluff. " Deke's on the landing up there. I figure he'll follow it around to the mine. He'll be waitin' for us there."

Princess started back up the trail.

"Better keep the dog back with you, son." Smith said. "Cain't have nothin' flusterin' Deke. I know he seen us all. He's gonna be upset enough as it is. Might cause him to do somethin' rash."

Smith waited until Gideon called the dog to his side, then stopped and faced his companions. "Listen, I couldn't ask for two finer friends than you two. I 'preciate y'all more'n I could ever tell you."

He swallowed hard. "We know what's gonna happen up there. Dunford's gonna kill me. An' if he's the coward I think he is, kill hisself. He's in a place where we can't get to him. The only chance I got to save Hattie is if neither one of you interferes. I'm askin' you—I'm beggin' you—let me go in there alone."

He paused, looked at the ground, and shook his head as if to clear his thoughts. "I gotta go along with Deke's scheme."

"Cain't do that, Smith. If you take a bullet we gotta be there to see Deke don't get away with it. But mebbe…" The sheriff broke off his response when Smith interrupted.

"When it's over, y'all take care of Hattie. Make sure she understands this was my choice. I'm makin' it. Nobody made me."

All three men looked up when thunder rumbled over the bluff. The wind picked up. Smith shivered against the chill.

Rain began falling. Smith hunched his shoulders and took a couple of hard breaths.

Once again, he started up the hillside, then stopped. "Sheriff, make sure the Dunford young'uns go to Marva and Conroy Fenton. Ain't nobody could love them kids more'n they do."

"I'll try, Smith, but we don't know for sure what'll hap…"

Smith interrupted again. "Gideon, you're a fine young man. Hoe a straight row, son. Give the Lord His rightful place in your life. An' take care of Darlin' and that young'un—you ever need anything, *anything at all*, you let Hattie know. She'll he'p you out." He swallowed hard as words failed him.

"Yessir, " Gideon answered softly.

Smith glanced back and saw the young man's eyes slide away.

"You and them dogs gonna make a name for yourself in Muhlenberg County. I'm… I'm proud to call you kin."

Smith looked up the trail. Already the rain was coming down the path in rivulets. He planted his bad foot on the wet path. "I reckon I cain't stop you from comin' with me, but either way, I'm goin' now. Hattie and the young'uns are waitin'."

Talk stopped as the men climbed toward the landing and the mine entrance. Around them lightning flashed and thunder rolled. The deadly showdown was just ahead.

Smith leaned down and picked up a large branch that lay on the path. He tossed it into the underbrush. *Lord, it's me, Smith. I'm sure needin' Your help again. You been mighty good to help me out. Much more'n I deserve. I'm ashamed of havin' to come to You for help so often, but Your Word told me to cast my cares on You, and I'm a castin' 'em."*

Under the darkening sky, he stumbled over a root. Clutching

the stick he used as a cane, he righted himself. He paused and surveyed the path, which leveled off just ahead. He glanced back. The sheriff, who had dropped back a short distance, was struggling up the path. Gideon and Princess followed behind.

Smith slowed his pace, but not his prayer. *Lord, You've given me almost three years with the sweetest woman ever created, not even exceptin' my own mama. And You've let me love and be loved by three of the sweetest little'uns I've ever laid my eyes on. I sure do thank You that I got to be their daddy for this little while. No matter what happens to me up here, please don't let 'em see it. Don't let 'em see Deke kill their daddy or hurt their mama. You know I want to be around to help Hattie raise 'em. But if'n it ain't in Your plan, then I know You and the Stoneworths can handle them just fine without me.*

Smith choked hard. He almost missed the hickory tree up ahead on the left—the one Deke had referred to in his letter.

The rain had eased to a steady drizzle. Lightning cracked and beyond the tree, Smith could see the black maw that was the entrance to the mine that ran back into the hillside. It opened out on the ledge above the old abandoned iron smelter and stone engine house.

Smith leaned against the tree with his left hand to catch his breath and slow his hammering heart. His eyes swept the mine entrance, watching for any movement, listening for any sound. *Lord, I don't reckon I've been so scared since I was in the Big War over in France. Didn't have near so much at stake back then. Help me. An'..., an' if'n You don't—for whatever your reason—please help Hattie,"* he pleaded. *"All she's ever done her whole life was love You, an' love other folks. That's what she was doin' when she brung Mamie an' the young'uns home with her. She don't deserve to die at Deke's hand. An' Mamie didn't neither. Please don't let him kill her, Lord. Don't let him...*

Smith didn't look back, but sensed the sheriff's presence right behind him. "This is it," he said quietly. "Now let me handle it. I'll talk to Dunford."

"If that's the way you want it, Smith."

"Deke, you there?" Smith yelled around the tree.

They stood stock-still, then heard Deke's voice.

"Yeah, but you ain't by yourself like I said." His voice echoed from the chamber. Based on Smith's years of working underground, he judged that Deke was not more than forty or fifty feet back in the mine.

"No, the sheriff's with me, but he ain't gonna try anything..."

"Deke," yelled the sheriff, "let me talk to you for a min..."

The deafening roar of a large-calibre revolver rumbled out and a bullet zinged from the mouth of the mine.

"Westerfield, shut your mouth! If I hear one more word out of you, I'm gonna shoot Delaney's woman. It'll be on your head. This ain't your fight. It's between me and Delaney. You ain't gonna talk me out of it."

Smith whirled around and grabbed the sheriff by the lapels. "He ain't gonna talk to you. Let me be! He's gonna kill her if'n you don't."

The sheriff shook Smith off like a small dog, then crouched behind the hickory tree. He raised his rifle to his shoulder and aimed toward the mine entrance. "Sorry, Smith," he said. "I had to try."

"Deke," Smith called, "you promise me, man to man, that if I step out there unarmed and let you shoot me down, you won't harm Hattie?"

"That's what I said, ain't it?"

"She's in there with you for sure?"

"Yeah—standin' right between me and you. She's gonna watch you die. You two ruined my life, and now you're gonna get what's coming to you—and she's gonna see it. Say something, woman."

"Mmmmmmmmph!"

Smith gasped when he heard the muffled cry of his wife. He clenched his teeth and slammed his right fist into his left palm. Fire gleamed in his eyes. Then he took two deep breaths to control his rage.

Deke laughed maniacally, "She's even got some *color* in her face. I done that for you, Delaney. You should see her!" he cackled at his own sick joke.

"Deke," Smith called. "I ain't steppin' in there 'til you send the young'uns out. Ain't no call for them to see what you got planned."

Deathly silence followed Smith's request. He waited. Nothing.

"Deke?"

"What?"

"Did you hear me?"

"Yeah."

"Let the young'uns go!"

Again, there was silence for a moment, then Deke answered, "I ain't got 'em. What are you tryin' to do Delaney? You tryin' to confuse me?"

Smith heard the ring of truth in Deke's words. He sagged against a tree, his mind racing. If the children weren't in the mine, where were they?

"What are you doin', Delaney?" Deke shouted.

"I want to see, Hattie."

"Nothin' doin'!"

"Look, I'm not steppin' in there, 'til I see her. Otherwise, how do I know you got her?"

Smith knew good and well that Hattie was in the mine, but he wasn't about to let Deke know that.

"You heard her a minute ago—quit stallin'.

"That coulda been you, fakin' it," Smith said.

Deke hollered back. "It warn't me, an' you know it. You'll see her when you step around the ledge. I ain't lettin' her go, and I ain't steppin' out with her where the sheriff can get me."

Smith closed his eyes. He had hoped that perhaps Deke, in his deranged mind, could be coaxed out to where the sheriff or Gideon could have gotten off a shot. Now, his last hope was gone.

"Okay, Deke, I give. I'm comin' in unarmed."

"Come on, Delaney. Step around the corner into plain sight. Then I'll give you a second to straighten up and stand tall for your lady to see."

"Gimme a minute to say my goodbyes."

"Make it snappy. I ain't draggin' this out all day!"

For a moment Smith stood with his cap in his left hand, running the fingers of his right hand through his hair. He turned to the officer. "Sheriff Westerfield, you're a good man. Proud to have known you."

"Smith, I hate this worse than…well, just about anything I can think of."

"Know you do." They shook hands.

"Gideon…" Smith looked past the sheriff, to where his young friend had stood. "Where's Gideon?" he asked.

"He turned back. Said he couldn't stand to watch you die. You been like a daddy to 'im. Told me so."

Choked by emotion he couldn't control, Smith squatted down and relaced the shoe with the built-up heel. "You tell 'im…tell him I don't mind him runnin' off. I'd rather it be that way. Tell 'im for me."

"I will." The sheriff's voice was thick.

Deke's voice echoed from the mine. "Time's up, Delaney. Quit stalling. I'm counting to ten. You'd better…"

"I'm coming." Smith stepped from behind the tree and limped toward the mine opening.

"I love you, Hattie." He called toward the mine. "Tell Dulcie and Jackie and Dalton I love them, too."

"Five, six, seven,…" Deke intoned.

Smith walked into the mouth of the mine. He could see them standing deep in the semidarkness. Deke, stood behind Hattie—his left arm clutched around her neck, a double-barrel shotgun in his right hand.

"Eight, nine,…"

Smith said, "Hattie, the Lord will take care…"

"Ten!"

Time locked into slow-moving frames. Smith saw the madman shove Hattie toward him, watched him swing the shotgun up and point it at her. *He's shooting her first!*

"No!" Smith screamed. He lunged forward, heard the roar of the first barrel and saw Hattie fall. A split-second later he felt the second blast hit. Then he saw nothing at all.

38

The hands that reached for Dulcie were as gentle as the face that went with them was black. And the voice was sweet pure molasses.

"Miss Dulcie—child, is that you? What you doin' out in this here storm?"

"Oh, Mr. Amos! Mr. Amos, I'm so glad...so glad it's you!"

Her arms went around his neck. "Gotta get to...Aunt Marva's. G...gotta find my daddy," she stammered.

He pulled his raincoat around her and enveloped her inside its folds. "What happened, Miss Dulcie. Where *is* your Daddy?"

"He w...went to work on Aunt Marva's h...house in Beech Creek. An' Mr. Dunford hit Mama! He took her. He took her away!"

"Oh, no! He hit Miz Hattie?"

"Yessir, and took her away. Gotta f...find Daddy. Gotta help Mama."

Dulcie spoke in fragments, her words rushing and tumbling over each other.

Mr. Amos Frazier gently lifted the frightened little girl and carried her toward the mule. "Of course we will. Sure will. Good thing me an' Charlie was walkin' home. I was leadin' him, 'cause he don't much like the lightnin'. You run right smack into me." He lifted her onto the mule and climbed up behind her, reaching his raincoat around her again.

"You might nigh made it to Beech Creek. Me an' Charlie'll take you the rest of the way. " He turned the mule around and moved past a huge elm that had been split by the lightning bolt. It smoldered and sizzled in the rain.

"You sure you know the way to Aunt Marva's house, Mr.

Amos? I gotta find my Daddy."

"Shore do. Young Brother Fenton's daddy been my friend a long time. Him and me went down in that mine with your daddy to save your Uncle Eldon, and your cousin Ben, and them others. Remember? I know right where we're goin.' You just rest."

The lightning had let up, and the mule plodded steadily through the now light rain.

"You...you reckon my daddy's gonna be mad at me for runnin' away from the others?"

Dulcie's tense little body slowly relaxed against his chest as Amos began talking softly. "No, ma'am. I reckon he's gonna be mighty proud. I ain't never seen a daddy that loves his children more'n yours loves you, Miss Dulcie. He's not gonna be mad at you. You can just bank on it. He'll take care of that Mr. Dunford, too, if'n I know Mr. Smith Delaney. Sure will. Yes, sir, he will. Don't you worry yourself none about that."

He nudged the mule's sides with his heels. Charlie moved briskly. "We'll get there in time. You just wait an' see if we don't. Why, might be, your daddy already knows, an' he's on his way. Did you ever think of that?"

Dulcie's head bobbed loosely on her neck as the mule picked its way down the path. She was so tired. And Mr. Amos had such a nice voice. He talked so sweet about her daddy. Dulcie's eyes fluttered—she forced them wide.

She leaned her head way back and looked up at Amos Frazier. "You reckon Daddy still loves me an' Jackie, even though he's got him a new baby?" Dulcie asked through chattering teeth. She had begun to shiver and couldn't stop.

"Giddup, Charlie!" Mr. Frazier said. Dulcie felt his legs move as he spurred the mule into a trot.

"'Course he does, honey. Why, Miss Dulcie, he thinks you hung the moon! Tol' me he couldn't love you more if you'd a-been borned his own flesh an' blood."

Dulcie shuddered violently. "Grandma Crowe, she says he don't love us. Wouldn't want us any more once Dalton got here."

Amos tightened his hold on the shaking child and hugged her

tighter. He spurred the mule again.

"Your old grandma—not meanin' no disrespect, you understand—your old grandma's all confused. Smith Delaney told me with his own mouth, 'Amos, my friend, you lookin' at the blessedest man on God's green Earth. I got Hattie, I got a new baby boy, and I got my sweet Dulcie, and fine little Jackie. Yessir, Amos,' said he, onliest thing in the world would make it better, would be if I could adopt Dulcie and Jackie. An' sure's the world, Amos, I'd give 'em my name in a minute, if'n they'd let me.' "

"You sure?" Dulcie twisted around to look at the miner's face.

"I'm tellin' you true! That's what he tol' me with his own lips. That's 'zactly what he said."

"He loves me," she said feebly. "He wants to adopt me."

She snuggled back against his chest and was quiet. After a little while her breathing became slow and steady and her head lolled to one side. She slept, her body still shivering.

Just as they reached the edge of Beech Creek, the sun broke through the clouds. Amos peeked down at the sleeping child, then quickly leaned his cheek against her forehead. It burned with fever.

When he pulled his mule up beside the porch at Marva's house, Dulcie felt him lift her off and pass her to Conroy.

I...I have to tell Uncle Conroy...I have to tell...

She heard Conroy say "Come on in, Mr. Frazier, tell us where you found this child—and we'll fill you in on what we know."

Amos lay his raincoat on the swing, and stomped his feet to shake the water off his trousers.

"You sure this is all right, Brother Fenton?"

"Absolutely. Make yourself at home." Conroy held open the door and ushered the man into the living room. "We'll get you a hot cup of coffee. You must be chilled to the bone. Have a seat. Be right with you."

Amos perched at the edge of the couch and waited.

Marva rushed behind Conroy with an armload of dry towels while he carried Dulcie into the bedroom.

"Smith loves me, Uncle Conroy..." Dulcie's fever-bright eyes bored into her uncle's. "He loves me an' Jackie."

"Of course he does, honey." He felt her brow. "You rest now."

"Where's Daddy? I want to tell him Smith loves me." She felt confused. "No, I want to tell him to help Smith find Mama. That's it! Gotta help Mama. Mr. Dunford hit her and took her away."

Marva and Conroy exchanged a glance over the tumbled little head.

"Conroy, get Mr. Frazier a cup of hot coffee while I dry Dulcie off and tuck her in."

Aunt Marva's hands were cool and dry when she brushed Dulcie's hair back off of her face.

"Let's get you out of these wet clothes, sugar. I have a dry towel for you, Dulcie, and one of Dorie's gowns.

"Conroy," she said as he started from the room, "You'd better bring some quinine."

Dulcie let Marva unbutton her dress and pull it over her head. She watched as Aunt Marva pulled off her shoes and peeled the wet socks from her feet. The rough towel felt good against her body.

"Where's my daddy, Aunt Marva?"

Marva bit her lip and blinked back tears. "He's gone to help your mama, honey."

Dulcie smiled. *Daddy will take care of Mama. Everything's going to be okay. Daddy's there.*

She was almost asleep when Conroy brought the medicine. Marva lifted Dulcie's head while she swallowed it. The quinine was awful, but she took it. It left a bitter, bitter taste in her mouth. The taste lingered even as she slipped into the dream world of semi-consciousness. Later, she thought she remembered Marva and Conroy on their knees at her bedside, praying. When they left the room, they left the door open. She heard their voices but couldn't make sense of anything they said. Something about a phone call from Paradise General Store. Smith and Sheriff Westerfield and Gideon went to the mine. And Dr. Wilson did, too. *Why would they go dig coal when Mama needs help? Maybe after Dr. Wilson finishes his shift at the mine, he'll come see me. And Daddy will come get me. He loves me. He loves me.*

Dulcie yawned. She could still taste the quinine in her mouth. *Daddy'll find Mama, then he'll come get me.*

The exhausted little girl felt her body sinking deeper and deeper into the featherbed. Far away, the phone rang again. But she couldn't wait and hear.

39

G*et up! Gotta get up! Hattie's down—gotta get up*! The thought echoed through Smith Delaney's mind. He tried to push himself up—but his arms were like rubber beneath him. He collapsed. Smith shook his head to clear the fog. He pushed himself up again. This time he was able to get up onto all fours. He made it to a sitting position and wiped his left hand across his throbbing face and brow. His fingers came away wet and sticky with blood. *He missed my eyes. But why don't he shoot again?*

Dunford's second shot had ricocheted off the ceiling of the mine and sprayed Smith with rock and buckshot—but the roof had absorbed most of the blast's power.

"Delaney, you okay?" he heard the voice of Sheriff Westerfield. The big man's massive paw gripped Smith's left arm and helped him to his feet.

"Gotta get to Hattie. Cover me, Sheriff," Smith croaked, stumbling forward. "Watch for Deke! Gotta get to Hattie."

He blinked several times and his vision cleared. Hattie lay on the floor of the mine. Smith staggered toward her. Then he saw Deke. Beyond Hattie, his crumpled body lay face down in semi-darkness. The double-barrel shotgun protruded from under him.

"Hattie, sweet Hattie," Smith crooned as he gathered her in his arms. She didn't respond.

"He missed her," said Westerfield. "I'm sure of it! Look, there's no blood on her! Missed her—an' just barely got you."

Smith continued to talk to Hattie as he gently removed the gag Deke had tied across her mouth. He leaned her forward and the sheriff cut the stiff cord that bound her wrists behind her back. Her arms fell limp.

"Wake up, Hattie, wake up. We're okay! Honey, wake up!"

Smith held her close—and felt her heartbeat!

"Here's some water, Smith. I brung it from the spring." Gideon stood beside, him holding the bucket they had left at the spring on Labor Day.

Smith yanked his bandana from his hip pocket, wet it, and began to bathe Hattie's face. He glanced at the sheriff, who was squatting beside Deke's prostrate form. "What happened?"

"You rounded the corner into the mine with your hands up, and stood there waitin' to be shot. I heard the crack of a rifle just a split second before the first shotgun blast—I looked out and there was Gideon crouching high on top of the stone wall of that old engine house. His rifle was at his shoulder and pointin' straight into the mine openin'."

Westerfield squatted by Deke and turned him over. "Dunford's dead. Gideon hit 'im with one shot right in the temple behind his left eye. Son, that was some shot! "

"Yessir," said Gideon, "I clumb up a tree leanin' against the buildin' to get on top. Got 'im with a Remington long rifle cartridge." Princess whimpered at the young man's side.

Smith shook his head. "We're beholden to you, son. Mighty beholden."

He continued to talk to his wife and to wipe her face with the wet cloth. Finally she moaned softly and rolled her head to one side.

"Hey, she moved a little—she's comin' around!" Smith exclaimed.

Westerfield looked at Hattie. "Bless her heart, looks like she had started to you—musta fainted. Look at those bruises. She landed face forward."

"No, sir," said Smith, anger boiling up inside. "That's the color in her face Dunford was laughing about. He done that to her. He beat her."

Smith glared at the corpse. "Sheriff, did you see what he done? He shoved her toward me an' raised the shotgun to shoot her in the back—that liar! But she fell—musta been right then that Gideon shot 'im. His shot caused Deke to jerk the gun upward—

the second blast bounced off the roof and grazed me."

The officer looked back at Dunford. "Got 'im with one clean shot. Stopped 'im in his tracks. Well done, Deputy McBride."

Hattie groaned, then blinked her eyes. After a moment they seemed to focus, then looked confused. "Smith, oh, Smith! Can't be heaven. You're bloody. Wouldn't be bloody in heaven! An' I smell brimstone!"

"No, you don't, Hattie." Smith shook his head and grinned. "That's just good ol' Airdrie spring water." Tears welled up in his eyes. "Take a big swig, sweetheart —you always said it was fine for what ails you." His hands shook as he held it to her lips.

Hattie drank, then wrinkled her nose and grimaced. She sat up and looked around. She was facing out of the mine into the slowly dimming sunlight.

"Oh, Smith, We're alive! We're alive!—" Suddenly, she cringed. Terror swept her features. "Where's Deke?"

"Don't have to be afraid of Deke, " said Smith, hesitating— "Where he is, he'd love a sip of this cool water. Wouldn't mind it smellin' like brimstone, neither. Don't worry none about Deke. What we gotta do is get home and find our young'uns."

Horror surged through Hattie. "Help me up, Smith, hurry! He didn't hurt our babies, did he?" Her voice filled with panic.

He lifted her to her feet and hugged her.

"Don't know. They was gatherin' walnuts when I left. Can you tell me what happened at the house this morning? Mebbe that'll give us a clue. The young'uns were gone by the time we realized Deke had you."

"But Dalton—they can't feed him!"

"Honey, Becky and Dulcie'll do the best they can with 'im. Likely have him at Radburn's just a waitin' for us. Annie'll be cooin' over 'im and tryin' to feed him concentrated milk or somethin'. The Lord who watches over the sparrows will watch over our little fellow—that's fer sure!"

"Hey, can we come in?" yelled a voice from just outside the mine opening. "It's me, Sheriff—it's me, Rainwater. We heard the shots. I got Doc Wilson—and some others."

"Yeah," called Westerfield. "Send the doc—the rest stay back..."

"Stay back, nothing!" boomed a loud voice. "My baby sister's in there, and I'm comin' in." Westerfield looked up and saw Forrest Stoneworth striding into the mine, followed by Doctor Wilson. A crack of thunder pealed, and rain began to fall on the men outside the mine. "C'mon in," said the officer. "Might as well have a party."

A swarm of men, most of them carrying guns, poured in from both sides of the mine entrance. Soon two members of the rescue team from Drakesboro's Black Diamond Coal Company carried a mildly protesting Hattie from the mine on a stretcher. Smith limped by her side, followed by an entourage of her brothers, nephews, and friends. Rain soaked them all.

Volunteers had cleared two downed trees from the old road to where Civil War General Don Carlos Buell's mansion once stood looking down on the Green River from the hill above the mine. There Dr. Wilson's car waited, as did a number of others. Hattie was soon tucked into the backseat of the physician's car to wait for him to return. Smith asked Forrest to have the people to give them some privacy, and climbed in beside her.

"Oh, Smith, we gotta hurry," she said as he closed the car door. "We gotta get to Dalton. That poor baby's bound to be starved—just bound to be!"

"Honey, Doc will get here as soon as he can. Won't take just a few minutes."

Hattie leaned against Smith.

He held her away from him. "Careful, honey, I'm covered in blood."

"I don't care!" Hattie gripped his hands. "We gotta find the young'uns…"

A snippet of remembered conversation wiggled its way out of her exhausted mind. "I think I know where they are!"

"Where?" asked Smith, sliding closer and cradling her against him. Both were soaked and shivering.

"Remember when Becky came to me to help with her mama?"

"How could I forget? That's what started this mess."

Hattie smiled broadly. "She said she'd left the other children at the little cabin—you know, the old log cabin by the spring at the base of Pa Rhoads Hill?"

"Sure do," he said.

"An' she told Marva that's where they *always* went when Deke was angry. Becky said they'd be safe there and wouldn't come out until she called them. They must have seen what Deke did to me. That's where they've gone—I'm just certain! They'd have shelter, and water." She paused, "But they wouldn't have anything for Dalton! Oh, Smith, I *do* wish Doctor Wilson and the sheriff would hurry."

Back in the mine, the doctor quickly examined Deke Dunford's body and pronounced him dead of a single gunshot wound to the head. Sheriff Westerfield and Deputy Rainwater found a straw mattress about thirty feet inside the mine. Next to it, leaned against the wall, were a high powered rifle, three loaded revolvers, and enough ammunition for Deke's guns for him to have withstood a week-long siege. The deputy got volunteers to help haul the body out and take it to Greenville. The doctor, accompanied by the sheriff, clambered up the hill to the waiting cars and the crowd milling around in the rain trying to figure out exactly what had happened.

Smith called the two men aside. "Could one of you take us home? My truck's waitin' there. So's Gideon's."

"Smith, beggin' your pardon," said Westerfield, "you got a passel of young'uns on the run and hidin' out somewhere—with that tiny baby. I'll be stickin' around 'til they come to light."

"Is that right?" asked the doctor. "The kids are gone and your little one's missing with the others?"

"That's about the size of it, Doc," Smith answered.

"I'm goin' too, then. No point in headin' home just to have y'all call me out again."

The doctor strode to his shiny black car and opened the back door. "Hattie, I'm moving you to the front seat. You look in the best shape of the two of you. Let me look at that shiner."

The doctor tipped Hattie's head back and gently probed the purpled skin around her eye. She winced, but didn't cry out. "Dunford got what was comin' to him," the doctor said through gritted teeth.

Finished with his cursory examination, the doctor turned to Gideon. "You drive. I'll climb in the back seat and examine Smith while we're en route to Drakesboro."

He helped Hattie out and opened the front door for her. Closing it briskly behind her, he waved Smith into the car and climbed in after him. He cocked Smith's head over to the side and gazed at the torn flap of skin above his ear.

"You've got one place still bleeding—blood's run down behind your ear and down your neck. That ear's nicked a bit, and you've got buckshot and slate particles in the left side of your face and buried under your scalp."

"I'll be fine, Doc. 'Sides, I ain't real excited about havin' you gouge around on my homely hide while Gideon bounces us along the washboard from here to Drakesboro."

"Well, I'm not about to let you die of lead poisoning or iron rust from buckshot," said the physician. "I know you. The minute this car stops, you're going to hit the ground running to find those children. So without the niceties of an operating room, we'll just have to take care of the matter as we roll along."

A short time later, Gideon guided the doctor's "mobile clinic" over the road toward Drakesboro. In the back seat, Smith gritted his teeth as the doctor probed and plucked to remove foreign objects from his face and scalp. In the propped-open trunk rode Gideon's prize hound, Princess.

40

Only a few miles separated Old Airdrie and Paradise from Drakesboro, but to Hattie it seemed a long journey. Gideon maneuvered the doctor's car over the rutted roads and around the curves with sureness, never taking his eyes off the narrow, twisting, turning ribbon of coal waste that made up the road's surface. It shone in the now-bright sun—tiny glints of light reflecting off the black shards. The hills and valleys swept around and behind them as they rushed toward Drakesboro—and the children who they hoped were hiding nearby in the small cabin at the base of Pa Rhoads Hill.

Hattie's nervous hands flew to her mouth as thoughts skittered here and there. What if Deke had snatched away the children before he'd come for her? No. He couldn't have. In his crazed rantings at the mine, he'd never mentioned them. But, could he have taken them? Surely not. Surely, God in His mercy wouldn't have let Deke hurt the children—hadn't He just delivered Hattie and Smith from the lion's den? Hadn't He held His hand on Gideon's trigger and claimed justice over the unjust? He would surely protect the children. Hattie prayed it was so.

She wound one long strand of hair around her forefinger, as she did when nervous, and then roughly shoved it back into the soft mass behind her ears.

Smith grumbled under Doc's probing fingers, and muttered something about "hamfisted healer." Doc roared with laughter and kept poking at Smith's scalp.

Behind them, a procession of trucks and battered old cars followed—Forrest and Eldon, Ben and Gene, along with friends who'd come to fight for one of their own. Each had the arsenal they'd thrown behind the seats and into their truck beds—to defend and protect. They hadn't been needed, but they'd come just the same. That's how it was. You took care of your own, and when you could, you defended your neighbor.

Somewhere in their blood, the history of wars in the highlands of Scotland, and the green hills of Ireland, and the shires of England, ran thick and raw. It lay shallow beneath the surface, gentled now, but ready—always ready. They were fighting men whose ancestors had warred and battled to keep what was theirs. Now they battled the mines, and drought, and crops that failed, and typhus and scarlet fever and poverty with the same fervency as that of their ancestors who fought the invaders of their lands. Today, victory was theirs. They had won the battle and now, with the same pride as the warriors of old, they were returning home to castles that were cabins, shotgun houses, and tarpaper shacks.

Gideon turned right at the corner where Mr. W.W. Bridges had built his stately home. In front of Radburn's store, Harwell blocked the road. He flapped his arms wildly to signal them.

Gideon pulled to the side and leaned out the window.

Harwell rushed to the car. "Paradise store called. Tol' us what happened up at Ole Airdrie. So good to hear it come out good."

He snatched his hat off of his head and turned it between his hands. "Your Dulcie's at Marva's place. She pert' near wore herself out getting' there in the storm—They couldn't make much sense of what she was a'sayin' so they put her to bed. Wanted you to know."

"Oh, thank goodness!" Hattie called.

"You mean that young'un went all the way to Beech Creek on foot?" asked Smith. "And by herself?"

"Sure did, and in that storm," said the storeowner. "Except I understand that Amos Frazier toted her the last little bit of the way."

"That child!" exclaimed Doc Wilson.

Gideon turned around in the seat. "What you want me to do, Smith? Head for Beech Creek an' Dulcie, or go on down to your place?"

Hattie bit her lip. "Our place, Gideon. If Dulcie's at Marva's, she's safe. We got to find the rest of 'em."

Smith grinned. "You heard the lady. Our place it is."

Gideon eased the car back onto the road and headed it toward the valley. Soon they plunged down the slope in front of the small house under the hill.

"Might as well keep going." Doctor Wilson said. "No point in changin' cars. Just drive as close as you can to the cabin. We likely got more than enough vehicles followin' behind to give each young'un their own ride back."

Gideon didn't argue. As Smith called directions, he swung the car onto the lane that ran to Miz Collier's house, turned right on the road to Jacksontown, then made another right on the road that led around toward Centralia Mine. "Pull off to the left by that row of silver-leaf poplars—see the old trail? Park there."

Smith hit the ground before the car rolled to a stop. Hattie was right behind him. On unsteady feet they rushed along the narrow path, with Gideon and Doc Wilson on their heels. They could hear car doors slamming as the rest of the entourage arrived on the road.

The small cabin appeared in the shadows ahead. In the gathering dusk, Smith called, "Children, you can come out now! It's all right!"

Five small heads appeared at the door and windows. Some as dark as shadows, the others as light as the morning sun. Jackie flew through the doorway first. Then Digger, Mary Claire and Dorie. Becky came last. In her arms she carried Dalton.

"Oh, look at you! Every blessed one of you!" Hattie exulted. She took the baby and hugged them all.

"Miz Hattie,"—Digger gulped hard and looked at the ground.—"We done lost Dulcie somehow. Stubbornes' woman-child I ever laid eyes on," he muttered.

Hattie laughed until the tears streamed down her cheeks. "She's fine, honey. Went to Marva's to get help. She's just fine."

Digger kicked at the grass that grew by the door. "Figured that's where she went to."

"You figured right, son," said Smith. "Let's go get her."

❧

The friends who'd joined the search returned to their homes. For the trip to Beech Creek, only the sheriff, the doctor, and Gideon McBride remained with Smith, Hattie, and the blood-kin Stoneworths.

Hattie crooned and clucked over Dalton as though she hadn't seen him in weeks. She modestly draped her shoulder with his blanket and nursed the baby as they went along. Smith leaned forward and draped one arm around her from his perch on the edge of the back seat.

"Never thought I'd get to see him again," he said, his voice thick with emotion. "All I could think of as I was climbin' up that hillside to the mine, was how I'd never get to tell him all the things I wanted him to know. How sweet his mama is, an' who his people are. Where he comes from, an' how to be a man. How to make his way..." Smith's voice faded as emotion choked him.

Hattie reached back with one hand and brushed her fingers down his cheek.

Doctor Wilson snatched his snowy handkerchief from his pocket and mopped his suddenly damp eyes. He blew his nose loudly. Stuffing the handkerchief back into his jacket, he cleared his throat.

"You're gonna be around a long time, Smith. Reckon the Lord isn't done with you yet. 'Course, if I have to keep stitchin' up your head..."

❧

Marva flew out the front door when the cars pulled up in front of her small house. She gasped at Hattie's bruised cheek and black eye, then raced to Forrest's car and gathered the Dunford children to her. Carrying Mary Claire on her hip, she rushed them all inside.

"Y'all come in! Hurry now. I want to hear everything!"

Smith said a few quiet words to Conroy. They gathered the Dunford children into the living room and told them of their father's death.

"So, he's dead, huh?" said Digger.

"Yes, son," Conroy answered.

"So, now we ain't got no people?"

"Digger, you have us, if you want us." Marva answered softly.

"What about the law?" Digger glared at the sheriff. "You aimin' to carry me an' my girls off?"

"Nope."

"You leavin' us here?"

"Yep."

Digger looked at Becky. "You reckon we should stick aroun' here a while an' see if'n we like it?"

"Reckon so," his sister answered.

Digger tugged at the strap on his overalls. He looked at the floor, then up at the ceiling. "You meanin' to make it legal-like? I mean, could we mebbe be Fentons 'stead of Dunfords?" he asked in a whisper.

Marva tightened her arms around Mary Claire. "If that's what you want, Digger, we'd be proud to have you."

"You too, Uncle Conroy?"

"Me, too, son." Conroy kissed the top of Dorie's blond head.

Digger draped one lanky arm around Becky's thin shoulders. "Reckon we'll give it a try, then."

Smith and Hattie tiptoed into the small bedroom off the kitchen. There, in the soft lamplight, Dulcie lay sleeping, tucked in the narrow bed with her ebony curls standing out against the white pillowcase.

Smith eased onto the edge of the bed.

"Dulcie, Daddy found Mama for you. I found her, darlin'," he whispered, leaning over her.

The little girl's dark eyelashes fluttered. She opened her eyes and sat up. She threw her arms around Smith's neck.

"Knew you'd find her, Daddy. Just knew you would!" she said.

Hattie dropped to her knees beside the bed and brushed the little girl's hair back off of her forehead. "You were so brave! I'm prouder than proud of you, darlin'."

Dulcie leaned against Smith's chest. "You ain't mad at me for runnin' away from Digger at the cabin? Even though he tol' me to stay?"

Hattie picked up one of Dulcie's hands and planted a kiss on her palm. "Not even a little bit."

Smith leaned down and lifted her into his arms. "Let's go home."

Dulcie wound her arms around his neck. "Will you keep me forever and always? An' not ever send me away? Even…even if I ain't really yours?"

Smith gazed down into her eyes. "Forever and always, Dulcie," he promised.

The little girl laid her sleepy head against his shoulder.

"Forever and always, amen," she said.

Epilogue

On a crisp December morning, Rebekah, Porter (Digger), Dorie and Mary Claire Dunford became Fentons. Marva and Conroy stood proudly behind their children as circuit court judge Craig Curtis made the adoptions legal. Happy tears rolled down Marva's cheeks.

Hattie and Smith, with Dalton in his daddy's arms, stood across the aisle watching the ceremony. Dulcie and Jackie stood with them.

The judge opened the second folder before him and scanned the first page. He cleared his throat, then directed his comments to Smith and Hattie.

"I have here a petition for the adoption of Dulcie and Jackie Stoneworth Crowe by Smith Delaney. Is that correct?"

Smith nodded.

"You understand, Mr. Delaney, that if I grant your petition, you will, for all intents and purposes, both legal and moral, be their father? That you will be responsible for their support until they reach the age of their majority?"

"Yes sir," Smith answered firmly.

"Mrs. Delaney, are you aware that he will have equal right to the children under the law? He will be your absolute equal in the decisions that affect their upbringing and their future? "

"Yes sir."

"And this is what you want?"

"Oh, yes, sir." Hattie said.

The judge steepled his fingers in front of his chin and turned his gaze to Dulcie. "How about you, young lady? Do you want Mr. Delaney to be your father?"

Dulcie smiled up at Smith, then nodded at the judge. "I want to be Dulcie Delaney. Then he'll be my daddy forever."

"That's exactly right. You'll have to mind him. You know that?"

"Yes, sir. I...I already mind him—'most always."

The judge laughed with the rest of the adults.

Jackie held onto the seat in front of him and solemnly peered over the top at the judge sitting high on the platform in his black robes. The little boy scooted onto his seat and swung his legs back and forth. He pushed himself up onto his knees and then stood up on the bench. Hattie put her arm around him. Judge Curtis winked at him. Jackie waved at the judge, who wiggled a few fingers in return.

Emboldened by the judge's friendliness, Jackie blurted out "Is you God?"

Hattie froze for a second, then clapped her hand over Jackie's mouth, her face flaming scarlet.

The judge threw back his head and laughed.

"No, son. Though when I'm rendering a judgement, some folks might think I am."

Jackie looked disappointed.

"Young man," the judge asked the boy, "Who is your daddy?"

Jackie tugged on Smith's sleeve. "Dat's him. An'...an' I'm gonna be jus' like him. The Bible says so."

Judge Curtis' eyebrows disappeared behind his hair. "Is that right?"

Jackie nodded hard. "John 5:20: '*For the Father loveth the Son and showeth Him all things that Himself doeth: and He will show Him greater works than these, that ye may marvel.*'"

Jackie paused and pointed one finger in the air as he continued, "Jus' wait. You gonna marvel somethin' fierce."

The judge grinned and leaned back in his chair. "Well, now. That's a pretty good Scripture, but I think that when the Lord spoke those words, He was talking about Himself as the Son and God as the Father."

Jackie bit his lip and frowned. " Mebbe so," he said. "But I heard the preacher say it, and my daddy shows me good things, too. He teached me to hull walnuts. An'...an' he's gonna he'p me build a doghouse for Pride. Mr. McBride gived him to us."

"Uh-huh."

An'...an' he's gonna teach Dulcie and Dalton, too."

"I see."

An'...an' he's nice." Jackie flashed a smile and nodded as he finished.

By this time Conroy was doubled over laughing. Marva had her handkerchief pressed to her mouth to hide her grin. Smith was beaming proudly. Hattie was looking at the ceiling, her sweet smile pasted on her face.

The judge suddenly seemed to realize he'd been debating Scripture with a toddler. He returned to the folder in front of him.

"As there is sufficient reason to believe that all parties are in agreement, and based on the written testimony previously submitted to the court, and by the testimony given here today—testimony I find *genuinely* compelling, I might add—I find that Dulcie and Jackie Crowe shall, indeed be the children of Smith Delaney, and will, from this day forward, be known as Dulcie and Jackie Delaney."

Dulcie cheered and threw her arms around Smith. He handed Dalton to Hattie and picked up his daughter.

"You're mine now, Dulcie," he whispered, spinning her in a circle. "Through thick an' thin, sunshine an' shadow. Just like you said, forever and always, Dulcie Delaney!"

Dulcie took his face between her small hands and pressed her nose to his. "Forever and always, Daddy!"

Glossary

There are three types of words in this novel that prove to be a challenge: mining terminology, slang in vogue in the thirties, and terms adapted from the mother tongues of settlers of Muhlenberg County. Someone suggested a number of years ago that if William Shakespeare should arise from the dead, he'd likely feel more at home, language-wise, in the mountains of Appalachia than anywhere else on earth. Muhlenberg County is not in Appalachia, but many of its settlers came from the mountains of Virginia and the Carolinas. This glossary will help you understand this novel's people of the 1930s as you share a bit of their lives.

Buell, General Don Carlos Civil War officer who, following the war, bought the Airdrie site on the Green River and lived in a mansion there for many years.

Dander Temper, anger, or level of irritation. "That stubborn old mule sure got my dander up."

Fetch Go, get, and bring back. "Fetch me that bucket of nails."

Fiddlesticks An expression of surprise, disbelief, or mild displeasure. "You sent him? Oh, fiddlesticks! By the time he gets back the ice will have melted. Forget about ice cream!"

Haint Ghost, apparition, wraith, specter or hobgoblin "Just as I passed the graveyard, a haint floated across the road ahead of me."

I'll be Jiggered An expression of wonder. "I'll be jiggered, Jenny, it's snowed on your birthday the last threee years.

Ort Ought or should. Combines in interesting ways:Orta = ought to; Ortn't = ought not.

Peaked (Pronounced Peek'-ed.) Thin, emaciated, unhealthy.
Peart Healthy, well. "Since I got this cough, I just ain't been feelin' peart at all."

Pert "Pretty" was often pronounced, "purty." But is was shortened to "Pert" when combined with "near" or "nigh" to mean "almost," or "nearly." "Honest, Tilly, when Edith found out that Ed was marryin' her sister, she pert nigh died."

Pillbug Common in dank, dark places, a many-legged little crustacean, perhaps the size of the smallest fingernail. It rolls into a ball when disturbed.

Reckon Consider, estimate, judge, assume. "Is Jim gonna join the union?" "I'm not sure—I reckon so."

Slack Very small pieces and particles of coal of limited marketability in the thirties. Often used to surface roadways.

Smidgen A small amount, a dab, a little bit.

Spencer seven-shooter This rifle was the first repeating weapon extensively used in warfare. Popular during the last half of the Civil War.

Swan Combines with "I'll" as an exclamation. "You surely don't mean it! Why—I'll swan!" Probably derived from Victorian times when a shocked lady might say, "Why, I'll swoon! I'll just swoon!"

Thrush (Thresh) A disease of the mouth and throat, often in infants. Usually characterized by white patches.
From the forthcoming

Forever and Always

Stoneworth Chronicles - III

"No. No. NO!" Smith Delaney shouted at his wife. "Hattie, Eunice Crowe is *not* comin' here to live!"

Hattie pushed her heavy dark hair off her shoulders and, facing him square on, answered quietly, "She doesn't have anywhere else to go."

"I don't care!" Smith slapped his open palm down on the kitchen table sloshing his coffee across its surface. "She ain't comin' *here*."

"Smith..."

"No! That woman's more trouble than a box full of copperheads—an' just as poisonous. An' she's *crazy!* She'll have you waitin' on her hand an' foot from sunup to sundown. She'll run you off your feet."

"She was Jack's mother," Hattie replied, referring to her first husband. "If he were still alive..."

"But he ain't. He's gone, an' ain't nothin' in the world gonna make me change my mind! Subject's closed." He picked up the latest *Grit* newspaper and snapped it open.

Hattie paced the small kitchen. "What will happen to her, then? Ferd is gone. She doesn't have *any*one to take care of her."

Smith peered over the top of the paper. "I'm sorry her brother's dead," he said flatly. "He was a nice man in his own way. But that don't mean you got to take on Eunice. Let someone *else* take her."

"That's just the point. There isn't anyone else. Not now—1936 is no time for an old woman to be without a place to rest her head. The county home is full with this Depression goin' on and on."

"Our home is full, too."

"But, honey..."

Smith threw the paper down, and stood up. He snatched

his cap off of the nail beside the back door. "Have you forgotten everything that woman has done to us? Have you forgotten what she's done to Dulcie? An' what she's tried to do to me?"

Hattie's gaze dropped to the floor. "No, of course I haven't. But how bad could it be? I mean, we'd be able to watch her every minute. She's just one old woman."

"Yeah. One *mean* ol' woman..." Smith said stepping up onto the screened in porch.

She threw her hands up. "What about 'Christian duty' and takin' care of widows and orphans?" she pleaded.

Smith turned back to his wife. "I know you think it's your mission in life to take care of every wounded soul who crosses your path. An' I've always supported you in that. But I'm drawin' the line at Eunice Crowe."

He poked his finger in Hattie's direction, "You are *not* bringin' Eunice into this house. I forbid it!"

Hattie watched his retreating back as he marched across the porch and slammed out the screen door.

Well, that went well, she thought angrily. She snatched the dishcloth out of the pan of soapy dishwater and wrung it out. Scrubbing hard at the coffee rings he'd left on the table, she fumed. *He forbids it, does he. He forbids me to bring Eunice into this house....*

A germ of an idea began forming in Hattie's mind. She rolled it over and over looking for flaws. A slow smile spread across her pretty face. *All right, Smith Delaney, I won't bring her into the house, but I am gonna bring her down here and take care of her. You just see if I don't!*

Would you like to know more about the extended Stoneworth and Delaney families and what happened before *Sunshine and Shadow*? Read ...

Turn Back Time

winner of the
2001 Benjamin Franklin
Award for Popular Fiction

It's an upbeat Depression-Era novel with mystery, adventure, and romance. Dulcie and Jackie are small children, but they play an important part, especially Dulcie. This novel is written for those who enjoy adventure with a touch of romance.

Is this novel for you? The judges for the Benjamin Franklin Awards are chosen from among top editors, writers, agents, and other leaders in the field of publishing.

About *Turn Back Time*, the Benjamin Franklin Award judges said:

"One of the best books I have ever read."

"Excellent description" **"Effective dialogue"**

"Well put together" ***"Great for all ages"***

"Well written" **"A keeper!**

"Grabbed me ... from start to finish"

Turn Back Time is the first of the Stoneworth Chronicles, that tell the story of Hattie Stoneworth Crowe, Smith Delaney, and their families. Don't miss it!

Check for this book at your favorite bookstore or copy the order form on the last page of this book.

Heirloom-quality children's picture books that make a difference!

ISBN 1-886864-00-4
$14.95

OVER is not UP! **By Dale Smith**
Just about every family has a child like Bitsie. When this little sleepy-head was called, she didn't get up, she just turned over—and OVER is not UP! The sun was up, the birds were up, and the flowers, even her pets—but not Bitsie. This book was a Benjamin Franklin Award national finalist. Its simple story line make it an ideal gift for children from two years to kindergarten. Illustrated by award-winning artist Donna Brooks. It isprinted on acid-free paper, as are all our picture books, so the child you get this book for will be able to pass it on to his or her children.

ISBN 1-886864-10-1
$14.95

Nighttime at the Zoo **By Dale Smith** is based on and includes, a lullaby that his mother sang to him when he was a child. It depicts children visiting a zoo at dusk as many animals get ready for the night. The music for the song appears on each appropriate page and on the back end papers. North Carolina "miracle artist" Gwen Clifford used colored pencils to draw the bright, detailed pictures. Many boys and girls around the nation and the world are going to sleep listening to this delightful song sung—or read—to them. It can become your family tradition, too.

Check for this book at your favorite bookstore or copy and send the order form on the last page of this book.

More life-enriching children's picture books.

ISBN 1-886864-08-X $15.95

The Rabbit and the Promise Sign **by Pat Day-Bivins and Philip Dale Smith** was named "Best Book of the Year" for children by the North American Book-dealer's Exchange. This charming Easter fable features magnificent illustrations by Donna Brooks. It is a story of assurance, hope, and love. The who receives this beautiful book will eagerly await the opportunity to see the "rabbit in the moon," and will remember the message of Grandfather Rabbit in the story. This highly reviewed and praised work is our best-selling children's book.

ISBN 1-886864-16-0 $15.95

Little Tom Meets Mr. Jonah, **by Philip Dale Smith and Pat Day-Bivins.**

Little Tom, a mischievous kitten who thinks he's big and tough, has an important lesson for every child. He disobeys his father, gets trapped in a box of fish, and ends up on board ship with Jonah, the character from the Bible. During the kitten's escapade he learns that thoughts lead to actions, actions have consequences, and that we're responsible for the results of our actions. He also learns how wonderful second chances can be! You will love the beautiful illustrations by Donna Brooks.

Check for this book at your favorite bookstore or copy and send the order form on the last page of this book.

Join Dulcie and Jackie Delaney, as teenagers, in a wild and wonderful adventure underground.

ISBN 1-886864-05-5
$9.95

Secrets of Rebel Cave

A Stoneworth Teen Adventure – I

Immediately after World War II, Dulcie and Jackie, along with Eugene and Poppy Stoneworth and two other teens, explore Rebel Cave in Tennessee to see if they can prove that Confederate soldiers hid out there during the Civil War.

What's behind the secret false wall they discover in the cave? And will Dulcie's great fear of mice, rats, and bats doom the expedition? Will her leadership and Jackie's phenomenal memory provide keys to solving an almost-century-old mystery?

The Stoneworth Teens meet and overcome many challenges and fears—and provide strong examples for today's youth as they face their fears, pressures, and prejudices. **An extensive resource section** supplements this historical novel. It has information about the Civil War and about caves: keys to safe exploration, how to locate nearby public caves, how to contact cave organizations, etc. Includes lists of books and web sites for further research. Contains thirty pencil sketches by gifted artist Susan Vaughn.

"Youth will delight in reading Secrets of Rebel Cave under their bedcovers with a flashlight...provided they can get the book away from their older brothers and sisters and their parents."
Henriette Anne Klauser, Ph.D., author, *Put Your Heart on Paper*

"This many-faceted book...will trigger dialogue about teamwork and relationships, dealing with emotions and prejudices, and often-forgotten aspects of our country's history."
Jean Bell, retired teacher, Chillicothe, MO

Get this first in the *Stoneworth Teen Adventure* series.

Check for this book at your favorite bookstore or copy the form on the last page of this book.

Order Form (copy this form)

You may order our books from your favorite bookstore or online source, or may order directly from Golden Anchor Press.

Fax to: 253-537-5323 Phone: 253-847-9441

Mail to: Golden Anchor Press
PO Box 45208
Tacoma, WA 98445

Website: http://www.goldenanchor.com

Please send the following books: I understand that I may return any product for a full refund—for any reason, no questions asked.

Number	Title	Cost
______	______________________________	__________
______	______________________________	__________
______	______________________________	__________

Shipping: 1st book $3.00, Each additional book $2.00

Name: ____

Address:____

City/State/Zip ____________________________________

Sales tax: Please add 8.4% for products shipped to WA addresses

Payment:: Check ___ Credit Card: Visa ___ Mastercard ___

Card number: _____________________________________

Name on card: ____________________________Exp. Date ___/___